Wallace Stevens and
the Idealist Tradition

Studies in Modern Literature, No. 24

A. Walton Litz, General Series Editor

Consulting Editor for Titles on Wallace Stevens
Professor of English
Princeton University

Other Titles in This Series

Wallace Stevens and the Idealist Tradition

by
Margaret Peterson

UMI RESEARCH PRESS
Ann Arbor, Michigan

Portions of chapter 4 appeared in an essay entitled "*Harmonium* and William James" in *The Southern Review*, Summer 1971, vol. 7 n. 3.

Quotations from the following works are reprinted by permission of Alfred A. Knopf, Inc.:

The Necessary Angel, Wallace Stevens, © copyright 1951 by Wallace Stevens

Opus Posthumous, Wallace Stevens, © copyright circa 1957 by Elsie Stevens and Holly Stevens

The Collected Poems of Wallace Stevens, Wallace Stevens © copyright 1954 by Wallace Stevens

Produced and distributed by
UMI Research Press
an imprint of
University Microfilms International
Ann Arbor, Michigan 48106

Library of Congress Cataloging in Publication Data

Peterson, Margaret Lee Wilson.
   Wallace Stevens and the idealist tradition.

   (Studies in modern literature ; no. 24)
   Revision of the author's thesis (Ph.D.)—Stanford
University, 1965.
      Bibliography: p.
      Includes index.
   1. Stevens, Wallace, 1879-1955—Philosophy. 2. Idealism
in literature.   I. Title. II. Series.

PS3537.T4753Z757 1983   811'.52   83-4996
ISBN 0-8357-1452-7

The point is that poetry is to a large extent an art of perception and that the problems of perception as they are developed in philosophy resemble similar problems in poetry. It may be said that to the extent that the analysis of perception in philosophy leads to ideas that are poetic the problems are identical.

Wallace Stevens

Contents

Preface

Although Wallace Stevens' stature as a major American poet is now assured, his poetry still presents interpretive problems which make responsible judgment difficult. This study is somewhat unorthodox in its dealing with those problems since it trespasses upon ground not usually associated with the criticism of modern poetry.

The subject which preoccupied Stevens throughout his career, and which he preferred to call the relation between reality and imagination, is properly an aesthetic-philosophical concern. It originated and developed within the tradition of Modern Idealism, and, beginning with Coleridge, it transformed the theory of poetry. While I have not undertaken any systematic account of that tradition, I have attempted to define in some detail its aesthetic implications as they affected Stevens and those writers who appear to have had most influence upon his thinking. The venture has not been undertaken without misgivings. It has required at certain points a more philosophical than literary approach, and I have been aware of my limitations in the former respect. I have been encouraged, however, by the fact that Stevens, himself, was not a trained philosopher, but that he nevertheless found himself increasingly drawn to the philosophical background of his subject. In so far as that background clarifies his poetry, its inclusion has seemed essential.

I wish to express my long indebtedness to Professor Yvor Winters as both teacher and friend. He initiated my interest in Stevens many years ago and saw my manuscript to completion shortly before his death. I am grateful also to Professors Charles Gullans and Douglas Peterson for many hours of patient listening, advice, and support.

1

Background: Stevens' Literary Reputation, His Generation, His Romanticism and Modernity

During an unusually long literary career, Wallace Stevens published only one small volume of prose, *The Necessary Angel* (1951).[1] With the exception of several short essays published after his death in 1955, the book contains all of his criticism of any significance.[2] The collection is in many ways disappointing. It is composed of essays which, except for one, were not intended for publication but were delivered as lectures for various occasions dating from 1942 to 1951. Stevens acknowledged that they were "contributions to the theory of poetry" rather than a clearly articulated aesthetic.[3] On the whole, they are repetitious and highly generalized. The prose itself is not remarkable for directness or coherence. It is suggestive rather than assertive; and it relies heavily upon illustrations impressive for their range, but often oblique in their relevance. The difficulties of style are increased by a sometimes cavalier disregard for the requirements of definition and logical connectives.

Granted its inadequacies, *The Necessary Angel* is an important book. The essays are united by what is now recognized as Stevens' single, pervasive subject: the relation between reality and the imagination. They are thus helpful in interpreting the poems, and they give Stevens' theory of poetry a reasonably clear intellectual context by documenting the influences, literary and non-literary, which appear to have had the most effect upon his thinking. This is a matter of interest. The question of Stevens' relation to his tradition has occasioned some remarkable speculation. He has been described as a Platonist, an eighteenth-century figure, a relic of the mauve decade, and an eminently modern poet. His poetry has been called metaphysical, symbolist, imagist, neo-romantic, and romantic-symbolist. Amid such a melange of labels, *The Necessary Angel* has provided the surest ground for agreement. For this reason it will be used here as a preliminary text, as the best means of approaching what is some-times obscure, and all too often liable to misinterpretation, in the poetry. The procedure gives undue importance to what is finally the unremarkable prose of a major American poet, but it is justified if it avoids some of the misunderstandings occasioned by the poetry itself.

Literary Reputation

Probably the most unusual feature of Stevens' literary career has been the startling revision of his reputation during the last two decades. It is now apparent that the poetry of *Harmonium* (1923), the book which established his early reputation, was understood only faintly during the twenties and thirties. The second book, *Ideas of Order,* did not appear until thirteen years later. Subsequent volumes — *The Man with the Blue Guitar* (1937), *Parts of a World* (1942), *Transport to Summer* (1947), *The Auroras of Autumn* (1950), *Collected Poems* (1954) and *Opus Posthumous* (1957) — successively clarified the early poetry.[4] Even so, much of the poetry, both early and late, remains difficult and at times obscure. Belated insights con-cerning *Harmonium* are still producing considerable critical activity.

The early reaction to *Harmonium* was best summarized by Gorham Munson's term, "dandyism." Stevens was described as a "virtuoso of the inane," a poet of "niggling sensuality," a "cavalier of beauty," the "hedonist par excellence of modern poetry."[5] Edmund Wilson dismissed him as "a charming decorative artist" with "a fascinating gift of words that is not far from a gift of nonsense."[6]

The "dandysim" charge was bolstered by the social consciousness of the thirties. A now celebrated example of the Marxist approach to Stevens was Stanley Burnshaw's review of *Ideas of Order,* which appeared in *The New Masses* of October 1, 1935. The review, which is actually a relatively temperate attack upon Stevens, owes its importance to Stevens' response to it in the poem "Mr. Burnshaw and the Statue." Burnshaw's judgment of *Harmonium,* however, is fairly typical of the period's intellectual left.

> It is remembered for its curious humor, its brightness, its words and phrases that one rolls on the tongue. It is the kind of verse that people concerned with the murderous world collapse can hardly swallow today except in tiny doses.[7]

Even sympathetic reviewers like Theodore Roethke took much the same tone: "It is a pity that such a rich and special sensibility as Stevens' should be content with the order of words and music, and not project itself more vigorously upon the present-day world."[8] There was, of course, some opposition to the view of Stevens as an effete sensibility. Howard Baker, among others, tried to point out his interest in "specific contemporary problems" and his use of Jungian archetypes. Although the evidence was not overwhelming, Baker's essay remains one of the earliest serious attempts to grapple with the interpretive problems of *Harmonium*.[9] With the publication of *The Man with the Blue Guitar* there were further sporadic attempts to improve Stevens' reputation by discovering signs, if not of social conversion, at least of humanitarian concern.[10] By the end of the decade, however, R. P. Blackmur's assessment in 1932 had not been radically altered:

> ...Mr. Stevens has a bad reputation among those who dislike the finicky, and a high one, unfortunately, among those who value the ornamental sounds of words but who see no purpose in developing sound from sense.[11]

After 1940 there was a growing awareness of Stevens as a serious and significant poet. The "dandy" tradition persisted, but among critics of any reputation he achieved major status. Since his award of the Bollingen Prize in 1949, three books have been devoted largely to exegesis of his poetry,[12] and in the last decade he has become one of the most discussed and highly admired poets of the country.

There have also been significant changes in critical approaches to the poetry. The early quest for humanitarian attitudes has been followed by efforts to establish Stevens as a humanist, albeit of a somewhat undefined sort. Hi Simons described his position in 1942 as "a humanism with an esthetic instead of a moralistic basis," and found it "better humored than the humanism of Babbitt and More."[13] A similar notion has been developed in recent years by Louis Martz, who stresses Stevens' admiration for "the wonder of human consciousness" and places him in the meditative tradition of Donne and Hopkins.[14] Another trend has been to exchange the "dandy" epithet for the ameliorative "comic." The newer version explains Stevens' aestheticism and detachment from social concerns as necessary prerequisites for his comic view. Robert Pack, observing that Stevens was "not so depressed as the rest of his generation, but rather more pleased with life than disappointed," devotes a chapter of his book to examining the poet's "comic spirit."[15] Samuel French Morse, attempting to locate him in some tradition, had earlier proposed the same approach by representing Stevens as an eighteenth-century figure who "reflects the Neo-classic doctrine of the superiority of art over nature." Morse anticipates Pack by concluding, "As a poet, then, Stevens is a comedian, and his poetry belongs to the tradition of comedy."[16]

Such divergent opinions reflect a certain critical malaise which seems to accompany most treatments of Stevens. Perhaps because the poetry is difficult, there has been until very recently an unwillingness to move beyond its more superficial features and a haste to affix a convenient literary label upon the slightest provocation. The comic elements—the incongruous titles, for example—are numerous and obvious. More often than not, however, a comic title is followed by a wholly serious poem. So too, when Stevens is called, as he often is, an eminently modern poet, the evidence is usually confined to poetic technique, frequently to diction alone.[17] The view of Stevens as a major poet but an amateur critic is fairly common, and it has encouraged the dismissal of his ideas about poetry in spite of the fact that those ideas are, directly or indirectly, the subject of most of the poetry. A number of critics during the forties felt that Stevens' preoccupation with theory was resulting in inferior poetry, but the criticism rather than bearing upon the theory itself, stressed its interference with the poetry. Randall Jarrell's lament that Stevens, in *Auroras of Autumn,* had developed the fatal habit of "philosophizing in verse,"[18] was followed by John Ciardi's judgment that "Stevens' true golden period ended with *Transport to Summer,*" after which he found it "more inviting to talk about his perceptions than to make them happen."[19] Jarrell and Ciardi sounded the note of critical orthodoxy—the dictum that poetry must deal concretely with immediate experience—which left Stevens' strongest defenders hastily tucking ideas out of sight at first encounter.

There is, finally, the criticism which is pertinent to this study: this is the criticism which has related Stevens' ideas to the romantic tradition and has regarded the poetry as the successful or unsuccessful (depending upon the critic) struggle with the problems of a romantic aesthetic. The most relevant critics are Frank Kermode, Louis Martz, Yvor Winters, R. P. Blackmur, and R. H. Pearce. Their views will be considered in some detail in later chapters. Briefly, Kermode, Pearce and Martz regard Stevens' poetry as representing a successful resolution of the problems of the romantic imagination. Yvor Winters finds what he early diagnosed as Stevens' philosophical "hedonism" (a manifestation of his romantic position) responsible for the decay of his talent after *Harmonium.* Blackmur is less specific, but seems to concur with Winters that Stevens' ideas—or lack of ideas—led to inferior poetry. Martz represents the compromise position, agreeing with Winters about the early poetry, but finding signs of recovery in the later.

That Stevens' position is essentially a romantic one cannot be seriously questioned. The issues which have engaged these critics are not reducible simply to an attempt to affix a romantic label. They are concerned with understanding the poetry in the light of Stevens' ideas about poetry, and in most cases with determining the effects of those ideas upon a major poet. They are clearly not in agreement, nor have they—except for Kermode — examined the body of Stevens' poetry in any consistent fashion. Kermode, the only one of the group to study Stevens at book length, has been limited by his primary aim — to introduce a difficult American poet to a British audience. Of the others, Winters' essay precedes the publication of the greater part of Stevens' poetry as well as *The Necessary Angel.* Martz, who deals with the poetry following *The Man with the Blue Guitar,* is interested in isolating what he regards as "meditative" elements; he is only by implication concerned with the critical problem. Taken as a group, however, these critics have focused upon what was, for Stevens at least, the real issue: a theory of poetry proposed as "the theory of life."[20] The subject will no doubt predominate in studies of Stevens for some time to come, and certainly it will be crucial in any final evaluation of his position in American poetry.

Stevens' Generation

The first sentence of *The Necessary Angel* is an appropriate introduction to Stevens' poetry as well as to his prose: "One function of the poet at any time is to discover by his own thought and feeling what seems to him to be poetry at that time."[21] The remark is itself a platitude of its time, yet in Stevens' case it carries unusual weight. In spite of his supposed detachment from contemporary concerns, there can be little question of his intellectual commitment to his age. Few poets have urged so insistently that the inadequacies of contemporary life determine the poet's function and give poetry its *raison d'être.* In a sense all of his prose is a single apologia for his preoccupation with the theory of poetry, and it is premised on the belief that for the modern mind poetry is the remaining hope of a desiccated culture, the surrogate of religious faith, a mode, even, of personal salvation. Unsympathetic critics have found it easy to reduce such sentiments to mere aestheticism and to label their author a decadent "purist" or a vestige of *fin de siècle* art-for-art's-sake. The supplication of poetry in the name of the "profound necessities of life today" is not a unique occurrence, however, in either nineteenth or twentieth-century literature. What is of more interest is Stevens' assessment of those necessities, and here he reflects the pessimism and skepticism characteristic of his generation. His frequent allusions to the "impoverishments" of American culture, to the modern "spirit of negation," to the "death of the Gods," to an "age of disbelief," and a culture "dominated by science" reflect the intellectual pessimism of the post-Victorian decades. Although this side of Stevens has been minimized, or perhaps simply taken for granted, it is important to recognize it as the motivating force of his aestheticism, and in particular, of his romanticism. Stevens, himself, recognizes it many times in the course of his prose.

> The spirit of negation has been so active, so confident and so intolerant that the commonplaces about the romantic provoke us to wonder if our salvation, if the way out, is not the romantic. All the great things have been denied....[22]

If he is, as some have thought, "less depressed" than the rest of his generation, one might perhaps remark that he seems quite as much obsessed. His skepticism is appallingly thorough. It is, as this passage indicates, the mainstay of his poetic, and it is the element in his poetry which more than any other relates him to his generation.

It may be that Stevens' long literary career and his belated recognition as a major poet have tended to place him in distorted perspective. It is a little startling to find a poet who dominates the poetry of the midcentury referred to as a *fin de siècle* figure. But it is true that in many ways he bears a closer resemblance to William James and Henry Adams than to the Lost Generation. He came to maturity in the first years of the century. He was twenty-one when the century began, studying at Harvard and contributing poems to the *Harvard Advocate*. He was forty-three, already a middle-aged lawyer of a Hartford insurance firm, when *The Wasteland* appeared. Eliot's poem was thought to have set the tone of the twenties. Only in recent years have critics begun to observe that Stevens' most famous poem, *Sunday Morning,* had already expressed it.

The biographical facts which are usually regarded as significant are those which relate Stevens to the poetry revival led by Pound and Eliot: his association with Harriet Monroe and *Poetry,* his contributions to *Others* and similar avant-garde publications, his admiration for Eliot, his friendship with William Carlos Williams, his interest in the French Symbolists.[23] The facts are relevant, and certainly, the influence of the modernist movements is unmistakable; but it is surprising how rarely Stevens alludes to contemporary poets and critics in his prose. More often his allusions are to figures involved in the intellectual developments of the period, Freud, Bertrand Russell, A. J. Ayer, Henri Bergson, Benedetto Croce. Of special interest are the recurrent references to Harvard's famous faculty members—to Henry Adams, William James, George Santayana, Irving Babbitt, and Alfred North Whitehead. The list recalls a period when the long struggle between science and art obtained a new intensity in sharply contested philosophical issues. A later generation, aware of the issues involved, may nevertheless find it hard to appreciate the sense of crisis that permeated that first quarter-century. Joseph Wood Krutch's *The Modern Temper* is one of the classic indicators of the intellectual mood and is useful as a kind of nihilistic compendium of the period. In a later preface, Krutch summarized his despairing thesis:

> The universe revealed by science, especially the science of biology and psychology, is one in which the human spirit cannot find a comfortable home. That spirit breathes

freely only in a universe where what philosophers call Value Judgments are of supreme importance. It needs to believe, for instance, that right and wrong are real, that Love is more than a biological function, that the human mind is capable of reason rather than merely of rationalization, and that it has the power to will and to choose instead of being compelled merely to react in the fashion predetermined by its conditioning. Since science has proved that none of these beliefs is more than a delusion, mankind will be compelled either to surrender what we call its humanity by adjusting to the real world or to live some kind of tragic existence in a universe alien to the deepest needs of its nature.[24]

Several of the essays of *The Necessary Angel* were written as much as twenty years later, but their pages are haunted by the same intellectual defeatism that is typical of the early decades. Science remained for Stevens the arch enemy, the denigrator of human values in general and of the arts in particular. He conceives of the contemporary mind in the same terms as Krutch: confronted by a world no longer responsive to its needs, distraught by political and social pressures, alienated from any belief and from its natural environment. It is a world in which "all the great things have been denied," in which "we remember perhaps that the soul no longer exists," that "the end of philosophy is despair," and that "we have poetry, because without it we do not have enough." In a passage reminiscent of Henry Adams, who was his contemporary if not of his generation, Stevens describes the changes in American life during his lifetime:

First, then, there is the reality that is taken for granted, that is latent and, on the whole, ignored. It is the comfortable American state of the eighties, the nineties and the first ten years of the present century. Next, there is the reality that has ceased to be indifferent, the years when the Victorians had been disposed of and intellectual minorities and social minorities began to take their place and to convert our state of life to something that might not be final. This much more vital reality made the life that had preceded it look like a volume of Ackermann's colored plates or one of Topfer's books of sketches in Switzerland. I am trying to give the feel of it. It was the reality of twenty or thirty years ago. I say that it was a vital reality. The phrase gives a false impression. It was vital in the sense of being instinct with the fatal or with what might be the fatal. The minorities began to convince us that the Victorians had left nothing behind.[25]

To subsequent generations, one of the curious features of this period must be the widespread acceptance of its intellectual and spiritual destruction. Stevens exhibits this in his repeated elaborations of the predicament of the modern artist: "Boileau's remark that Descartes had cut poetry's throat is a remark that could have been made respecting a great many people during the last hundred years...."[26] But it is primarily in his references to science that the pessimism of the period is evident. Such references tend to be simply a cataloguing of ideas that the poet is bound to resist. Freud superseded Pascal in undermining the imagination. Logical positivism furthered the process by relegating art to the study of illusion. The distrust of the connotative values of language, initiated in the scientific movement of the seventeenth century, was revived by the twentieth. Modern physics, by adducing the quantum theory, abetted modern philosophy in the dissolution of matter. Finally, and most important, in the wake of its triumph over religion, science has focused upon the concept of man, of human nobility.[27] The recourse for art is summed up in one of the late essays.

> If we escape destruction at the hands of the logical positivists and if we cleanse the imagination of the taint of the romantic, we still face Freud. What would he have said of the imagination as the clue to reality and of a culture based on the imagination? Before jumping to the conclusion that at last there is no escape, is it not possible that he might have said that in a civilization based on science there could be a science of illusions? Moreover, if the imagination is not quite the clue to reality now, might it not become so then? As for the present what have we, if we do not have science, except for the imagination? And who is to say of its deliberate fictions arising out of the contemporary mind that they are not the forerunners of some such science?[28]

The notable feature of this passage is the all-inclusive dichotomy between science and art. The opposition is fundamental to Stevens' thinking. In a "culture based on science" the imagination is given exclusive salutary power. Its functions are associated here with "escape," "illusion," "deliberate fictions"—in short, with a conscious retreat to an imaginary world invincible to science.

It is helpful to return at this point to Krutch, this time to his conclusions regarding the state of modern philosophy:

> Certain minds, convinced that the triumphs of science were spiritually barren, set out to combat some of its deductions and to win for the humanistic conclusions of pure thought the right to assert the existence of spiritual verities denied or neglected by science. Instead of accomplishing this purpose the majority of these minds have ended, either by surrendering their freedom to dogmatic authority, or by retiring from the real world which they could not remold into some realm of Possibility whose purely fictional character they were willing to admit in exchange for the right to arrange those fictions into patterns more satisfactory than that which their triumphant enemy had revealed in all-embracing Nature. But when the subject matter of metaphysics is thus considered to be not what *is* but what *might* be, it becomes pure art, and the admission that the human spirit finds a home in art alone is exactly the admission which distinguishes modern despair.....[29]

Given the alternatives—dogmatic authority or a fictional world—Krutch would have found Stevens' choice of the latter, in contrast to Eliot's choice of the former, a typical reflection of the philosophical despair of his generation.

Romanticism and Modernity

Stevens' emphasis upon the poet's contemporaneity, coupled with the obvious modernity of his poetic style, has tended to obscure his more fundamental alliance with the romantic tradition. There are probably other reasons why the subject has not encouraged critical discussion. One is the difficulty of disengaging the romantic from the modernist tradition. There is also the imprecision of the romantic label and the highly charged connotations the term has acquired in some quarters. On the other hand it is misleading to suggest without qualification that Stevens' poetry is typically modernist. This is true whether modernist poetry means, in Mr. Allen Tate's sense, poetry that drives from the "revolution" in American poetry associated with Pound and Eliot,[30] or, more broadly, in Mr. J. V. Cunningham's sense, poetry that is "consciously different" from the preceding tradition.[31] In either sense Stevens' poetry is unquestionably modernist. But with respect to his major subject, the theory of poetry which his poems and prose elaborate, he is just as unquestionably romantic.

As a way of emphasizing this distinction, it is helpful to recall the literary situation at the time Stevens' first poems were beginning to appear. Lord David Cecil recently described the period as it culminated during the First World War:

> With the coming of peace...young writers felt less than ever able to rise above the discord of the romantic situation. What was the use of building citadels of imagination into which to retire from the onslaught of the hideous world? The world simply invaded them and broke them up. The romantic situation had become the romantic predicament. All the poet could do was to confront it, examine it, expose it. A mood of wry, unhopeful curiosity pervaded the mental atmosphere. To find words for it poets turned to the new modes of expression devised by Eliot and Yeats.[32]

Stevens shared with his contemporaries the breakdown in post-Paterian aestheticism and the exposure of the romantic predicament led by such influential spokesmen as Irving Babbitt and T. S. Eliot. The attendant reforms in American poetry did not constitute a total revolution in aesthetic theory, however. The Imagist movement, for example, aimed primarily at correctives in style rather than a re-examination of the intellectual tradition informing romantic doctrines. Edmund Wilson's comment that after Eliot romanticism meant "vague emotions vaguely expressed" is indicative of the focus of attack upon romanticism. The predominant concerns were negative in nature—the avoidance of emotional excess, the elimination of vapid abstractions, rhetorical spiritualizing, and sentimentality. The underlying philosophical issues of the romantic predicament tended to be submerged under the more superficial preoccupation with such stylistic reforms. Through T. E. Hulme, the Imagist movement did attach itself to new philosophical concepts deriving from Henri Bergson, but Bergson himself was fully within the aesthetic-philosophical tradition of romanticism, and Hulme's philosophical interests did not extend to a re-evaluation of that tradition. He was, like Pound, advocating a theory of composition aimed at "accurate, precise and definite description" as opposed to the "sloppiness" of romantic attitudes and diction. He thus contributed to the identification of the romantic label with stylistic imprecision, at the same time he was urging the retention of a fundamentally romantic aesthetic.[33]

Stevens was not unique in his awareness of this situation, but he parts company with most of his contemporaries in refusing to accept the romantic predicament as the modern dilemma which poets must tacitly accept and try to live with. He elected to defend the intellectual tradition of romantic poetry and to explore its basic assumptions. His prose and poetry alike show that the choice led to an increasingly narrow focus upon the core of the problem, the epistemology of the Kantian aesthetic as it was formulated primarily in Coleridge's theory of the imagination. Ultimately, the problem is an inextricable part of the epistemological issues descending from Kant and his German successors to modern idealism. These are subjects, however, for later chapters.

It is difficult, then, to distinguish with much precision between Stevens' romanticism and his modernity. The subject raises an issue by now a little threadbare: the extent to which modern criticism derives from the English Romantics of the early nineteenth century. Stevens has undoubtedly proved something of an embarrassment to those of his contemporaries who, having abandoned the problems of the romantic predicament, would prefer to forget them. He has a knack for converting a fashionable critical formula into something not quite so fashionable, something that sounds, it may be, like Shelley or Poe. Conversely, his attitude toward various modernist schools is notably detached; at most he offers sympathy toward all but adherence to none.

These characteristics emerge from one of the earliest essays, "The Irrational Element in Poetry." Ostensibly, the essay celebrates the contribution of modernist movements in defending the irrational in poetry. By irrational, Stevens apparently means all that is subjective, and hence for Stevens inexplicable in poetry—the definition is typically vague. In the course of the essay, however, Stevens offers with approval a general description of modern poetry as "poetry in which not the true subject but the poetry of the subject is paramount."[34] This might accord with Eliot's discussion some years earlier of poetry in which "truth ceases to matter," or I. A. Richards' theory of poetry as "pseudo-statement,"[35] but Stevens manages to defend the theory in terms as reminiscent of Poe as of Valéry:

> When we find in poetry that which gives us a momentary existence on an exquisite plane, is it necessary to ask the meaning of the poem? If the poem had a meaning and if its explanation destroyed the illusion, would we have gained or lost?[36]

This notion sounds remarkably like Poe's famous contention that lyric poetry should create momentary illusions of ideal beauty. The resemblance to Poe may well be explained by Stevens' admiration for the French Symbolists, themselves deeply influenced by Poe, but Stevens' flair for turning modernist theory back upon its unfashionable sources is consciously cultivated. Few modernists would appropriate, as he does in another essay, Shelley's description of the imagination, calling it "that imperial faculty whose throne is curtained within the invisible nature of man."[37]

In contrast, Stevens' references to modernist schools suggest only qualified approval. The imagist creed is treated as needlessly restrictive: "If you are an imagist, you make a choice of subjects that is obviously limited."[38] Mallarmé and Rimbaud are praised as "portentous influences" in giving the irrational "a legitimacy it never had before."[39] But Mallarmé's "pure poetry" is implicitly rejected along with the "pure poetry" of Henri Brémond and the surrealists. By comparison, his own position sounds remarkably conservative.

> Pure poetry is both mystical and irrational. If we descend a little from this height and apply the looser and broader definition of pure poetry, it is possible to say that, while it can lie in the temperament of very few of us to write poetry in order to find God, it is probably the purpose of each of us to write poetry to find the good which, in the Platonic sense, is synonymous with God. One writes poetry, then, in order to approach the good in what is harmonious and orderly.[40]

The passage is hardly a part of modernist canon, and it is oddly at variance with the notion that poetry may be a momentary illusion calculated to give us "momentary existence on an exquisite plane." It sounds very much like Santayana's formulation of poetry at the turn of the century, poetry which must become "the high Platonic road," the surrogate of religion which substitutes Platonic good for God "because the soul that receives that harmony welcomes it as the fulfillment of her natural ends."[41] Such passages are useful reminders that the modernist reforms in American poetry were events of Stevens' maturity, and that he was never so closely allied with the experimental revolution in American poetry as some have supposed. The modernist reforms, especially the reforms in style, are fully evident in the earliest volume of poetry, *Harmonium*, but these are often superimposed upon attitudes that suggest earlier and deeper ties with Harvard at the end of the century. The combination is perceptible in Stevens' aloofness from the doctrinaire zeal of modernist schools, and in an attitude which has affinities with the kind of spiritual *laissez faire* of Santayana's early aesthetic creed. It is better, as he remarks in this early essay on modernist poetry, not to "profess rigidly" or to be anything "in particular," but to "elect to remain free and to go about in the world experiencing whatever you happen to experience."[42]

The essays of *The Necessary Angel* document Stevens' subsequent recourse to basic romantic principles centered in his theory of the imagination. The theory itself will be considered in subsequent chapters. It is necessary at this point, however, to clarify certain misunderstandings that have been occasioned by Stevens' use of the term "romantic." He uses the term in both a favorable and unfavorable sense, and, to the bewilderment of several critics, the dual connotations are never explained in the course of *The Necessary Angel.* The distinction originates in a 1935 review of Marianne Moore's poetry. Miss Moore's imagery is described approvingly as "romantic," with the following explanation:

> At this point one very well might stop for definitions. It is clear enough, without all that, to say that the romantic in the pejorative sense merely connotes obsolescence, but the word has, or should have another sense.... True, when Professor Babbitt speaks of the romantic, he means the romantic. Romantic objects are things, like garden furniture or colonial lingerie or, not to burden the imagination, country millinery.
>
> Yes, but for the romantic in its other sense, meaning always the living and at the same time the imaginative, the youthful, the delicate and a variety of things which it is not necessary to try to particularize at the moment, constitutes the vital element in poetry. It is absurd to wince at being called a romantic poet. Unless one is that, one is not a poet at all..... Just what it means, Miss Moore's book discloses. It means, now-a-days, an uncommon intelligence. It means in a time like our own of violent feelings, equally violent feelings and the most skillful expression of the genuine.[43]

The reference to violent feeling in a time of violent feeling scarcely prepares the reader for the citation of Eliot as "the most brilliant instance of the romantic." Surely Mr. Eliot, an advocate of violent feeling, but a notorious opponent of the "romantic" on his own terms, must have "winced" a little. The review concludes with Stevens again worrying the term:

> The romantic that falsifies is rot and that is true even though the romantic inevitably falsifies: it falsifies but it does not vitiate. It is an association of the true and the false. It is not the true. It is not the false. It is both. The school of poetry that believes in sticking to the facts would be stoned if it was not sticking to the facts in a world in which there are no facts: or some such thing.[44]

The passage is characteristic of Stevens' stylistic mannerisms, his evasiveness and fondness for paradox, as well as his offhand reversion to skepticism. The possibility that when Professor Babbitt considered the romantic he was thinking of garden furniture may also give one pause. But the defensiveness with which the romantic label is advanced is significant, as is the distinction between an obsolescent and a modern romanticism. The distinction clarifies later discussions of the subject.

The first essay of *The Necessary Angel* invokes the romantic tradition in open defiance of its disrepute among the modernists. Interspersed with quotations from Bergson, Croce and Charles Mauron, are quotations from Coleridge's *Biographia Literaria* and Wordsworth's *Preface to the Lyrical*

Ballads. The function of the imagination is illustrated by a citation from Wordsworth's "London." It seems necessary to stress that these citations do not necessarily indicate the critical naïveté of which Stevens is sometimes accused. The juxtaposing of moderns and romantics is intended to expose the agreement between them and the hypocrisy of the modernists who deny it. If romanticism means escapism, for example, so does the modernist position:

> ...how is it possible to condemn escapism? The poetic process is psychologically an escapist process. The chatter about escapism is, to my way of thinking, merely common cant.[45]

The choice of spokesmen for the modernist viewpoint is no doubt biased, but the charge that contemporary criticism traffics surreptitiously in principles it overtly condemns has much to be said for it.

In later essays, Stevens usually defers to the prevailing connotations of "romantic," using it pejoratively:

> The imagination is one of the great human powers. The romantic belittles it. The imagination is the liberty of the mind. The romantic is a failure to make use of that liberty. It is to the imagination what sentimentality is to feeling.[46]

The comment is not developed. It has given support to critics like Louis Martz who argue that Stevens abandoned his early romantic views some time in the forties, emerging from this "middle period" toward a position which is regarded, depending upon the critic, as either more traditional or more modern.[47] Similar evidence is made of another passing remark that the imagination must be cleansed of its romantic "taint" and that "it is not worthy to survive if it is to be identified with the romantic."[48] On neither occasion, however, does Stevens indicate any distinction between his own theory of the imagination and romantic theory. The references to sentimentality and the taint of obsolescent romanticism reflect the stylistic reforms of the Imagists. Beyond this the passages give evidence of nothing more than the defensiveness with which Stevens advocates a theory of imagination which, in spite of its modernist elements, is largely indistinguishable from its romantic predecessors.

This would seem to be supported by one of Stevens' last essays in which he returns to his original distinction between obsolescent and modern romanticism. His defense of the romantic on this occasion is a restatement of his original comments in the review of Marianne Moore's poetry:

> It looks like something completely contemptible in the light of literary intellectualism and cynicism. The romantic, however, has a way of renewing itself. It can be said of the romantic, just as it can be said of the imagination, that it can never effectively touch the

same thing twice in the same way. It is partly because the romantic will not be what has been romantic in the past that it is preposterous to think of confining poetry hereafter to the revelation of reality. The whole effort of the imagination is toward the production of the romantic. When, therefore, the romantic is in abeyance, when it is discredited, it remains true that there is always an unknown romantic and that the imagination will not forever be denied.[49]

The passage was written in 1951, four years before Stevens' death. It is the conclusion of some three decades of struggle with the problems of the romantic aesthetic, and it profits from a greater sophistication. It concedes the cynicism that attended the exposure of the romantic predicament, and it does not propose that the romantic faith can be made intellectually defensible. Rather, it asserts what Stevens had asserted at the beginning: that there is no alternative for art. This is of interest in the light of the increasingly popular notion that Stevens' later poetry represents the evolution of a new theory of the imagination and the resolution of his aesthetic problems. One should notice that the argument here reverts to the traditional either/or proposition of the romantic predicament: either accept the imagination or confine poetry to "the revelation of reality." Reality means, of course, the reality of the scientific viewpoint; it means as Stevens had said some twenty years earlier, "sticking to the facts in a world in which there are no facts."

The same opposition between reality and the imagination is assumed in most modern criticism, but rarely in terms of an absolute dichotomy. The opposition, with its attendant difficulties, is more often veiled by that happiest of subterfuges, the assurance that the imagination affords "insights into reality," a phrase which may mean anything or nothing but which connotes something superior and valuable. In the case of Stevens the dualism has to be recognized; it is the basic dualism which governs his thinking, necessitates his acceptance of the romantic faith, and initiates the epistemological concerns that are the subject of his poetry.

For the literary historian the problem is all too familiar: once reality is delivered over to science, the mind is isolated. Reality becomes the objective world, exclusive of the mind, and scientific truth becomes absolute, even with the skeptical provision that "there are no facts." The poet is left with his unaided imagination, unable to make any valid claim upon the real world. He accepts, as Stevens sometimes does, the proposition that "reality is true, and the imagination is false, whatever else may be said of it."[50] His refuge becomes not reality but unreality, and the imagination becomes "the means by which we import the unreal into the real."[51] Such has been the historical development of modern poetry based upon the art-science antithesis initiated with the romantic theory of imagination. Historically,

Stevens is a descendant of the philosophical father of this tradition—
Coleridge. Since it is Coleridge who initiates the epistemological concerns
which are relevant to Stevens, their relation is the subject of the next two
chapters.

Coleridge and the Idealist Tradition

That Stevens' preoccupation with a theory of the imagination is reminiscent of Coleridge has been remarked by several critics. Mr. Kermode, who
is one of the few to stress the nineteenth-century origins of Stevens' aesthetic, refers to Coleridge in passing as "Stevens' direct ancestor."[1] Even
Robert Pack, whose study of Stevens neglects the tradition almost entirely,
notices that Stevens observes Coleridge's distinction between imagination
and fancy.[2] Most typical perhaps is William York Tindall's comment that
Stevens' interest in the imagination is "that of Coleridge and Baudelaire,"
but since Stevens never decided whether he was a romantic "the labels do
not matter."[3]

It is surprising that the obvious similarities between the two poets have
been given so little attention. It may be that since I. A. Richards' renova-
tion of the Coleridgean imagination, Coleridge's importance to modern
criticism is so widely acknowledged that the subject no longer elicits much
interest.[4] A passing comparison to Coleridge, like a comparison to Donne,
has become a conventional practice in literary name-dropping, an assurance that the modern critic or his modern poet has traveled through the
best historical circles. But in the case of Stevens, there is justification for
stressing the singular importance of Coleridge.

In Coleridge, the opposition between science and art, the opposition
that dominates subsequent aesthetic theory, takes up philosophical ground.
As the first English poet to give the romantic aesthetic its philosophical
bearings, Coleridge remains a major expositor of the romantic predicament. His relevance to modern criticism has been acknowledged at least
since Babbitt and has been periodically reexamined. There is, for example,
Mr. M. H. Abrams' study of romantic aesthetic in *The Mirror and the
Lamp*. Abrams' thesis is that the chief contribution of romantic criticism to
modern theory was its development of an aesthetic based upon a revolutionary concept of mind. In place of the traditional view of the mind as a
passive reflector of the external world (the Lockean mirror), romantic

critics substituted a "projective and creative mind" (the Coleridgean lamp). While he traces important eighteenth-century precedents, Abrams attributes this revolution in critical thought to Coleridge:

> In all essential aspects, Coleridge's theory of mind, like that of contemporary German philosophers, was, as he insisted, revolutionary; it was in fact, part of a change in the habitual way of thinking, in all areas of intellectual enterprise, which is as sharp and dramatic as any the history of ideas can show.[5]

The union of a theory of mind with a theory of poetry meant, as Abrams thoroughly documents, a radical change in subsequent tradition. Issue will be taken later on with some of his conclusions about Coleridge. There is no quarrel, however, with his major thesis nor with the statement with which he introduces his study: "The development of literary theory in the lifetime of Coleridge was to a surprising extent the making of the modern critical mind."[6] The relation of Stevens to Coleridge, as it will be developed here, assumes the same principle of continuity but in a somewhat different focus.

The theory of mind which unites both romantic and modern aesthetic traditions derives, as Coleridge indicates throughout the *Biographia Literaria,* from the German idealists, primarily from Kant. It is also through the German philosophers that modern aesthetic became implicated in the epistemological problems of philosophical idealism. And it is here, as a revolutionary theory of knowledge rather than a revolutionary theory of art, that the full implications of the Coleridgean aesthetic are realized.

Philosophical idealism admits of course of many variations—Platonic, Berkeleyan, Kantian, and a number of modern variants. The foundations of "modern idealism" are usually attributed to Berkeley (at least in the English tradition) as the precursor of Kant, but it is Kant who is the universally acknowledged father of modern idealism. The term, "modern idealism," then, should be understood here to refer to the broad philosophical tradition descending from Kant to the present. Its distinguishing feature is the acceptance of a common epistemological theory. This is the theory that the knowable world, the sensible world, the world of objects, does not exist independent of the mind. Modern idealism thus represents the epistemological antithesis of modern realism, sometimes called "naive realism," which takes as its base the theory that the world of objects is ultimately independent of any knowledge of its existence.[7] To put the distinction more simply: When a realist enters the room, he assumes that the table he sees is the same table that was in the room before he entered; when an idealist enters the room, he assumes that the table he *sees* did not exist until he entered the room and perceived it. It does not follow that the idealist believes that there was nothing at all in the room before he entered—here a variety of explanations are possible. He maintains only that the object he *sees* is wholly the product of mental activity, an objectification of the mind's content, a mental creation. The relation between the mental table and a physical table external to the mind permits a wide range of explanation. At one extreme, the subjective idealist may deny any necessary relation at all, committing himself to a pure solipsism in which there is no reality beyond the individual mind. The more conservative or "objective" idealist insists upon the interdependence of mind and matter, subject and object. The *Encyclopaedia Britannica* elaborates upon this more common interpretation.

> Idealism as a philosophical doctrine conceives of knowledge or experience as a process in which the two factors of subject and object stand in a relation of entire interdependence on each other as warp and woof. Apart from the activity of the self or subject in sensory reaction, memory and association, imagination, judgment and inference, there can be no world of objects. A thing-in-itself which is not a thing to some consciousness is an entirely unrealizable, because self-contradictory, conception.... It is in becoming permeated and transformed by the mind's ideas that the world develops the fullness of its reality as object.[8]

Needless to say, epistemological idealism has had profound influence upon the development of modern philosophy. To the question of whether the nature of reality is knowable, it directed attention from the external world to the mind as percipient. As one of its twentieth-century proponents somewhat understated the matter, it gave "a privileged position to mind."[9] The cost of that privilege, however, was that the mind's hold upon a physical world had become extremely precarious. Once the reality of an independent physical world was regarded as an outmoded illusion, the question became whether the reality of a mental world was not also illusion. Thus the privileged position of mind has involved modern philosophy in a preoccupation with theories of knowledge from which it has yet to recover. H. H. Price remarked some years ago that the problem had so dominated English philosophy that it was referred to by continental philosophers as the English "national pastime."[10] The preoccupation is understandable. At the epistemological level, what is at stake is a common sensible world, a common object of knowledge and thought, the loss of which means solipsism. At the metaphysical level, the stake is material reality, the loss of which means a metaphysical monism in which all reality is mind. The ultimate problem, however, is the epistemological one, for once the reality of an independent external world is excluded from a theory of knowledge, it is obviously difficult to sustain that reality at an ontological level. In both respects, modern idealism has found its inherent danger to be the solipsistic predicament of mind alone.

Finally, there is the manner in which idealism has taken up residence in modern aesthetics. Here, the significant figure is Coleridge and, as Abrams says, his "revolutionary theory of mind." The theory of a "projective and creative" mind is, of course, an aesthetic restatement of epistemological idealism, of the doctrine that the sensible world is the product of mental creativity; and the transposition of this doctrine from philosophy to aesthetics is formally accomplished by Coleridge. The subsequent development of nineteenth-century aesthetic, which is the concern of Mr. Abrams' book, need not be considered here. In anticipation of later chapters certain twentieth-century developments should be mentioned.

The first is the peculiarly congenial ground afforded modern idealism by the twentieth-century interest in psychology, especially in the unconscious. In his analysis of modern aesthetic in the *Grammar of Motives,* Mr. Kenneth Burke has stressed the close connection between idealism and psychology.

> Because of its stress upon agent, idealism leads readily into both individual and group psychology. Its close connections with epistemology, or the problem of knowledge is due to the same bias. For to approach the universe by asking ourselves how knowledge is possible is to ground our speculations psychologistically, in the nature of the knower.[11]

Second, there is the diffusive character of aesthetic idealism in contemporary literature, its accretion of diverse sources and influences, and its varied expression. Here again, Mr. Burke offers a good illustration of its diversity:

> The variants in esthetic theory stress such terms as "sensibility," "expression," "self-expression," "consciousness" and the "unconscious." The Crocean philosophy has been prominent as a bridge between metaphysical and esthetic idealism. In his preface to *The Protrait of a Lady,* Henry James gives us a characteristically idealistic statement when referring to "the artist's prime sensibility" as the "soil out of which his subject springs" and which "grows" the work of art. Here a book is treated as an act grounded in the author's mind as its motivating scene....[12]

Had Burke chosen an illustration from modern poetry, he might have used Eliot's famous description of the poet's mind as a catalytic agent or, for a more extreme position, Wallace Stevens' much quoted reference to the imagination as "the one reality in this imagined world." But behind such modern variants, at the core of the matter, is the far more celebrated quotation from the fourteenth chapter of the *Biographia Literaria.*

> The primary imagination I hold to be the living Power and prime Agent of all human Perception, and as a repetition in the finite mind of the eternal act of creation in the infinite I AM.[13]

These quotations, spanning some century-and-a-half, attest to the flexibility of aesthetic idealism. The theory of the world-building power of the artist has accommodated almost as much variation as its epistemological counterpart in philosophy, ranging from Coleridge as its conservative pole to the French Symbolists at its radical extreme. The tradition has been the aesthetic harbor of both romantic faith and modern skepticism. This is nowhere more apparent than in the modern rediscovery of Coleridge by critics who, excluding Coleridge's "eternal act of creation in the infinite I AM," have had no difficulty endorsing its "repetition in the finite mind."

Finally, the tendency of twentieth-century critical theorists has been to divorce aesthetic idealism from its philosophical sources, to regard the principle of the creative mind simply as a compositional theory. The consequence has been the development of the notion of autonomous art corresponding to the solipsistic predicament which remains the inherent problem of philosophical idealism. So viewed, aesthetic theory can become little more than an emphasis upon subjectivity, non-rational mental processes, and undefinable "aesthetic" values. At worst, it becomes a support for pure relativism and artistic irresponsibility. Reduced to a mental process independent of a common sensible world, artistic creation becomes a solipsistic pursuit, unmitigated by common experience or preestablished artistic standards. These are dangers which confront any modern poet who subscribes to some variation of aesthetic idealism. If he chooses to avoid them, to defend the relevance and value of his art, he may find himself in intellectual quicksand. He may agree with Alfred North Whitehead that "with the exception of those who are content with themselves as forming the entire universe, solitary amid nothing, everyone wants to struggle back to some sort of objectivist position."[14] But the history of modern philosophy would indicate that the struggle back is not easy, as would the example of his famous predecessor Samuel Coleridge.

The subject of Coleridge's alliance with German idealism is well-worn ground. It will be necessary, however, to trace one or two beaten paths in order to show how, in Abrams' phrase, a "revolutionary theory of mind" initiated the epistemological problems underlying modern aesthetics.

To begin, then, with Coleridge: The series of oppositions by which romanticism is commonly schematized can be attributed to a variety of causes. Generally, the opposition of art to science and scientific rationalism is considered primary. The resulting polarities, which with few modifications remain the modern ones, posit on the one side reason, fact, matter, truth, denotation, objectivity; and on the other side imagination (or intuition), emotion, spirit, "higher" truth (or insight), connotation, subjectivity. Coleridge chose to regard the romantic oppositions in terms of the Cartesian dualism of mind and matter (subject and object). Having made the ominous discovery that the poet's problems were the philosopher's problems, he traced the Cartesian evolution into two antithetical traditions: empiricism and idealism. Under duress from science, art was naturally gravitating toward idealism. What Coleridge found in German idealism, however, was not an escape from science but the hope of compromise. It was Kant who offered the greatest hope "for establishing and pacifying the unsettled, warring, and embroiled domain of philosophy."[15] To this same end, Coleridge's quarrel with Hartley became an attack upon the empirical tradition of English philosophy reaching back to Locke, and also an attempt to avoid the more radical forms of idealism, epitomized for him by Berkeley, but reaching back to Plato and forward to the post-Kantian Fichte. His aim was to establish, as Kant had tried to do, a middle ground which could effectively unite the antithetical Cartesian factions.

Upon this middle ground he hoped to erect his aesthetic. The key stages in its development, in so far as they can be extracted from the tortuous progression of the *Biographia,* begin significantly with the statement of the epistemological problem:

> To the best of my knowledge Des Cartes was the first philosopher, who introduced the absolute and essential heterogeneity of the soul as intelligence, and the body as matter.... The soul was a *thinking* substance; and the body a space-filling substance. Yet the apparent action of each on the other pressed heavy on the philosopher on the one hand; and no less heavily on the other hand pressed the evident truth, that the law of causality holds only between homogeneous things, i.e. things having some common property; and cannot extend from one world into another, its opposite.[16]

Hence Coleridge concludes that the empirical tradition of science cannot explain the intelligibility of its own world, which is wholly the world of matter; whereas idealism — that is, the metaphysical idealism of Berkeley — destroys the physical world by spiritualizing matter as mental phenomena in order to make it intelligible.

Accepting Descartes' *cogito, ergo sum* as the ground of philosophical certainty, Coleridge followed Kant onto psychological ground, regarding the problem as one of knowing rather than of being. The mind itself must furnish the principle by which matter and mind, objective and subjective, could be reconciled:

> Both conceptions are in necessary antithesis. Intelligence is conceived as exclusively representative, nature as exclusively represented; the one as conscious, the other as without consciousness. Now in all acts of positive knowledge there is required a reciprocal concurrence of both, namely of the conscious being, and of that which is in itself unconscious. Our problem is to explain this concurrence, its possibility and its necessity.[17]

What was required for this concurrence was a faculty similar to Kant's faculty of "sensible intuition," which established perception as a compromise between matter and mind. For Coleridge, this faculty was the Primary Imagination, the seat of consciousness and the "Agent of all human Perception." It is here, as Abrams says, that a revolutionary theory of mind enters literary theory. Perception becomes a creative activity. As Coleridge, himself, summarized it, "The pith of my system is to make the senses out of the mind — not the mind out of the senses, as Locke did."[18] But it is also the point at which modern aesthetic assumes Kant's epistemological legacy.

According to Kant, the mind passively recorded sense data, but actively interpreted the data in terms of time and space to yield perception. Time and space, however, were merely *a priori* mental "conditions," having no existence outside the mind. They were the necessary, albeit unreal, conditions which the mind had to impose upon sense data in order to construct the empirical world of appearances or phenomena. Coleridge, for good reason, tried to avoid these conclusions. One of the significant passages in the *Biographia* is that in which he recognizes the implications of following Kant.

> In spite therefore of his own declarations, I could never believe, that it was possible for him to have meant no more by his *Noumenon,* or THING IN ITSELF, than his mere words express; or that in his own conception he confined the whole *plastic* power to the forms of the intellect, leaving for the external cause, for the *materiale* of our sensations, a matter without form, which is doubtless inconceivable.[19]

What Coleridge recognizes is that Kant's creative mind denied the possibility of a knowable world. If the intellect was the formal principle imposed upon sense data, then sensible reality exclusive of the mind was nothing but a chaos of sense data. This was the fatal paradox of the Kantian compromise: perception was grounded empirically in sense data, but knowledge was grounded idealistically in mental phenomena. Ultimately all thought had to rest upon the sensible world, but ultimately the sensible world was unintelligible. Thus, for Kant, the true nature of things had to reside in an unknowable world, the unconditioned (without time and space) world of things-in-themselves:

> To avoid all misapprehension, it is necessary to explain, as clearly as possible, what our view is regarding the fundamental constitution of sensible knowledge in general.
>
> What we have meant to say is that all our intuition is nothing but the representation of appearance; that the things which we intuit are not in themselves what we intuit them as being, nor their relations so constituted in themselves as they appear to us, and that if the subject, or even only the subjective constitution of the senses in general, be removed, the whole constitution and all the relations of objects in space and time, nay space and time themselves, would vanish. As appearances, they cannot exist in themselves, but only in us. What objects may be in themselves, and apart from all this receptivity of our sensibility, remains completely unknown to us.[20]

Coleridge turned to Schelling, who by stressing the identity of subject and object in an indissoluble perceptual act, had hoped to be rid of the epistemological question.

> During the act of knowledge itself, the objective and subjective are so instantly united, that we cannot determine to which of the two the priority belongs. There is here no first, and no second; both are coinstantaneous and one.[21]

The question of priority was scarcely the important one. If there is no first and no second, then we can never know the nature of the first; and consequently we can never distinguish an external reality from our mental interpretation of it. And how then can we trust our mental interpretation? Coleridge had seen the trouble at the beginning. He had pointedly assured his readers that there was no trouble at all. It was true, he admitted, that the realist position was metaphysically untenable. It could not be otherwise, for knowledge had been grounded in the mind of the knower by the acceptance of the Cartesian *cogito*. In order to maintain some grasp upon the external world, the realist position had simply to be assumed. The assumption could be made easier, however, if it were regarded not as a groundless one, but as already implicit in the self-evident *cogito* of the idealists:

> Now the apparent contradiction, that the former position, namely, the existence of things without us, which from its nature cannot be immediately certain, should be received as blindly and as independently of all grounds as the existence of our own being, the transcendental philosopher can solve only by the supposition, that the former is unconsciously involved in the latter; that it is not only coherent but identical, and one and the same thing with our own immediate self-consciousness.[22]

A realist would have understandable difficulty in comprehending how the external world could be granted an independent existence by virtue of its being "unconsciously involved" in his own self-consciousness. Coleridge, who is here following Schelling, adopts the two crucial epistemological developments of German idealism after Kant. If mind was to supply the criterion of certainty, i.e. the consciousness of the thinking self, it was natural to conclude that the certainty of an external world depended upon its identification with mind. Moreover, as with self-consciousness, this identification of knower and known was possible only in immediate experience.

> If, therefore, this be the one only immediate truth, in the certainty of which the reality of our collective knowledge is grounded, it must follow that the spirit in all the objects which it views, views only itself. If this could be proved, the immediate reality of all intuitive knowledge would be assured.[23]

The implications of this doctrine, with its dual emphasis upon identification and immediacy will be recurrent themes in subsequent chapters. It is sufficient here to note that Coleridge was well aware that his position was dangerously close to the egocentric predicament of Berkeleyan idealism. He would have understood better than many of his interpreters the full meaning of Professor Gilson's remark: "Everyone is free to decide whether he shall begin to philosophize as a pure mind; if he should elect to do so the difficulty will be not how to get into the mind, but how to get out of it."[24]

Coleridge did what he could to forestall the collapse of his aesthetic into a metaphysical monism. He argued that the existence of objects external to the mind is "unconsciously involved" in the idealistic notion of consciousness, and he rejected Kant's theory that the sensible world supplied nothing to perception but unarticulated sense data. Beyond this he could only abandon the role of philosopher to plead in the name of common sense that "it is the table itself which the man of common sense believes himself to see."[25] Just so, of course, Samuel Johnson declared he had refuted Berkeley by kicking a stone — but Johnson was not at the time proposing an aesthetic based upon the assumption that it was not, in truth, the real stone that he kicked.

Thus Coleridge in the summary "theses" upon which he proposes to base his aesthetic, concludes that the problem raised by Kant as to the external ground of the phenomenal world is not properly the concern of the transcendental philosopher.

> The transcendental philosopher does not inquire, what ultimate ground of our knowledge there may lie out of our knowing, but what is the last in our knowing itself, beyond which *we* cannot pass.[26]

And since we cannot pass out of the mind, upon which "the reality of our collective knowledge is grounded, it must follow that the spirit in all the objects which it views, views only itself."[27]

In addition to its inherent difficulties, Kant's theory of perception had disastrous implications for reason. For Kant, the rational faculty, composed of the Understanding and Pure Reason, was limited to the organization and unification of sense phenomena. It might suffice for practical purposes, but on the one hand, since it had no basis in the real world of physical objects, it could tell nothing about their actual nature; and on the other hand, its efforts to transcend the sensible world as a speculative instrument, to determine the ultimate nature of things through metaphysical dialectic, was illusory. In so far as ideas are independent of the sensible world (given *a priori*), they are regulative only, not constitutive, and their application does not extend beyond the sensible world.[28] The empirical limitations which Kant thus imposed upon knowledge, pointed out to his successors the necessity of a new faculty. Since the whole system rested

upon its epistemological base—its revolutionary theory of a creative mind—
it could not be opened out at the bottom. The alternative was to open it at
the top, and for this purpose Kant's "Pure Reason" became the faculty of
pure (intellectual rather than sensible) intuition, empowered to do exactly
what Kant had insisted it could not do—transcend the limitations of time
and space by the immediate apprehension of an absolute or ultimate reality.
It was empowered "not merely to imagine, postulate or believe in, but to
know, with the most indubitable kind of knowledge, a realm of realities
other than that of sense-experience, and not subject to the categories and
laws which hold good of the sensible world."[29]

The importance of this faculty, beyond the fact that it provided access
to an absolute reality beyond appearances, was that in transcending the
world conditioned by time and space it also transcended the law of causality to which Kant's theory of knowledge was committed. For Kant, no
freedom could be allowed to a temporal world in which every event was the
necessary result of antecedent causes. Yet since freedom was a necessary
postulate of his treatment of morals in the second Critique, the *Critique of
Practical Reason,* Kant had to grant the knowledge of one thing-in-itself,
the Noumenal Self or Ego, which in a non-temporal realm was capable of
freedom, although in the temporal world it could not be.[30] This difficult
conception of a self that was inwardly free yet outwardly (in its visible
actions) committed to the mechanistic laws of the universe led naturally
enough to the notion that freedom was manifested only as mental activity
or "creativity." Moreover, since the source of this freedom lay in a non-
temporal reality, the mind had to have a faculty capable of apprehending
that reality. Thus the distinction between the Understanding, the rational
faculty governing sense perception, and the Pure Reason, as the intuitive
faculty of a supersensible realm, became for Coleridge, like many others, a
fundamental distinction based on a difference in kind rather than degree.

> Until you have mastered the fundamental difference, in kind, between the reason and
> the understanding as faculties of the human mind, you cannot escape a thousand diffi-
> culties in philosophy. It is pre-eminently the *Gradus ad Philosophiam.*[31]

In his reference to this distinction Coleridge repeatedly stresses the inherent
incompatibility of the two faculties. In *Aids to Reflection* he observes that
"the test of the truth of Reason is that it cannot be translated by the understanding"; it is a "truth *beyond* conception and inexpressible."[32] In the *Lay
Sermons* he remarks that not only do the "doctrines of the pure and intuitive reason transcend the understanding," but they "can never be contemplated by it, but through a false and falsifying perspective."[33] In *Table
Talk* the abrogative power of the higher faculty is stressed. The notions of
the Understanding are "contemplated" by the Reason, "and, as it were

looked down upon from the throne of actual ideas, or living, inborn, essential truths."[34] It is also evident that the incompatibility of these two faculties derives from the incompatibility of their respective worlds, the one being mechanistic and the other being organic, the timeless realm of the "universal," the "all," the "One." Understanding, Coleridge explains, is concerned with concepts as they relate merely to the "particular and individual," whereas Reason is appointed to consider "the individual, as it exists and has its being in the universal."

> The reason on the other hand, is the science of the universal, having the ideas of oneness and allness as its two elements or primary factors.... The reason first manifests itself in man by the tendency to the comprehension of all as one.[35]

Thus Coleridge, appealing to "the Immediate in everyman," joined the bargainers with Kant for whom pure intuition supplied the only satisfactory escape from a temporal mechanism. But the crucial problem, especially for the artist, was not so much the ascent of the transcendental summit, as the problem of reclaiming some hold upon a sensible world. One should not have to return like the Ancient Mariner to fix an impatient audience with the tale of what he had seen. The empirical basis of Kant's epistemology, remained, however, an unnegotiable barrier; one returned to the same world he had left, the world of science, mechanism, and specious appearances, where objects, as Coleridge said, "are essentially fixed and dead."[36] From this viewpoint, the effort to unify matter and mind, object and subject, appeared to have ended by dramatizing their incompatibility. Coleridge's recourse, paralleling the continental reaction, was to aesthetics, specifically to Schelling's theory of the *natura naturans*. Schelling's theory was an attempt to restore the impaired connection between mind and the physical world by proposing that both mind and nature partook in some mysterious way of a common spiritual realm. But since the spiritual forms of nature could not be inherent in specious appearances, they had to find their true subsistence in the mind. Thus appearances became related to mind as symbol to reality, and the poet stepped in to save the metaphysician. By meditating upon the symbol, supplied by the primary imagination, the secondary imagination "dissolves, diffuses, dissipates, in order to recreate" the true reality. Coleridge provides the identifying formula of romantic aesthetic:

> Now so to place these images [of nature] totalized, and fitted to the limits of the human mind, as to elicit from, and to superinduce upon, the forms themselves the moral reflections to which they approximate, to make the external internal, the internal external, to make nature thought, and thought nature—this is the mystery of genius in the Fine Arts.[37]

One should notice how thoroughly idealized the procedure has become. Nature is treated not as external reality but as appearance, a perceptual "image"; as image it is "fitted to the limits of the human mind," after which moral reflections are intuited either from the image or the mind itself, and the two are mentally identified or fused. As Coleridge says, nature becomes thought; but thought does not become nature in the sense of a reality external to the mind. Reality is the end product of three creative acts, perception, intuition, and the artistic transformation by which they are fused. A more explicit account of this view of the relation between mind and nature occurs in *Anima Poetae.*

> In looking at the objects of Nature while I am thinking, as at yonder moon dim-glimmering through the dewy window-pane, I seem rather to be seeking, as it were asking for, a symbolical language for something within me that already and for ever exists, than observing anything new. Even when the latter is the case, yet still I have always an obscure feeling as if that new phenomena were the dim awaking of a forgotten or hidden truth of my inner nature. It is still interesting as *a word—a symbol.* (italics added)[38]

This is the typical post-Kantian pattern of German philosophy which Kenneth Burke has described:

> In any event, from the time of Fichte the pattern of idealism pure and simple was set. With varying terms such philosophers as Schelling, Hegel, and Schopenhauer traced the geneology of the objective world from the subjective, treating nature as an externalization or expression of spirit somewhat as a poem may be called an externalization of the poet. Nature being thus viewed as the incarnation or embodiment of mind, the pattern was edifying in Fichte, esthetic in Schelling, optimistic in Hegel, and pessimistic in Schopenhauer.... [39]

The instigation of this pattern meant, as another writer has characterized it, the "steady devaluation of the created [i.e., physical] world" and the concomitant "promotion of the aesthetic faculty to the minister of the Absolute."[40] Nature was relegated as Coleridge saw to an "interesting symbol." A further difficulty was that the same mind that had created that symbol had to defend its reality as certain and then repudiate its reality (as the ground of our merely "notional understanding") in order to recreate it in accordance with its own certainty of a higher reality. Coleridge eventually recognizes in the *Biographia* that his aesthetic had slipped from an epistemological to a metaphysical idealism, but given Kant's epistemology, there seemed to be no other way to relate sensibility to intelligence.[41] Shawcross, who focuses upon this philosophical dilemma in his introduction to the *Biographia,* points out that Coleridge was never able to find in Schelling's *natura naturans* a solution short of pantheism on the one hand, materialism on the other.

Thus Schelling's spiritual intuition of a spiritual reality becomes the merely intellectual apprehension of a bare abstraction; and nature, deprived of its animating principle is opposed to intelligence in an absolute antithesis, of which each term precludes and yet necessitates the other. The materialistic implications of such a conception were bound, sooner or later, to reveal themselves to Coleridge. In later years he wrote of the *Transcendental Idealism:* "The more I reflect, the more convinced I am of the gross materialism of the whole system!" The same conviction led him, in 1818, to class Schelling with Spinoza among the pantheists; and this because "the inevitable result of all consequent reasoning in which the intellect refuses to acknowledge a higher or deeper ground than it can itself supply—and weens to possess within itself the centre of its own system—is Pantheism."[42]

These are conclusions that modern criticism, so heavily invested in Kantian aesthetic, has strenuously resisted. The dominant modern position, which will need to be considered presently, is that art is autonomous, and hence aesthetic stands independent of philosophy. But the autonomy of art is simply an extension of the conclusion at which Coleridge arrives here—the solipsism of the mind. The mind is isolated the moment one accepts the Kantian theory of perception and tries to construct from it more than the empirical world of appearances.

From this philosophical structure, Coleridge comes, then, to the deduction of his aesthetic faculty, the Secondary Imagination, and it is important to notice that in the *Biographia* and elsewhere this faculty is united to Pure Reason. As a joint faculty of the supersensible the Imagination serves to objectify or "externalize" the otherwise inexpressible truths of the Pure Reason:

... that which neither refers to outward factors, nor yet is abstracted from the forms of perception contained in the understanding, but which is an educt of the imagination actuated by the pure reason, to which *there neither is nor can be an adequate correspondent in the world of the senses*—this and this alone is—an idea.[43]

And in *Table Talk,* the two faculties provide the same distinction between men of talent and men of genius which underlies the extensive discussion of genius in art in the *Biographia.* "Talent, lying in the understanding, is often inherited; genius, being the action of reason and imagination, rarely or never."[44] Men of mere talent differ from men of genius because they are content to appropriate and apply the knowledge of others; unlike men of genius they are unable to objectify the truths of their "own living spirit" (i.e. the truths of Pure Reason):

While the former rest content between thought and reality as it were in an intermundium of which their own living spirit supplies the *substance,* and their imagination the ever-varying *form;* the latter must impress their preconceptions on the world without, in order to present them back to their own view with the satisfying degree of clearness, distinctness, and individuality.[45]

The description of genius here anticipates Coleridge's later adaptation of Schelling in which he concludes that the function of intelligence is to "objectize itself" and to "know itself in the object."[46] More interesting, however, is his reference to an "intermundium" between substance and form which only the power of genius can resolve. Thus it is only the genius who possesses the power to make "nature thought, and thought nature."

After all the arguments of the *Biographia,* Coleridge's revolutionary aesthetic, with its revolutionary theory of mind, left him still haunted by the dilemma of Berkeley. In "The Art of Poesy" he comes to this somewhat remarkable conclusion:

> For all we see, hear, feel and touch the substance is and must be in ourselves; and therefore there is no alternative in reason between the dreary (and thank heaven! almost impossible) belief that everything around us is but a phantom, or that the life which is in us is in them likewise; and that to know is to resemble, when we speak of objects outside of ourselves, even as within ourselves to learn is, according to Plato, only to recollect....[47]

With the admission that the substance of sense must lie "in ourselves," a long metaphysical road seemed simply to lead back to Berkeley, who as Coleridge had said "removes all reality and immediateness of perception, and places us in a dream world of phantoms and spectres, the inexplicable swarm...in our own brains."[48] Without rational sanctions, without an external world that was meaningful or knowable, Coleridge's promised ground of certainty became the romantic faith in the "mystery of art." Ultimately, the secondary imagination could stand only upon a faith in its divine sanction. Coleridge in his later years concluded that the epistemological problem had no solution. The relation between mind and the external world "is a mystery which of itself should suffice to make us religious; for it is a problem of which God is the only solution."[49] And God would not deceive us. But as some pious philosopher once replied to the same argument, men had always proved capable of doing that for themselves.

The difficulty with the theory of divine sanction, of course, is that it left the poet no way of distinguishing between the "eternal act of creation," and his own creative enterprise. Left to spiritualize a world from which spiritual reality had withdrawn, the imagination took over the functions of divinity. A pious critic like Coleridge might pay lip service to his divine sanction, but when he sought the true world-building power there was no place to look but in his own mind. The consequences for Romantic poetry have been summarized by C. M. Bowra:

> The fact is that the Romantics are concerned with a mystery which belongs not to faith but to the imagination. It is not something outside themselves which they try to realize, but something which they create largely by their own efforts. Even when they feel them-

selves in the presence of "eternity," it is not entirely external, but has many connections with their own selves. Their approach to the Beyond and the invisible powers which enclose the visible is determined by their conviction that in the last resort the only reality is mind, and that even the universal mind is manifested in individual minds.[50]

Mr. Bowra is describing what he finds to be characteristic of romantic poetry generally. He is not concerned with Coleridge's struggle with Kant. It is Coleridge, however, who worries away at the core of the problem, and who explains why it is that "in the last resort the only reality is mind." Behind what is often regarded as mere pretentiousness — the elaborate arguments for the imagination's objectivity, the claims to a "corrected" realism, the contempt for Fichte, the ridicule of Berkeley — lies the growing surmise that if in "the last resort" the only reality is mind, it is because in the first resort the only reality was mind, the Cartesian *cogito.*

> That which we find in ourselves is (gradu mutato) the substance and the life of all our knowledge. Without this latent presence of the "I am," all modes of existence in the external world would flit before us as coloured shadows, with no greater depth, root, or fixture, than the image of a rock hath in a gliding stream.... [51]

In modern theory the need for divine sanction would be replaced by the doctrine of autonomous art, ruled over by its proper divinity, the poet himself. Before this development, however, aesthetic idealism reached its radical extreme with the French Symbolists, by whom the creative mind was charged with the destruction of the world of appearances. The Symbolists represent the ultimate fruition of idealist assumptions, the conscious derangement of those faculties which Kant and his successors had consigned to empirical modes of knowledge, perception and "understanding." It is noteworthy that an earlier Frenchman, Flaubert, had anticipated something of this development when, with the Devil as his spokesman, he tempted his Saint Anthony:

> Mais les choses ne t'arrivent que par l'intermédiare de ton esprit. Tel qu'un miroir concave il déforme les objets; — et tout moyen te marque pour en vérifier l'exactitude.
>
> Jamais tu ne connâitras l'univers dans sa pleine étendue; par conséquent tu ne peux te faire une idée de sa cause, avoir une notion juste de Dieu, ni même dire que l'univers est infini, — car il faudrait d'abord connâitre l'Infini!
>
> La Forme est peut-être une erreur de tes sens, la substance une imagination de ta pensée.
>
> A moins que le monde étant un flux perpétuel des choses, l'apparence au contraire ne soit tout ce qu'il y a de plus vrai, l'illusion la seule réalité?
>
> Mais es-tu sûr de voir? es-tu même sûr de vivre? Peut-être qu'il n'y a rien! [52]

The road to modern skepticism would appear, in this passage at least, to be paved with Kantian theory. The mind is conceived as a deforming mirror, the inescapable intermediary between man and an external world.

Thus the external world can afford him no means of certainty. If he turns to the spiritual world for reassurance, he finds that here, too, certainty is beyond the reach of his finite mind (limited, as Kant maintained, by the conditions of time and space). As a consequence, form (for Kant, the mental interpretation of sense data) may be no more than a trick of perception; and the notion of a reality behind the phenomenal world may be a mere illusion. Flaubert's passage is a remarkably concise summary of the basis laid by Kant for the subsequent development of modern skepticism. It is not a great distance from the Devil's sinister conclusion—"Peut-être qu'il n'y a rien!—" to Mallarmé's celebrated remark that after having found Nothingness, he had found the Beautiful.

The Symbolist movement is usually regarded as a foreign development which was never fully assimilated into English and American traditions in spite of its considerable influence. The movement was, nevertheless, a significant manifestation of nineteenth century idealism under the increasing stress of empiricism and skepticism. It is important to recognize the continuity of this tradition, especially since Stevens is more often associated with the Symbolists than with Coleridge.[53] Stevens was not a Symbolist, however, and for the purpose of isolating the epistemological problem with which he was concerned, Coleridge is the relevant figure.

Before considering the relation between Stevens and Coleridge, something should be said about the adaptation of Coleridge's aesthetic in modern criticism. It is commonly observed that no other figure has had so much influence upon modern criticism. One should not suppose from this, however, that the problems raised by the *Biographia,* those which have been outlined here, have been settled to everyone's satisfaction, or even that their resolution remains a pressing concern. The procedure has been, rather, to avoid such matters altogether by the simple expedient of extracting Coleridge's theory of the imagination from its philosophical context and of elaborating upon it as a self-contained aesthetic. The imagination has come to be regarded as a floating faculty, a unique mental solvent which, although unrelated to anything itself, is capable of relating everything else.

The beginning of this formulation can be traced to I. A. Richards' influential book *Coleridge on Imagination.* Richards acknowledges the importance, for Coleridge, of his philosophical structure; in fact he suggests that Coleridge's defection from idealist principles was connected with the decline of his artistic powers:

> Coleridge, as "the years matured the silent strife," became more and more held by the attitudes consonant with the Realist doctrine, less and less able to recover his earlier integral vision of the poet's mind. But the feeling that whatever he had to say was half

the truth, that there was another half, irreconcilable but equally required, haunted him.[54]

He goes on, however, to dismiss the realist-idealist conflict as an unreal issue. The trouble, he explains—with what is a modern extension of Kantian logic—is that Coleridge mistook his ideas about the external world for facts, and that when ideas are mistaken for facts they are believed in. Such beliefs "as Coleridge's own history shows, can become gross obstacles to the return of 'the philosophic imagination, the sacred power of self-intuition.'"[55] Presumably Richards believes in his own ideas, here, and it is somewhat ironic that their first famous elaborator should have been Immanuel Kant.[56] In any event, the argument supplies the logic behind Richards' transference of Coleridge's aesthetic to psychological ground:

> What I shall try to do, so far as I can, is to use Coleridge's metaphysical machinery *as* machinery, disregarding the undeniable fact that Coleridge himself so often took it to be much more. I shall take his constructions, that is, as 'concepts of the understanding' (to use his terminology) and use them, not as doctrines to be accepted, refuted or corrected (however great the temptations) but as instruments with which to explore the nature of poetry. Only later . . . shall I attempt to reduce them from such concepts to the 'fact of mind' from which they come.[57]

With such discarding of its original philosophical freight, the Coleridgean imagination assumed its modernized form and its central position in modern criticism. Cleanth Brooks has said, for example, that the criteria of modern criticism derive from a single fundamental principle—Coleridge's principle of the imagination's "reconciliation of opposites." These criteria, as Abrams, along with others, has observed, "have been cut loose from their roots in Coleridge's metaphysical principles and from their context in a highly developed organic theory of art. . . ."[58] Descending from Richards, the school of New Criticism has flourished, one might say, by adopting the theory of the Coleridgean imagination as a working hypothesis, uncontaminated by metaphysical problems and transcendentalist subterfuges. It has done so by appropriating the skeptical heritage of its own intellectual tradition, by using a skeptical "critique" to justify, as Richards does, the dismissal of its philosophical sources, of the very assumptions which have proliferated its critical dogmas. The danger may be that in losing sight of its intellectual sources, with their attendant problems, textual criticism descending from Richards may proportionately lose sight of its traditional functions. The important issue at present is whether such criticism, within the self-imposed isolation of its aesthetic, can avoid intellectual stagnation. The evidence of the last few decades suggests that criticism confined to textual analysis is limited to a quest for increasingly complex methodologies at increasingly superficial levels.

The same reluctance to tap the sources of modern aesthetic is reflected in contemporary scholarship. Even Mr. Abrams, whose book on romantic aesthetic corroborates in its major thesis the approach taken here, exhibits the same preference for isolating the Coleridgean aesthetic. Unlike Richards, Abrams takes no notice of Coleridge's own misgivings about his philosophical structure. He does notice, however, that Richards, by dismissing Coleridge's idealist principles, was actually trying to make the aesthetic more congenial to his own empiricist viewpoint. Since Abrams finds the resolution of such philosophical disagreements "exceedingly dubious," he proposes another standard. For the empiricist or Aristotelian, Coleridge's insistence upon an idealist basis may appear irrational; however,

> the crucial difference lies in the choice of the initial premisses (often, if I have not been mistaken, the analogical premisses) of our reasoning, and the validity of the choice is measured by the adequacy of its coherently reasoned consequences in making the universe intelligible and manageable. If this criterion incorporates our need to make the universe emotionally as well as intellectually manageable, is not that the most important requirement of all?[59]

The "coherency" standard is undoubtedly the most acceptable standard to most modern critics, but Mr. Abrams does not bring the Coleridgean aesthetic to that test. He represents it as a rational and coherent system, defending it from its "degeneration" in the hands of Coleridge's contemporaries, from the "short-sighted" criticism of Pater, from the irrationality charged by "Irving Babbitt and others after him," and from any dependency upon a supersensible reality. This last issue, since it raises the philosophical question, is the significant one; and here Abrams' treatment is ambiguous. He observes, for example, that the degeneration of Coleridge's crucial distinction between imagination and fancy was due to a lack of philosophical understanding on the part of his contemporaries:

> Even when we turn to those contemporaries who were poets or critics by profession, we find little support or understanding of what Coleridge aimed to achieve by his theory of imagination.... Not infrequently, we also hear echoes of Coleridge's antithesis between fancy and imagination, but the distinction is usually desultory and tends to collapse entirely, because unsupported by the firm understructure of Coleridge's philosophical principles.[60]

A similar confusion can be found among the Victorians, who according to Abrams converted "poetry into a kind of religion," whereas "Coleridge very carefully kept science, poetry, and religion distinct by attributing each, primarily to its appropriate faculty of understanding, imagination and reason."[61] Surprisingly, this distinction of faculties establishes, just as it does for Richards and Brooks, the independence of Coleridge's aesthetic from both religion and the support of a supersensible reality. It is thus that Abrams argues against Bowra's thesis, quoted earlier, that romantic aesthetic was dependent upon a transcendental Beyond:

> A recent writer has even built a book concerning English romantic poetry around the thesis that the major poets "agreed on one vital point: that the creative imagination is closely connected with a peculiar insight into an unseen order behind visible things." It is clear that a salient and distinctive aspect of romantic theory was a recourse to the imagination.... But it is, I think, ultimately misleading to put Blake and Shelley, instead of Wordsworth and Coleridge, at the intellectual center of English romanticism, and consequently to make the keystone of romantic aesthetics the doctrine that the poetic imagination is the organ of intuition beyond experience, and that poetry is a mode of discourse which reveals the eternal verities. Coleridge, translating almost literally from Schelling, says that art imitates the *natura naturans,* the 'spirit of nature'; but in context, this turns out to be a way of saying that the 'idea,' or generative element in poetic composition, accords with that in external nature, in such a way as to insure a likeness between the evolving principle of a poem and what is vital and organic in nature. Coleridge does not make special cognitive claims for poetry. In his philosophy, it is specifically the reason, not the secondary imagination, which is 'the organ of the supersensuous,' with 'the power of acquainting itself with invisible realities or spiritual objects,' with the result that religion and poetry remain distinct. Reason may co-operate with imagination, so that some religious statements are poetic, and the truth of 'invisible realities' sometimes finds expression in poetry; but this is an incidental question of subject matter, and not a matter of the essence of poetry.[62]

Under this passage the whole romantic problem appears to be quietly submerged. In the first place, the *natura naturans* is more than a compositional principle, and Abrams admits as much when he says that it *insures* a likeness between the poem and the external world. It is hard to see how a compositional principle can insure a likeness to anything unless it first corresponds to something itself. But where is the "organic and vital" likeness which Mr. Abrams attributes to nature? This is the Kantian world; it is still the world of Descartes, to the extent that "objects (as objects) are essentially fixed and dead." Mr. Abrams appears to have wandered off into Bergsonian gardens. At least he appears to have forgotten that his own thesis concerns the fact that there *was* no vital and organic principle in Locke's nature and the romantic aesthetic was an effort to supply the missing principle. He earlier acknowledges, in fact, that Coleridge's compositional principle was in reality a metaphysical principle: "Coleridge's lecture 'On Poesy or Art' (1818) is grounded on Schelling's metaphysics of a psychonatural parallelism, according to which the essences within nature have a kind of duplicate subsistence as ideas in the mind."[63] There is a further difficulty in explaining what the secondary imagination is doing at all in Coleridge's system, if it is not the organ of "invisible realities" and if Coleridge makes no "special cognitive claims" for its creative activity.

Again, Mr. Abrams writes earlier, speaking of Coleridge's theory of the reconciliation of opposites:

> The dynamic conflict of opposites, and their reconciliation into a *higher third,* is not limited to the process of individual consciousness. The same concept serves Coleridge as the root principle of his cosmogony, his epistemology, and his theory of poetic creation alike.... The imagination, in creating poetry, therefore *echoes the creative principle underlying the universe.*[64] (italics added)

It is hard to see how any faculty can echo God's creative principle or produce from opposites a "higher third" without invoking something beyond a visible reality and entailing a particular kind of cognition. If the imagination echoes the creative principle underlying the universe, one must assume that such a principle exists as an invisible reality, and if that principle resides in a "higher third," inaccessible by means of perception or reason (intuitive or otherwise), then the imagination must assume a "special cognitive" function. Unfortunately, many modern critics are so accustomed to thinking of the imagination simply as "a process of individual consciousness" that they have difficulty conceiving of it as a metaphysical principle, as an aesthetic process capable of functioning as the essential binding agent in an otherwise unrelated cosmological structure. Once that structure is removed, however, the creative imagination is deprived both of its function and its justification as Coleridge understood these. This is what has occurred in the modernization of the imagination, which is purportedly based simply on Coleridge's single definition of the "essence" of poetry as a mental "reconciliation of opposites." Construed psychologistically, Coleridge's philosophical problems are excluded as simply as Abrams here excludes a supersensible reality as "an incidental question of subject matter, and not a matter of the essence of poetry."

The next chapter, which concerns the consequences of the modernized imagination as it appears in Stevens, should justify the attention here given to Coleridge's original philosophical structure.

3

Coleridge and Stevens:
The Transcendental Legacy

> As poetry goes, as the imagination goes, as
> the approach to truth, or, say, to being by
> way of the imagination goes, Coleridge is
> one of the great figures. (*N. A.*, 41)

Stevens' debt to the Coleridgean aesthetic is acknowledged implicitly in the title of his collected essays. The "necessary angel" derives from one of his own poems in which the imagination, personified as the "angel of reality," describes herself as "the necessary angel of earth / Since, in my sight, you see the earth again."[1] The reference identifies Stevens' poetic as descendent from the tradition of the angelic imagination for which Allen Tate, in an essay on its American sources in Poe, has provided the label "angelism."[2] Like Poe's angel, Stevens' angel shares the same spiritual bower as Coleridge's Teutonic one. As the faculty for the recovery of reality from the despiritualized world of science, it depends upon the same philosophical tradition, functions in essentially the same way, and involves the same problems. The one great difference is that Stevens' angel, being a modern one, lacks transcendental support, and without such support, or some equivalent form of mysticism, the Coleridgean imagination leads inevitably to a solipsistic aesthetic.

In so far as Stevens accepts these consequences, he can be identified with the central tradition of modern criticism. As Frank Kermode has said, "Stevens' problems are the problems also of modern criticism," and his recourse to the imagination "has become everybody's."[3] On the other hand, he is distinguished from his contemporaries by his frank acknowledgment of his nineteenth-century sources, his focus upon the essential romantic doctrines, and his efforts to sustain a faith akin to the romantic faith in the validity of poetry. All this is suggested by the first essay of *The*

Necessary Angel, in which Stevens proposes as his preliminary definition of poetry: "It is an interdependence of imagination and reality as equals."[4] The meaning of this proposition is not, as some critics have assumed, self-evident. It is frequently cited as evidence of Stevens' nonromantic bias, his realistic "respect for facts." It is more certainly evidence of the distinguishing assumption of aesthetic idealism, and given that assumption, the meaning of the term "reality" becomes a point in question. The confusion of modern criticism, as Babbitt once observed, is largely due to the failure "to define, above all, the words real (or realism) and imagination, not only separately but in their relation to one another."[5] What Babbitt seems to have had in mind, and what Stevens' criticism illustrates, is that behind most modern formulations lies Coleridge's "coalescence of subject and object" and the imagination's unique power to "make the internal external, the external internal." Coleridge's problems with the angelic imagination, however, become considerably more complex when the imagination is deprived, as it is in Stevens, of its transcendental support.

The extent to which the Coleridgean legacy is preserved by Stevens is best illustrated in a relatively late essay, "The Imagination as Value" (1948), an essay containing his most explicit account of the creative process. The key passage is one that offers nothing unfamiliar to the modern critic, but it is of interest for the historian of ideas in that it is an excellent example of how the Coleridgean imagination, after a century and a half, looks in modern dress.

> If the imagination is the faculty by which we import the unreal into what is real, its value is the value of the way of thinking by which we project the idea of God into the idea of man. It creates images that are independent of their originals since nothing is more certain than that the imagination is agreeable to the imagination.... This may suggest that the imagination is the ignorance of the mind. Yet the imagination changes as the mind changes. I know an Italian who was a shepherd in Italy as a boy. He described his day's work. He said that at evening he was so tired he would lie down under a tree like a dog. This image was, of course, an image of his own dog. It was easy for him to say how tired he was by using the image of his tired dog. But given another mind, given the mind of a man of strong powers, accustomed to thought, accustomed to the essays of the imagination, and the whole imaginative substance changes. It is as if one could say that the imagination lives as the mind lives. The primitivism disappears. The Platonic resolution of diversity appears. The world is no longer an extraneous object, full of other extraneous objects, but an image. In the last analysis it is with this image of the world that we are vitally concerned.[6]

The passage illustrates how the Coleridgean scheme, divested of its transcendental superstructure, is adapted to a radically idealistic context. In place of the transcendental "ideal" the imagination now imports the "unreal" into the real. Coleridge's "repetition in the finite mind of the eternal act of creation in the Infinite I AM" becomes the projection of "the idea of God into the idea of man." The images which Coleridge's poet created "out of his own mind," but which were capable of assimilating him to nature, are now simply "independent of their originals." The principle of self-determination, the imagination's conformity to "laws of its own origination," is restated in the notion that "the imagination is agreeable to the imagination" (agreeable in the precise sense of "conforming to"). The example of the shepherd's "easy" use of the image of his dog borrows rather obviously from Coleridge's dismissal of Wordsworth's "common man," who uses mere fancy in perceiving already fixed associations. By the same token Stevens' "man of strong powers" for whom "the whole imaginative substance changes" is Coleridge's "self-sufficing" genius, the man of a truly creative imagination. The ascension from primitivism to the "Platonic resolution of diversity" is an ubiquitous notion in the realistic tradition, but is paralleled by Coleridge's use of the Platonic scale: "The object of art is to give the whole *ad hominem;* hence each step of nature hath its ideal, and hence the possibility of a climax up to the perfect form of a harmonized chaos."[7] Finally, the world of "extraneous objects," Coleridge's "unrelated particulars," ceases to be extraneous; the world is synthesized as a mental image, that coalescence of subject and object in which the external becomes internal.

The recasting of the Coleridgean aesthetic in these terms deprives the imagination of its original metaphysical function and any claim to objective validity. There is now no spiritual reality, no vital principle, no underlying unity or order external to the mind. There is simply matter, unrelated particularity. What the mind intuits is mind. In place of the transcendental access to invisible realities, an "idea" of god projected into an "idea" of man creates an "idea" of the world. None of these ideas, however, has any external source or significance; they begin as they end, in the mind of the poet. The romantic faith in the poet's unique power to pierce the veil, to have, as it is now euphemistically phrased, "imaginative insights into reality," becomes a meaningless anachronism, a literary husk deprived of its metaphysical core.

The solipsistic implications of the creative process, as Stevens here describes it, leave him no alternative but to accept the absolute autonomy of art. For a skeptic as thorough-going as Stevens, however, acceptance would be tantamount to despair. The contention that art is a "way out" of the modern predicament has to be accompanied by some modicum of faith in the relevance of art. In his later years his awareness of the solipsism to which his aesthetic threatened to reduce him is clearly evident. In his posthumously published essays he calls for an "act of faith" in reality, a belief that the poet is able to "see what he wants to see and touch what he wants to touch."[8] He elaborates upon Jean Paulhan's phrase "la confiance. . . au monde" as the phrase which more than any other has "penetrated to our needs."[9] The problem of establishing a valid relation between mind and the external reality is rehearsed in poem after poem, and the possible ways of resolving it become pervasive themes. This vacillation before seeming alternatives of an intractable problem becomes, in fact, an intellectual mannerism as characteristic as the mannerisms of his style. In order to understand the problem it is necessary to consider in some detail the distinguishing assumptions which characterize, for Stevens as well as for modern criticism generally, the transcendental heritage of aesthetic idealism.

The Liberating Faculty

Ever since Coleridge attributed the development of his aesthetic to his reaction against Hartley's mechanistic psychology, there has been a tendency to regard Coleridge's own theory of mind as a defense of the mind's active and self-determining powers. The Coleridgean imagination, it is said, asserted the principle of creative freedom, hence abrogating the merely passive functions assigned to the mind by the empirical tradition. Thus I. A. Richards writes:

> Against both Primary and Secondary Imagination is set Fancy—which collects and re-arranges, without re-making them, units of meaning already constituted by the Imagination. . . . The passage from the conceptions of the mind's doings as Fancy to that of the creative Imagination is the passage from Hartley to Kant.[10]

The implication here is that the principle of self-determination by which the mind remakes the physical world was the principle by which Kant abrogated the deterministic psychologies of the empirical tradition. For Kant, however, the principle of self-determination was not a liberating principle in any philosophical sense. Even though the mind created the phenomenal world, its creations had to retain the necessitarian basis given it by the empirical tradition; otherwise the phenomenalist epistemology could not accommodate science as a legitimate enterprise. In order to establish the objective reality of appearances Kant called upon the law of efficient causality. Agreeing with Hume that appearances were themselves united by nothing more than their sequential order, he posited causality as the necessary and universal rule operative through the Understanding. All perception, in so far as it was objective, had to conform to the law of efficient causality; that is, every event was to be interpreted as proceeding from antecedent events—as the necessary effect of antecedent causes. Only by regarding this rule of the Understanding as universal, Kant held, could the objective reality of appearances, as opposed to the mind's subjective apprehension of them, be distinguished. And only by this rule could an otherwise arbitrary succession of appearances be given empirically valid relationships.[11]

Kant's theory of knowledge was, then, both mechanistic and deterministic. The notion of a creative mind did not, for him, constitute an escape from determinism so far as the sensible world was concerned. Rather, Kant implicated the mind as cooperating in the sensationalism of Locke and Hume and subservient to the Humean concept of causality. This created an impasse between his theory of knowledge and his theory of moral consciousness, for as A. C. Ewing among other philosophers has observed, "since phenomenal causality is in Kant's view merely necessary succession. . . it gives no opportunity for freedom which is yet an indispensable postulate of ethics, at least so Kant would add."[12]

This conflict between freedom and determinism has interesting ramifications in Kant's treatment of aesthetics in the *Critique of Judgement*. Here poetry is described as the product of Understanding and imagination. It is the process by which the concepts of the Understanding are given sensible representation by a freely creative imagination. The Understanding retains here its mechanistic ground and hence represents the objective faculty "in conformity to law"; but the imagination manifests its freedom by self-determination, by a "free harmonizing" which "cannot be brought about by any observance of rules, whether of science or mechanical imitation, but can only be produced by the nature of the individual."[13] It is here, in the contrast between a mechanistic faculty and a freely creative one, that the core of Kant's entire aesthetic is to be found. In order to give precedent to the free side of the equation, poetry had to be conceived as primarily a matter of individual and unique sensibility. And since the free faculty was the wholly subjective faculty, Kant could claim for it no more than "merely an entertaining *play* with ideas" (Kant's italics).[14] Moreover, in order to claim the reader's attention, the poet was required to disguise his play with a pretense of seriousness. Poetry was, Kant concluded, the art "of conducting a free play of the imagination as if it were a serious business of the understanding."[15] It was an unhappy situation, for Kant no less than his successors was sure that poetry was a more serious affair than his principles would seem to admit. It is not difficult to see, however, that Kant's emphasis upon a free imagination, upon creative "play," upon the spontaneity and originality of genius, as well as upon the purposelessness or disinterested pleasure of aesthetic experience, are the compensatory features of a necessitarian theory of knowledge. In many of these references to the freedom of the imagination, Kant hovers about the notion that art may appeal to a higher truth than his cognitive faculties could supply. With Coleridge, that notion is explicitly formulated; freedom becomes identified with escape from mechanism by means of radical creativity, by πoιησιs (poiesis) as distinguished from μoρφoσιs (morphosis). In this new formulation radical creativity is dependent upon two essential features: an idealist context capable of establishing the validity of mental addenda to perceptual reality as "higher truth"; and a faculty or faculties whose activity is self-determining, that is, governed by an innate organic principle rather than the principle of efficient causality. The classic criticism of these doctrines is probably still that of Irving Babbitt, who emphasized above all their focus upon irrational mental processes. Babbitt's criticism has been reiterated often enough. There is one point, however, that has peculiar relevance for twentieth-century aesthetic and particularly for Wallace Stevens. This is the point that while Coleridge's aesthetic was, as Pater observed, "part of the long pleading of German culture for things behind the veil," its practical effect was "an interest in the elusive phenomena that are off the center of normal consciousness."[16]

> The originality of the creator was conceived almost from the start not only as spontaneous, but as something over which he had little control. "An original," we read in Edward Young (1759), "may be said to be a vegetable nature.... It grows, it is not made." For "vegetable" Coleridge, in the wake of the Germans, substituted "organic"— still an epithet to conjure with.... Here is the point of departure for the distinction between genius and mere talent of which the early romantics made so much. According to Hazlitt "talent is a voluntary power, while genius is involuntary." In short the man who knows what he is about is not a genius. The contrast between the organic and spontaneous and the merely imitative and mechanical is closely connected with the predominant interest in the unconscious, as compared with the conscious, which has assumed so many forms from the eighteenth century down to psychoanalysts.[17]

The natural connection between epistemological idealism and the modern interest in psychology and the unconscious has been mentioned earlier. Babbitt's comment, however, indicates how this connection is appreciably strengthened by the aesthetic formulation which tied together freedom, creativity, and an organic principle of mind. The connection of these terms is commonly assumed in modern criticism, but it is important to clarify their meaning in terms of the underlying philosophical motivations. Otherwise, the notion of a creative mind may be confused with the notion of freedom through self-determination, whereas neither is necessarily implicit in the other. Kant's theory of perception posited a creative act of mind, but it did not make that act a free act. The objectivity and, for Kant, the validity of perception and understanding were in fact based upon the argument that they could not act freely but were governed by irrevocable conditions and laws. In so far as Kant succeeded in effecting a new order, it was by virtue of perpetuating an old one. His concession to empiricism was a commitment to a necessitarian theory of knowledge which could be mitigated only at transcendental altitudes. He gave philosophic affirmation to what had been the foregone conclusion of the empirical tradition, namely, that if the physical world could be known in any way other than the empirical, it could not be known at the normal level of consciousness (assuming this to be the level of common perception and rational activity). If poetry was to have cognitive value, if it was to be a "serious business" rather than "entertaining play," it had to lay claim either to something above or below that level. Such is the philosophical predicament behind Babbitt's charge that the Coleridgean aesthetic meant the migration of art to the periphery of consciousness. Babbitt's proposed corrective, the establishment of "a theory of imagination that seizes what is normal and central in human experience" has yet to be achieved. It may be wondered, after some thirty years of exhaustive discussion, whether the normal and central in human experience will ever be exhumed from a transcendental theory of the imagination, or from related modern inquiries into psychology and linguistics. So long as a common sensible world is relegated to empirical interpretation, art would appear to have no recourse but to an uncommon world constructed by unique mental processes. To reject this division may require a certain philosophical innocence, but it seems unlikely that art can focus upon the central in human experience while it abjures reliance upon a common sensible world.

In Stevens' aesthetic, the stress of this problem is more than evident. His most vehement defense of the imagination is that it can and must produce what is central in human experience. His divorce from Symbolist aesthetic is made explicitly upon this issue.

> The poet is constantly concerned with two theories. One relates to the imagination as a power within him not so much to destroy reality at will as to put it to his own uses. He comes to feel that his imagination is not wholly his own but that it may be part of a much larger, much more potent imagination, which it is his affair to try to get at. For this reason, he pushes on and lives, or tries to live, as Paul Valéry did, on the verge of consciousness. This often results in a poetry that is marginal, subliminal. . . . The second theory relates to the imagination as a power within him to have such insights into reality as will make it possible for him to be sufficient as a poet in the very center of consciousness. This results, or should result, in a central poetry.[18]

This might have been Babbitt writing of Coleridge and the transcendentalists. But against the central imagination that Stevens proposes stand the empirical assumptions to which his aesthetic is committed. The impasse is evident throughout his criticism. The imagination is invariably described as the "liberating" faculty, opposed to a deterministic world. The escape from systematic and rational modes of inquiry is identified with an escape from causal relationship to self-sufficiency and freedom. These notions appear as early as "The Irrational Element in Poetry," in which freedom is equated quite simply with escape from the rational:

> The incessant desire for freedom in literature or in any of the arts is a desire for freedom in life. The desire is irrational. The result is the irrational searching the irrational, a conspicuously happy state of affairs, if you are so inclined.[19]

In *The Necessary Angel,* the irrational becomes identified with the imagination, the faculty of "psychological escapism." "The Noble Rider and the Sound of Words" is an extended defense of the imagination as the only remaining source of liberty for modern man. The existence of the faculty is the sole guarantee of human nobility since it "is not an artifice that the mind has added to human nature," but a faculty which simply by its existence protects the mind from external domination:

> It is a violence from within that protects us from a violence without. It is the imagination pressing back against the pressure of reality. It seems, in the last analysis, to have something to do with our self-preservation....[20]

Subsequent essays refer to the imagination as "the liberty of the mind" and, in that familiar romantic phrase, "the only genius." It permits "the extension of the mind beyond the range of the mind" and it evinces "the determination not to be confined."[21]

The antithesis between a deterministic world and a liberating imagination tends to produce an oversimplified dialectic in which critical judgments are difficult. Freud, for example, is cited as one of the enemies of modern poetry and is dismissed with the remark that by favoring reason over the imagination, Freud advocated a "surrender to reality."[22] Similar dismissals of science, philosophy, and rational disciplines in general—to the neglect of any values which might attend them—have understandably irritated a number of critics. Even Mr. Ransom, a notably sympathetic critic, has observed in his discreet fashion Stevens' "serene neglect of everything common." A surrender to reality, however, usually means nothing more or less for Stevens than a surrender to determinism, and the absoluteness of the equation makes qualification irrelevant. This is reflected in a curious way by his great admiration for Santayana. Santayana is praised in prose and in the poem "To An Old Philosopher in Rome," but he is praised not as a philosopher, given to the life of reason, but as an exemplar of the life of the imagination. The prose passage, which concerns Santayana's retirement to monastic seclusion, has been badly misunderstood and is worth examining:

> In life one hesitates when one speaks of the value of the imagination. Its value in arts and letters is aesthetic. Most men's lives are thrust upon them. The existence of aesthetic

value in lives that are forced on those that live them is an improbable sort of thing. There can be lives, nevertheless, which exist by the deliberate choice of those that live them. To use a single illustration: it may be assumed that the life of Professor Santayana is a life in which the function of the imagination has had a function similar to its function in any deliberate work of art or letters. We have only to think of this present phase of it, in which, in his old age, he dwells in the head of the world, in the company of devoted women, in their convent, and in the company of familiar saints, whose presence does so much to make any convent an appropriate refuge for a generous and human philosopher. To repeat, there can be lives in which the value of the imagination is the same as its value in arts and letters.... [23]

Mr. Louis Martz finds this passage indicative of a radical change in Stevens' development. According to Martz it represents the abandonment of Stevens' earlier hedonism and solipsism for a new "admiration for the power of thinking, for the constructive power of deliberate choice." [24] Mr. Martz seems to assume that there is something reassuringly traditional about "thinking." Actually, the passage elaborates upon the typically idealistic equation: reality and determinism versus imagination and freedom. The parallel drawn between imagination in art and in life is solely in terms of its liberating power. Santayana illustrates that deliberate choice is possible, but what is meant by choice is not, as Martz assumes, the traditional meaning; it is not choice between rational alternatives or courses of action. The choice is between the determinism of an external world and the freedom of the inner world, the mental world of imagination. Santayana chooses the latter; he lives "in the head of the world." The convent, nuns, and saints are "appropriate" symbols not in any religious sense, but in the sense that they evince the existence of spiritual or "imagined" values which have successfully resisted reality.

A related application of the same ideas occurs in the posthumous "A Collect of Philosophy" (1951). Stevens concludes his discussion of philosophers by turning rather unexpectedly to Planck, who is a "much truer symbol of ourselves." His interest is in an account by André George of one of the physicist's last papers, "The Concept of Causality in Physics." According to George, Planck rejects in this paper his previous belief in absolute causality, accepting the view that causality is merely a working hypothesis. George offers a rational explanation for Planck's revision, but, characteristically, what Stevens sees in all this is a sign of visitation from his necessary angel.

George says, finally, that this conclusion is far away from the rigid concept, firmly determinist, which seemed up to now to constitute Planck's belief. He calls it a nuance, but a nuance of importance, worth being signalized.

I think we may fairly say that it is a nuance of the imagination, one of those unwilled and innumerable nuances of the imagination that we find so often in the works of philosophers and so constantly in the works of poets. It is unexpected to have to recognize even in Planck the presence of the poet. [25]

It is a little difficult to suppose that Planck was persuaded by nothing more than an inspired poetic moment to abandon the determinist convictions of a lifetime. If passages such as these entail an obvious straining for the point, they are all the more significant; they illustrate the extent to which Stevens' critical intelligence was constricted by its controlling assumptions. Santayana's escape from the world, Planck's escape from causality are similar triumphs of freedom. Stevens' approach to science and philosophy, like his approach to the external world, often appears limited to a search for flaws in the deterministic order of the universe. This in turn helps to explain the almost religious fervor of his preoccupation with the imagination. At seventy-five, accepting honors for his collected poetry, he remarked that he regarded his achievement to be not in the poetry so much as in the discovery of "the power over the mind that lies in the mind itself, the incalculable expanse of the imagination." Such, he concludes, is the only true satisfaction for the poet who "lives in the world of Darwin and not in the world of Plato."[26]

The dread of an external reality, of a world composed of forces that threaten at every moment to overwhelm the individual, is so strong in Stevens as to suggest neurosis. It may be true, as many have observed, that his devotion to the life of the imagination is reflective of *fin de siècle* aestheticism. It is certainly true that his skepticism and anti-intellectualism reflect the intellectual hysteria of the early decades of the twentieth century. There is no need to discount environment or even natural temperament. But however one accounts for these characteristics, it is important to recognize that they are accommodated and enforced by a theory of poetry which still retains the philosophical molding of Coleridgean aesthetic.

Faculty Psychology

The notion that freedom resides in creativity divorced from causal relationships issues in the incorrigible dualism of reason and imagination which has characterized critical thought since Coleridge. Coleridge's own efforts to resolve the antithesis have been repeatedly examined, but the examinations, usually based upon selective quotation from the *Biographia*, have not led to any unanimity of opinion. M. H. Abrams, who reopened the question some years ago, asserts that the irrationalism of Coleridge's aesthetic has been greatly exaggerated. His position is fairly typical of the descendents of the Richards school who refuse to allow the philosophical dimensions of the problem. It rests on the argument that if Coleridge declared reason and imagination to be reconcilable, then they must in fact be so.

Coleridge's constant and most emphatic iteration, in fact, is that poetry brings "the whole soul of man into activity"; that the imagination is "first put in action by the *will* and understanding, and retained under their irremissive though gentle and unnoticed, control"; and that "great as was the genius of Shakespeare, his judgment was at least equal." When Clarence D. Thorpe defended the thesis that no critic ever "had more to say for the value of intellect and reason than Coleridge," he pointed to a side of Coleridge's theory that Pater, like Irving Babbitt and others after him, totally overlooked.[27]

The manner in which Coleridge reconciled reason and imagination, however, is never explained. Abrams contends that the best solution is to be found in the theory of organic law. He cites Coleridge's statement that Shakespeare was not a lawless genius because genius acts under "laws of its own origination"; and concludes that "the solution is that genius, however free from prior precept, is never free from law...."[28] This would seem to be an evasion rather than a solution. The question is not whether the imagination is free from law, but whether the law is ascertainable, predictable, purposeful, comprehensible—in short, rational. No amount of evasion can conceal the basic incompatibility of the mechanistic and organic principles which distinguish, for Coleridge, rational and imaginative processes. It would seem more reasonable to ask, not whether the two faculties are incompatible, but why they should be, and this is a matter to be decided in terms of first assumptions. The crucial point is once again the empirical basis of the Kantian theory of mind. It is only when Coleridge follows the logic of his own assumptions that his comments are relevant to the subsequent development of literary theory. This he does when he insists upon the self-sufficiency of both Pure Reason and the creative imagination, both governed by intuitive principles:

> For even as truth is its own light and evidence, discovering at once itself and falsehood, so it is the prerogative of poetic genius to distinguish by parental instinct its proper offspring.... Could a rule be given from without, poetry would cease to be poetry, and sink into a mechanical art. It would be μορφοσις not ποιησις. The rules of the imagination are themselves the very powers of growth and production.[29]

The distinction is basic to Coleridge's faculty psychology. It separates those faculties which are subservient to the empirical world from those which are independent of it, which furnish their "own light and evidence." There is no way here to reconcile Understanding, which is subservient to the deterministic laws governing the sensible world, with either the imagination or the intuitive intellect, which must retain its self-sufficiency in order to retain its liberty.[30]

Stevens' discussions of the relation of reason and imagination show an interesting development. The development, however, is within this same context and is governed by the same assumptions. In the early essays he describes the imagination primarily in terms of emotion, accounting for the uniqueness of its creative process by the unique "sensibility" of the artist. The inadequacy of this doctrine is that it does not presuppose a distinct mode of cognition. It is incompatible with the notion of freedom through creativity inasmuch as the unique sensibility of the artist is reducible to a deterministic psychology. In 1945, Kenneth Burke, in the course of demonstrating "how deeply 'scientism' has permeated modern thought," makes just this point about what was then Stevens' most recent essay, "The Figure of the Youth as Virile Poet." Burke first notes the idealist context of Stevens' poetic:

> The autumn, 1944 issue of *The Sewanee Review* contains an essay by Wallace Stevens that is quite to our purposes. Written with all the deftness and subtlety of Stevens' poetry, it speaks of poetry in precisely the idealist cluster of terms we have been examining in this section. The importance of "personality" is stressed. Poetry is derived from an "indirect egotism." "Nervous sensitiveness" is basic, for the poet's morality is "the morality of the right sensation."[31]

Burke goes on to observe that in spite of this typical "idealist cluster," grouped under the usual unifying concept, "imagination," Stevens' remark about the morality of the poet ends "on the most scientist term of all: 'sensation.'"[32]

Three years after Burke's remarks, Stevens wrote the passage analyzed at the beginning of this chapter, in which he adapts the Coleridgean imagination to a radically idealistic context. In a subsequent essay, "The Relations Between Poetry and Painting" (1951), he is ready to abandon the doctrine of "sensibility" for Coleridge's faculty scheme:

> Yet if one questions the dogma that the origins of poetry are to be found in the sensibility and if one says that a fortunate poem or a fortunate painting is a synthesis of exceptional concentration (that degree of concentration that has a lucidity of its own, in which we see clearly what we want to do and do it instantly and perfectly), we find that the operative force within us does not, in fact, seem to be the sensibility, that is to say, the feelings. It seems to be a constructive faculty, that derives its energy more from the imagination than from the sensibility. I have spoken of questioning, not denying. The mind retains experience, so that long after the experience...the faculty within us of which I have spoken makes its own construction out of that experience. If it merely reconstructed the experience or repeated for us our sensations in the face of it, it would be memory. What it really does is to use it as material with which it does whatever it wills. This is the typical function of the imagination which always makes use of the familiar to produce the unfamiliar.[33]

The final sentence, of course, recalls Coleridge's account of the plan for the *Lyrical Ballads,* which was to demonstrate the power of the imagination to conjoin the familiar and unfamiliar.[34] The issue is the same one that underlies Coleridge's extended criticism of Wordsworth's *Preface*. Coleridge's irritation with Wordsworth's definitions of poetry and poetic diction — his doctrine of "essential passions," and words used "in a state of excitement," — is due to Wordsworth's failure to derive these from a single, governing concept of the essence of poetry. That essence had to establish, for Coleridge, a constructive power which could not be reduced to the poet's emotional response to sensation: "For the property of passion is not to *create*," he explains, "but to set in increased activity."[35]

Coleridge was rightly annoyed with Wordsworth's failure to grasp the importance of this distinction; it was not a minor quibble. To explain poetry in terms of causal relationships between the mind and an external world was to reopen the issue with Hartley. The question was whether to risk the reduction of the creative process to a deterministic psychology, or to insist upon its noncausal, self-determining essence and to grapple with the resultant problems of irrational art.

This is the problem that Stevens comes back to repeatedly. He never clearly decides between alternatives, preferring as he says to speak "of questioning not denying." In this passage, however, he acknowledges that the doctrine of "poetic sensibility" is insufficient to sustain his belief in free creativity. He clearly prefers the self-sufficient imagination which "does whatever it wills," to the imagination which reconstructs remembered sensations, that is "emotion recollected in tranquillity." The motive is apparent when, a page later, he remarks that since the imagination must produce the unfamiliar, it would seem to require "an effort of the mind not dependent on the vicissitudes of the sensibility."[36] One should also notice that the creative act is accompanied by its familiar requirements, spontaneity and intuition. The imaginative synthesis occurs at the moment that has "a lucidity of its own" and in which one creates "instantly and perfectly." Also, there is the customary relegation of memory (and by implication, fancy) to its passive function as a copyist of experience. With this much of the Coleridgean formula established, the position of reason is fairly predictable.

Stevens' attitude toward reason varies between antipathy toward scientific reason and a skeptical tolerance toward speculative reason. Usually he regards reason simply as the tool of science, epitomized for him by such deterministic interpreters of reality as Freud, Planck, and Ayer. In this sense, the dichotomy between reason and imagination is assumed to be absolute — as when he says, referring to the imagination, "Only the reason stands between it and the reality for which the two are engaged in a struggle."[37] With the dichotomy in force, poetry's traffic with rational activity is carried on under the "imaginative" disguise that is characteristic of much modern criticism. Abstraction, reflection, evaluation, even logical argument are processes subsumed by the imagination. Reason becomes mainly a term of convenience, used as a pejorative to justify dismissal of any argument or idea unfavorable to the imagination. Thus he goes on to describe the struggle between reason and imagination as an "academic struggle," which those who live in the imagination may regard as "merely a bit of academic junk." When the same rational processes are favorably implicated in poetry they become "imaginative thought," or as he calls them on one occasion, "the miraculous kind of reason that the imagination sometimes promotes."[38] Thus Freud, when preferring reality to illusion, speaks with the "voice of the intellect," whereas Planck's abandonment of absolute causality in physics is a "nuance of imagination" indicating "the presence of a poet."

On a few occasions, when he appears to be thinking of speculative reason primarily, he implies the possible compatibility of reason and imagination. The most he is willing to concede, however, is that they are not inherently antithetical, although as independent faculties their concurrence is accidental. It is worth noticing how, on such occasions, the argument is contained within a radically idealistic context. In the following passage, for example, compatibility arises not from a common purpose, nor from any consideration of the particular faculty's authority or validity. It arises simply from the concurrent "satisfaction" of both faculties.

> Since we expect rational ideas to satisfy the reason and imaginative ideas to satisfy the imagination, it follows that if we are sceptical of rational ideas it is because they do not satisfy the reason and if we are sceptical of imaginative ideas it is because they do not satisfy the imagination. If a rational idea does not satisfy the imagination, it may, nevertheless, satisfy the reason. If an imaginative idea does not satisfy the reason, we regard the fact as in the nature of things. If an imaginative idea does not satisfy the imagination, our expectation of it is not fulfilled. On the other hand, and finally, if an imaginative idea satisfies the imagination, we are indifferent to the fact that it does not satisfy the reason, although we concede that it would be complete, as an idea, if, in addition to satisfying the imagination, it also satisfied the reason.[39]

One might well complain that this dialectical exercise in tautological generalities satisfies neither. It is a good illustration, however, of how the mind may become trapped in its self-sufficiency. Not only the mind, but the separate faculties are self-sufficient, each functioning as judge, witness and advocate within its own domain. The oppositions so rigorously spelled out in this passage are not merely Stevens', however; they are wholly within the central tradition of modern criticism. One can find their antecedent in I. A. Richards' theory of poetry as "pseudo-statement," and in the subsequent development of psychologies of belief or credibility as a critical standard. The peaceful coexistence of faculties, each indifferent to the satisfactions of the other, is a characteristic manifestation of the post-Kantian distinction between empirical and intuitive faculties.

In his last years Stevens makes sporadic efforts to withdraw the free license of the imagination. His interest in philosophy and his admiration for philosophers such as Whitehead and Santayana are paralleled by a disenchantment with the irrational excesses of modern literature. By 1948, the irrationalism he had once called a "conspicuously happy state of affairs" has become a cause for uneasiness. In "The Imagination as Value" he confronts the problem of prescribing limits to the imagination:

> The disposition toward a point of view derogatory to the imagination is an aversion to the abnormal. We see it in the common attitude toward modern arts and letters. The exploits of Rimbaud in poetry, if Rimbaud can any longer be called modern, and of Kafka in prose are deliberate exploits of the abnormal. It is natural for us to identify the imagination with those that extend its abnormality. It is like identifying liberty with those who abuse it. A literature overfull of abnormality and, certainly, present-day European literature, as one knows it, seems to be a literature full of abnormality, gives the reason an appearance of normality to which it is not, solely, entitled. The truth seems to be that we live in the concepts of the imagination before reason has established them. If this is true, then reason is simply the methodizer of the imagination. It may be that the imagination is a miracle of logic and that its exquisite divinations are calculations beyond analysis, as the conclusions of reason are calculations wholly within analysis.[40]

Whatever distinction lies submerged under the misty modernity of "normal" and "abnormal," the distinction between reason and imagination abides in the clarity of long established tradition. The imagination is distinguished from mere abnormality because it is capable of intuitive truth, of concepts "before reason has established them." Coleridge called it truth "that is its own light and evidence"; and referred to it as a "higher logic."[41] Without access to an invisible reality, to an existing realm of higher truths, the validity of this appeal rests solely upon the authority of the poet's own imagination, which is free, as Stevens says, to do "whatever it wills." The nature, source, and validity of its intuitive power are no longer legitimate questions, but it is difficult to square the notion that the imagination's "exquisite divinations" are "beyond analysis" with Stevens' belief that the poet should operate at the "center of consciousness." What is apparent, however, is that Stevens is concerned in his later essays with aligning reason and imagination, even though that alignment must rest upon a faith in miracle. The possibility that the imagination is a "miracle of logic" and the reason "simply the methodizer of the imagination" represents a balancing act upon a precariously fine distinction. But there is no alternative. Any attempt to "methodize" the imagination means what it meant for Coleridge—to "sink into a mechanical art." Once this is granted, it is hard to avoid the reduction to absurdity: the truth shall set you free, provided you do not understand it.

As always with Stevens, such vacillations and contradictions have to be understood in terms of underlying assumptions, and in most cases these have not changed significantly since Coleridge. One begins by supposing that the demons of the empirical world — from Hartley to Ayer — can be exorcised only by the idealist incantation, *"poiesis."* The liberating faculty in a deterministic world is the imagination, whose self-sufficiency rests upon its ability to transcend sensible reality and rational processes. The imagination thereby assumes an unavoidably defensive role, that of steady retreat before the encroachment of the so-called "empirical" faculties, perception and reason. And since these furnish the causal relations between man and the external world, between mind and whatever may be external to it, the retreat of the imagination will be away from, not toward, the center of consciousness.

The alternative is to place the imagination in the role of the aggressor; to charge it with the actual destruction of the empirical faculties. This is the method undertaken by the Symbolists, who aimed at the disorientation of sense perception (as, for example, in synaesthesia) and the subversion of rational processes. It is significant that Stevens, dissociating himself from the Symbolist aesthetic, becomes increasingly concerned with the relation of sense perception and reason to the imagination. His efforts to respect the former pair without violating the independence of the imagination indicates his closer affinity with Coleridge than with either the Symbolists or their American ancestor Poe. His adaptation of Coleridge's faculty psychology is part of his effort to reinstate poetry in the "center of consciousness" as the "sum of our faculties." It is a reassertion of Coleridge's claim that the imagination "brings the whole soul of man into activity." But one cannot assume that the intention is equivalent to the achievement.

Radical Creation and the "Phantom Aesthetic"

A final way in which Stevens illustrates the consequences of the Transcendentalist legacy concerns the doctrine of the nonutility or purposelessness of art. The theory that the end of poetry is the experience of pleasure divorced from intellectual or practical interests was long ago characterized by I. A. Richards as the "phantom aesthetic" of modern criticism. Richards summarizes the theory, stressing its Kantian origin.

> All modern aesthetics rests upon an assumption which has been strangely little discussed, the assumption that there is a distinct *kind* of mental activity present in what are called aesthetic experiences. Ever since 'the first rational word concerning beauty' was

spoken by Kant, the attempt to define the 'judgment of taste' as concerning pleasure which is disinterested, universal, unintellectual, and not to be confused with the pleasures of sense or ordinary emotions, in short to make it a thing *sui generis,* has continued.[42]

The phantom aesthetic, Richards finds, originates with Kant's reduction of all mental faculties to the tri-partite division of his *Critiques: Pure Reason, Judgment,* and *Practical Reason.* By assigning aesthetics to the *Critique of Judgment,* Kant isolated art from rational and utilitarian concerns:

> Truth was the object of the inquiring activity, of the Intellectual or Theoretical part of the mind, and the Good that of the willing, desiring, practical part; what part could be found for the Beautiful? Some activity that was neither inquisitive nor practical, that did not question and did not seek to use. The result was the aesthetic, the contemplative, activity which is still defined, in most treatments, by these negative conditions alone, as that mode of commerce with things which is neither intellectual enquiry into their nature nor an attempt to make them satisfy our desire.[43]

Richards conveniently ignored the antiempirical motives behind Kant's distinctions. (Notice that he avoids that area in this passage by implying that Kant's isolated aesthetic was a chance misfortune, the accident of a tidy mind that needed a place for everything and everything in its place.) His purpose was to reduce aesthetic "pleasure," as formulated by Kant, to psychological explanation. The undertaking betrays the kind of philosophical confusion in which modern criticism is implicated. What Richards was actually proposing was the application of scientific methodology, based on individual and group psychology, to an idealist aesthetic which had been perpetuated by the effort to escape scientific methodology.[44]

Kant's phantom aesthetic is, as Richard implies, however, an assertion of the principle of discontinuity. By positing aesthetic experience as an end in itself, Kant established its value as independent of the sensible world and hence of determinism. Aesthetic judgment, he explained, "makes possible the transition from the realm of the concept of nature to that of the concept of freedom."[45] The necessity of this doctrine is recognized both in the modern notion of purposeless art, and the notion that creativity begins with a subjective state. One might cite for example Mr. Eliot's remark that the poet "begins with a feeling." A mental experience without causal relations leads to the work of art which becomes a mental experience without affectual relations. As Coleridge explains, "Poetry also is purely human; for all its materials are from the mind, and all its products are for the mind."[46] Thus in the effort to avoid causal necessity, art becomes artificially isolated, confined to the transmission of states of mind, inexplicably produced in the poet, inexplicably valued by the reader. Stevens, denying any intellectual or social obligations on the part of the poet, reveals the same motive with refreshing candor:

The truth is that the social obligation so closely urged is *a phase of the pressure of reality* which a poet (in the absence of dramatic poets) *is bound to resist or evade today*.... What is his function? Certainly it is not to lead people out of the confusion in which they find themselves. Nor is it, I think, to comfort them while they follow their readers to and fro. I think that his function is *to make his imagination theirs* and that he fulfills himself only as he sees his imagination become the light in the minds of others.[47] (italics added)

In the world of common experience, of course, the poet like everyone else assumes that his emotions arise from causes and affect his actions. But the effort to confine art to states of mind, to psychological origins and ends, is dictated by the epistemological base of Kantian aesthetic. With a mechanistic world on the one hand, and a creative faculty on the other, any causal relation between the two implicates creativity in mechanism. Art can be reduced, as Mr. Kenneth Burke remarks, to Stevens' "morality of the right sensation."[48]

In the same manner, Stevens' effort to annex comprehensible values to poetry shows the frustrating dependence upon negative definition which Richards complains of. Eventually, he comes to admit that the effort is futile "because poetic value is an intuitional value and intuitional values cannot be justified."[49] The admission, however, is not one that Stevens was ever able to accept. What might not trouble the skeptic, continued to haunt the poet; and his poems are devoted, like those of his romantic predecessors, to endless illustrations of changes wrought on appearances by the imagination, to the repeated assertion of values which can be neither specified nor accounted for.

Implicated in the indefinable character of the phantom aesthetic, is the transcendental emphasis upon radical creativity. An intuitional value might not be subject to demonstration, but Coleridge could at least account for its novelty. He could assume that an intuition presupposes the existence of something to be intuited. There were possible answers to such questions as: If poetry is a unique mode of cognition, what is the object of cognition? If it is a creative act, what is the nature of the radically new? If it is a mental addendum to reality, what relation does it have to reality? Without recourse to invisible realities, modern criticism has for some thirty years endeavored to explain the creation of a new "something" spontaneously conceived from nothing. A book of recent years, Mr. Murray Krieger's *The New Apologists for Poetry,* is a good example. Addressing himself to what he regards as the unifying problem of literary criticism over the past several decades, Mr. Krieger explains: "These discussions...seek to answer this question: to what extent is the poet literally creative—that is, to what extent does he add to the materials provided him by the world—and to what extent is he passive, an amasser and combiner of the experience he has discovered in the world?"[50] One should notice the alternatives provided: creativity or passivity — ποιησις or μορφοσις. The idealistic solution triumphs with the posing of the question, and it is no surprise that Mr. Krieger offers one more reworking of the doctrine of organic form. Unfortunately, the absence of philosophical support in modern usage deprives the term "organic" of its original implication of radical creativity. As one critic has remarked in an interesting account of the development of the organic theory, "organic" has come to be simply an intensive: "organic unity" means "lots of unity" and "organic form" means "lots of form."

> But the truth of the matter is this, that the idea of organic unity in art is descended from very *hochphilosophisch* forbears, from attempts to resolve the fundamental enigmas of the universe by proclaiming the oneness of spirit and matter.... To fail to understand the metaphysical nature of the theory of organic unity, is to fail to understand its very essence.[51]

The essence of the theory, he adds, is "a recourse to those idealistic philosophies which asserted the innateness of knowledge." Such was the meaning of the term for Coleridge; the organic principle of the Imagination was not only the principle of creativity, it was the "very power of growth and production." With the productions of the imagination something new entered the sublunary world, something having metaphysical relation to that world — the relation of the ideal to the real, spirit to matter, the One to the many. When T. E. Hulme complained that Coleridge's aesthetic "let in the infinite," the term "organic" entered its modern phase, becoming as Babbitt said, "an epithet to conjure with." In modern usage it usually implies that the poem has been magically transported to a world of nondiscursive meanings, but how and what are questions left to psychologists and linguists rather than philosophers. The critic is committed to the theory that creativity is manifested by organic unity, but since this unity is by definition inexplicable, he tends instead to focus upon linguistic novelty. In the end novelty supplants the missing metaphysical principle as the only discernible or analyzable evidence that the poet is not a passive "combiner."

The notion of organic unity would appear to be the equivalent of what Stevens calls the "idea of order," that is, of the unification of particulars according to an intuitive principle of the imagination. Thus when echoing Coleridge's theory of imaginative fusion, he says that "the whole imaginative substance changes" and there is a "Platonic resolution of diversity." He is trifling a bit with a traditional rhetoric, since he is not a Platonist; the unity he refers to is a psychological phenomenon only. But the transcendental legacy, which originally imputed to the imagination an access to a higher plane of reality, still evokes in modern phrasing a meaning no longer there. So, too, Stevens' account of the mysterious fusing power, the imaginative synthesis which was for Coleridge the mystery of Genius, is almost a paraphrase of Coleridge. Of the modern poet, he says,

> ...his own measure as a poet, in spite of all the lovers of truth, is the measure of his power to abstract himself, and to withdraw into his abstraction the reality on which lovers of truth insist. He must be able to abstract himself, and also to abstract reality, which he does by placing it in his imagination.[52]

Passages such as this last are frequently cited as evidence that Stevens' theories represent the abandonment of the romantic imagination and the discovery of a new kind of imagination which incorporates the humanistic virtues. For Louis Martz the clue to this new imagination is that it operates "in the very center of consciousness" and so composes "a world of value and order." Martz dates the emergence of this new view from the publication of *The Man with a Blue Guitar* in 1937. From this point on, he sees Stevens developing "toward a position thoroughly established in his prose essays and later poetry: that 'the poet must get rid of the hieratic in everything that concerns him,' that he must abolish 'the false conception of the imagination as some incalculable *vates* with us.'"[53] Accordingly he finds that for Stevens the "object of admiration is now human," a change he adduces largely from Stevens' admiration for Santayana. The passage he is commenting upon has already been examined.[54] It will be recalled that Martz sees in this passage Stevens' new admiration for the "power of deliberate choice." But Stevens is not praising deliberate choice as Martz understands it; he is denying its existence.

Since Martz is a Renaissance scholar, when he comes to the nineteenth and twentieth-century poets, he sees familiar words—"order," "value," "reality," "thought," "choice"—and he assumes that they carry traditional meanings or that the differences in meaning are so slight as to be irrelevant. He reads Stevens' praise of Santayana as he would read Greville's praise of Sidney.

Martz's misunderstanding of Stevens raises the point at issue in this study: the assumption that literary criticism can afford to ignore philosophy. A remarkable example of what can happen in this respect is an essay by Samuel French Morse. Mr. Morse has edited Stevens' *Opus Postumous* and a book of Stevens' selected poems, for which he has supplied extensive introductions. He has written several essays on Stevens and is currently at work on a critical biography. In one essay, Morse proposes that Stevens is really a neoclassic poet, in spirit if not in letter. He is neoclassical because (1) like Pope, he "has a sense of a universal order that art 'discovers' rather than devises" and (2) his idea of the artist improving on nature "reflects the neoclassic doctrine of the superiority of art over nature."[55] Morse does not explain what Pope understood by these doctrines, nor how Pope's understanding may have differed from what Coleridge, or Shelley, or for that matter, Sidney, understood by the same notions. The point is this: both Morse and Martz assume that the discovery of order can be identified as a literary principle irrespective of any concern for the kind of universe which supplies that order—Aristotelian, Hobbesian, Kantian. When such distinctions are disregarded or confused, Stevens can be related to any period in the tradition, which is pretty much what has happened. Stevens' aesthetic, however, derives from the transcendental framework it assumed with Coleridge. It differs in that it lacks the God and the supersensible reality which supported, at least in theory, the mysterious elements of Coleridge's creative faculty and the romantic claim to "higher truth." In this sense it may be described as post-Romantic, but it is not a new phase of humanism nor a reassertion of humanistic values, nor does it aim at the creation of "a world of value and order." It aims at the creation of imaginary worlds which are valuable because they satisfy our psychological needs and in so doing, attest to "the power of the mind over the mind itself." If one begins from the standpoint of modern skepticism, this may be the best aesthetic formulation possible. Before that can be decided, we shall need to agree upon what it means and why.

4

Modern Variations Of
Aesthetic Idealism

"We do not know what is real and what
is not." ("An Ordinary Evening in New
Haven")

Only in the last decade has Stevens' interest in philosophy and his use of
philosophical concepts received much notice. The question of whether or
not he was a philosophical poet has been raised, along with the possibility
that his interest in the insolvable problems of existence was merely an
extension of his aestheticism. It is apparent that his traffic with philosophy
was carried on with something of the air of irresponsible dilettantism. His
reference to Kant, for example, is fairly typical:

> The philosopher thinks of the world as an enormous pastiche or, as he puts it, the world
> is as the percipient. Thus Kant says that the objects of perception are conditioned by the
> nature of the mind as to their form. But the poet says that whatever it may be, *la vie est
> plus belle que les idées.*[1]

Even when confined to his central theme, the creative process of the imagination, his critical comments betray an eclecticism that does not pretend
to more than superficial coherence. In philosophy the ideas that interested
him most were those dealing with the problem of knowledge, specifically
those which modified the basic idealist epistemology. Since the problem of
knowledge is an ubiquitous concern among modern philosophers, it is
scarcely possible to single out those writers who may have been significant
influences. It is possible, however, to establish the general context of
Stevens' interest through those philosophers with whom he was acquainted,
those to whom he refers on several occasions and whose ideas on aesthetic
theory, and the problem of knowledge generally, are related to his own.
For this purpose, the most useful figures are I. A. Richards, Benedetto

Croce, Henri Bergson, William James, and George Santayana. Since the influence of Richards and Croce upon modern aesthetic is widely recognized, Stevens' appropriation of some of their theories is not particularly noteworthy. They will be considered here together as representative theorists illustrating Stevens' relation to the central tradition of modern aesthetic. The subsequent discussion of Bergson, James, and Santayana will bear more specifically upon the problem of knowledge. The purpose here will be to indicate the general philosophical context upon which Stevens drew for variations of aesthetic theory. It seems necessary to stress that the discussion of these figures is not aimed at establishing influences (although in the case of Bergson and Santayana the appropriation of certain ideas appears to be a matter of direct influence), but of familiarizing the reader with the area of Stevens' interest in modern philosophy. It is difficult to specify relevant ideas in an area in which Stevens managed to be unspecific with remarkable consistency. The most that can be hoped for is some grasp (admittedly limited) of the relation between Stevens' aesthetic problems and the modern development of the problem of knowledge as it bears upon the idealist tradition.

I. A. Richards and Benedetto Croce

In a late essay Stevens characterized the period of modern art as "a time in which the search for the supreme truth has been a search in reality or through reality or even a search for some supremely acceptable fiction."[2] The last choice, that of a "supreme fiction," which is referred to as early as *Harmonium,* is usually thought to be Stevens' choice and to represent a definitive aesthetic theory. Robert Pack, for instance, devotes a chapter to explaining such a theory, concluding that it refers to a belief in some kind of oversoul which "exists beyond change" and can be identified with "knowledge of the eternal."[3]

Actually, the representation of poetry as play, a game, a fiction, a myth, or even "pseudo-statement" is common in the literary tradition from Baudelaire and Schopenhauer to Valéry and Santayana and I. A. Richards. As substitute for the "higher truth" of the Romantics, such terms usually stress that poetry is subjective or "created" truth, dependent upon the mind rather than external reality. They do not imply that poetry is a lie or even, necessarily, an invention in the sense of something the poet simply "makes up." They merely indicate an idealist bias (in the epistemological sense). Thus in the listing of alternatives, Stevens opposes the "supreme fiction" to a search for truth "in reality or through reality," indicating an aesthetic subjectively based upon the mind as opposed to one claiming objective validity. Since art does not claim objective validity, it may be accepted (in "a culture dominated by science") as frankly fictional. This is such a commonplace notion that it is difficult to account for the excitement that Stevens' particular phrasing has occasioned.

Under this general heading of "supreme fiction," then, Stevens elaborates upon a variety of modern aesthetic theories, theories which exhibit compatibility at a general level although as often as not they are incompatible in their specific formulations. A good example of this kind of appropriation is "The Noble Rider and the Sound of Words." In this first essay of *The Necessary Angel,* Stevens explores two popular criteria of poetry regarded as "supreme fiction": credibility and linguistic existence. Unlike the classic Aristotelian theory of probability, which stressed a rational relation between motive and action, the modern requirement of "credibility" is rooted in psychological probability. It tends, in short, to place emphasis upon the psychological response of an audience rather than upon a relation between mind and external reality. I. A. Richards, who is probably the single most important exponent of the theory, provides a characteristic statement of it in *Principles of Literary Criticism:*

> Many attitudes, which arise without dependence upon reference, merely by the interplay and resolution of impulses otherwise awakened, can be momentarily encouraged by suitable beliefs held as scientific beliefs are held. So far as this encouragement is concerned, the truth or falsity of these beliefs does not matter, the immediate effect is the same in either case. When the attitude is important, the temptation to base it upon some reference which is treated as established scientific truth is very great, and the poet thus easily comes to invite the destruction of his work.... The attitude for the sake of which the belief is introduced is thereby made not more but less stable. Remove the belief, once it has affected the attitude; the attitude collapses. It may later be restored by more appropriate means, but that is another matter. And all such beliefs are very likely to be removed; their logical connections with other beliefs scientifically entertained are, to say the least, shaky.[4]

Richards' terminology belongs to the peculiar perlance of modern semantic analysis and may confuse the uninitiated. By "belief" he means anything capable of statement, anything to which the mind may give, as he says, "intellectual assent." It is the equivalent of what is normally meant, in standard usage, by one's ideas, one's thoughts or formulated opinions (intellectual assent being implicit in the use of a possessive). For Richards, all beliefs either refer to an object or are "objectless." The former, since they are statements capable of empirical verification, are "scientific statements." Any other idea about the external world, since it has no object, is an objectless belief; it is in fact no idea or belief at all but merely an "attitude" that has been incorrectly formulated. All such ideas, if they are "important," are "very likely to be removed" by science (with some help, one might add, from analytical semanticists). For example, the statement "All men are created equal" or "All men possess inalienable rights" is an objectless belief; it is merely an attitude incorrectly formulated. The significant point, however, is that the poet who relies upon such "objectless" ideas threatens the credibility of his emotion or attitude. For this reason, Richards allows that the poet may employ "trivial" beliefs, since these, even if scientifically untrue, do not usually interfere with a poem's credibility.

The implications of this position are fairly clear. Presumably a major poet is concerned with important attitudes. He should not use "important" ideas, if nonscientific, to support his attitude; it is hardly likely that he will use trivial ideas to support it; and it is fairly certain he will get little emotional assistance from scientific "statements of fact." The poet's job would appear to be limited to the expression of attitudes by the emotional treatment of physical detail. But even here, according to Richards, he should not suppose that his emotions are really dependent upon external references. His attitudes are psychological in origin and, beyond whatever practical necessity they may have, their justification is wholly in terms of psychological needs. The supposed relation between one's emotions and the external world is for Richards not merely an illusion, but a damaging one:

> Actually what is needed is a habit of mind which allows both reference and the development of attitudes their proper independence. This habit of mind is not to be attained at once, or for most people with ease. We try desperately to support our attitudes with beliefs as to facts, verified or accepted as scientifically established, and by so doing we weaken our own emotional backbone. For the justification of any attitude *per se* is its success for the needs of the being. It is not justified by the soundness of the views which may seem to be, and in pathological cases are, its ground and causes.... Opinion as to matters of fact, knowledge, belief, are not necessarily involved in any of our attitudes to the world in general, or to particular phases of it. If we bring them in, if, by a psychological perversion only too easy to fall into, we make them the basis of our adjustment, we run extreme risks of later disorganisation elsewhere.
>
> Many people find great difficulty in accepting or even in understanding this position. They are so accustomed to regarding "recognised facts" as the natural basis of attitudes, that they cannot conceive how anyone can be otherwise organised.[5]

The poet has been carefully wrapped here, in a self-contained psychology. Not only his ideas but his emotions have no basis in the external world. Reality has merely a specious value. It tricks the gullible, or rather the credulous, into accepting the poet's emotion. To return, however, to Richards' theory of "objectless belief": Shelley's *Adonais* illustrates what happens when the poet attaches emotions to unreal objects:

> Thus when, through reading *Adonais,* for example, we are left in a strong emotional attitude which feels like belief, it is only too easy to think that we are believing in immortality or survival, or in something else capable of statement, and fatally easy also

to attribute the value of the poem to the alleged effect, or conversely to regret that it should depend upon such a scientifically doubtful conclusion.[6]

In the "Noble Rider and the Sound of Words" Stevens adapts the psychology of credibility to a broader historical setting, beginning with Plato rather than Shelley. The essay develops from a discussion of Plato's figure of the charioteer traversing the heavens, a figure expressing the nobility of the soul. Stevens remarks that while the figure creates an immediate emotional response, "suddenly we remember, it may be, that the soul no longer exists and we droop in our flight...." He concludes that whereas Plato was "free to yield himself" to his imagination, history has produced psychological changes: the modern poet must accept another notion of poetry—

> The imagination loses vitality as it ceases to adhere to what is real. When it adheres to the unreal and intensifies what is unreal, while its first effect may be extraordinary that effect is the maximum effect that it will ever have. In Plato's figure, his imagination does not adhere to what is real.... The case is, then, that we concede that the figure is all imagination. At the same time, we say that it has not the slightest meaning for us, except for its nobility.... What has happened, as we were traversing the whole heaven, is that the imagination lost its power to sustain us. It has the strength of reality or none at all.[7]

The theory, which in Richards gives an idealistic aesthetic an underpinning of psychological determinism, involves Stevens in a curiously confused argument for historical determinism. The notion, for example, that Plato was free to yield himself to his imagination is presumably based upon a modern definition of reality, an empirical reality which Plato would have been the last to accept. On the other hand, Plato appears during the course of the discussion to share the modern viewpoint: "The existence of the soul, of charioteers and chariots and of winged horses is immaterial. They did not exist for Plato, not even the charioteer and chariot;..."[8] But Plato, whatever his view of charioteers, did believe in the existence of the soul and this is a matter of some significance in considering Plato's freedom to yield to what is "wholly the poetry of the unreal." The ambiguity of the entire argument seems to center in the ambiguous meaning of "reality," which is in turn the result of portraying the artist and his audience as historically subservient to the human race's "progressive mental states." As Stevens follows this line of development through Verrocchio, and Cervantes to modern American artists, the discussion becomes in fact a discussion of changing realities. ("It is not that there is a new imagination but that there is a new reality.") The modern reality comes to include social, political, religious and intellectual changes, none of which seems to be implied in the reality by which Plato's figure is judged.

Of all Stevens' essays, this is the one most widely quoted and admired. Yet it is, as Mr. Kermode has observed, "a little marred by some thin passages on the history of ideas,"[9] and more important, it never really engages its theme, the relation between imagination and reality. The discussion of Plato's charioteer is frequently cited as evidence of Stevens' unromantic devotion to fact. Such a reading assumes that the requirement of "adherence to reality" assures the poet of some objective norm or standard of truth, but the passage does not deal with the "truth" afforded by reality; it deals with the "strength of reality"—that is, its power to sustain an illusion, to lend it credibility.[10] The value of Plato's figure lies for Stevens, as it would for Richards, in the feeling or attitude toward human nobility, and the problem is to sustain that feeling not by an "objectless belief" in the existence of the soul but by convincing physical detail. When a work of art accomplishes this, Stevens says, "we regard it, in the language of Dr. Richards, as something inexhaustible to meditation."[11]

The importance of this standard of credibility, treated historically in terms of changing psychological states, becomes evident as the essay develops farther. The ambiguous use of the word "reality" is openly exploited. Quotations from Joad and Bergson are used to present reality as construed by rational disciplines: Bergson reduced reality to a perceptual flux; modern physics has resolved matter into "vibrations, movements, changes"; philosophy has "dismissed the notion of substance"; and natural science accepts the illusion that reality is "a collection of solid, static objects extended in space."[12] The quotations are intended, of course, to imply that the nature of reality cannot be grasped by rational means. All reason is reductive; we murder to dissect. By contrast the imagination comprehends reality in its restored fullness.

> The subject matter of poetry is not that "collection of solid, static objects extended in space" but the life that is lived in the scene that it composes; and so reality is not that external scene but the life that is lived in it. Reality is things as they are.[13]

A statement so reassuringly confident of the wholeness and value of poetry seems to demand nothing more than happy acquiescence, but it is an excellent example of how what appears so often in Stevens to be a philosophically innocent, common sense statement is ripe with dilemma. Reality is moved here, almost unnoticeably, from the realist to the idealist perspective. Reality is "not that external scene" but the life of the mind. When Stevens adds to this one of the themes of a later essay, that "if we live in the mind we live in the imagination," it would seem that reality is to be identified with the imagination, and by extension with poetry. Yet the contradictory theme to which he repeatedly returns is that "the imagination is false, whatever else may be said of it, and reality is true."[14] Thus in the above quotation reality is redefined as things "composed" by the mind, and a few pages on, the wholeness of that composition begins to diminish. Developing the Crocean theory of poetry as intuition become expression, Stevens concludes that the poet has been concerned with life "except as the intellect has had to do with it." He next elaborates upon the Crocean theory of language, approaching Croce's habit of regarding words themselves as providing expression with a kind of mystical existential validity:

> The deepening need for words to express our thoughts and feelings which, we are sure, are all the truth that we shall ever experience, having no illusions, makes us listen to words when we hear them, loving them and feeling them, makes us search the sound of them, for a finality, a perfection, an unalterable vibration which it is only within the power of the acutest poet to give them.[15]

At this point reality appears from the extreme viewpoint of subjectivist idealism, limited to "our own thoughts and feelings." Finally, referring to Croce's remark that "language is perpetual creation," Stevens reduces the reality of poetry to words themselves. "Poetry is a revelation in words by means of words," and "a poet's words are of things that do not exist without the words."[16]

The flexibility of the "supreme fiction"—once granted an idealist basis—is evident. Within a few pages the reality of poetry is diminished from "things as they are" to words about things that do not exist. The process suggests something, however, of the continuity (at least, superficial continuity) of modern criticism. Croce's version of the transcendental aesthetic was introduced by Spingarn in 1911. In essence, it presented a reinterpretation of Kant's *Critique of Judgment* along lines more amenable to modern skepticism. Croce replaces both Kant's incorporation of Understanding in the aesthetic process, and the post-Kantian incorporation of Pure Reason, with "form." "Form" is in turn defined as "expression."[17] In effect, this reduced the transcendalist aesthetic to a linguistic existentialism. Croce thus eliminated the epistemological concerns which had preoccupied Coleridge by the rather simple process of eliminating everything but the poem. Sensation, mind, and poem are conceived as a single evolving process, and the quest for truth or reality ends in the autonomous work of art, the only existential "thing," an effect without distinguishable causes. Poetry becomes objectified sensation, the mind of the poet being treated as the necessary purifying or formalizing medium through which the poem passes on its way to realization. The process, as Croce describes it, suggests Eliot's and Valéry's notion of the poet as catalyst:

> In the aesthetic fact, expressive activity is not added to the fact of the impressions, but these latter are formed and elaborated by it. The impressions appear as it were in expression, like water put into a filter, which reappears the same and yet different on the other side.[18]

In place of a solipsistic mind, one has the autonomous poem—words which refer to nothing but themselves. One has, in a more familiar phrase, the poem that cannot mean but can only be.

As with Richards, Croce's aesthetic is inconsistent with some of Stevens' favorite theories. That the poet contributes to the poem only formally is not consonant with Stevens' view elsewhere that the poet abstracts and idealizes his material. So too, Richards' scientific approach to the poetic process in terms of the "interplay of impulses" in the "central nervous system" could hardly be more antithetical to Stevens' idealist bent of mind. It is of passing interest to recall, also, Richards' unveiled contempt for Croce, whose "appeal has been exclusively to those unfamiliar with the subject."[19] Yet the influence of Croce did much to set the stage for Mr. Richards' school of New Criticism. When poetry is reduced to words about things that do not exist without the words, the critic has little choice but to confine his labors to the words themselves.

To conclude: Stevens' treatment of theories for which Richards and Croce may be taken as representative, illustrates the difficulty of identifying his "supreme fiction" with anything more specific than the current generalities of modern criticism. Certainly it cannot be regarded as an articulated aesthetic theory, either with respect to its coherence or its distinctiveness. His prose demonstrates his habit of borrowing from writers often widely spaced over the same intellectual tradition, and of availing himself of sympathetic ideas which on closer inspection resist assimilation. Croce and Richards, however incompatible their specific theories, are nonetheless representative of the major direction that aesthetic idealism has taken. Beginning with the theory of the interdependence of imagination and reality, the movement has been progressively away from a dependence upon external reality and toward the remaining alternatives, mind and language. For the relation between Stevens' supreme fiction and modern criticism generally, Croce's "science of expression" and Richards' "psychological theory of values" are crucial texts.[20]

Bergson, James, and Santayana

Although Stevens' comments upon poetry often reflect the subjectivist extreme to which the theory of "supreme fiction" can be taken, the possibility of restoring art to a search for truth "in or through reality" involves him in the efforts of modern philosophers to reassert an objectivist position. Of the most relevant philosophers, Bergson, James and Santayana, Bergson's importance is undeniable. Alfred North Whitehead, who regarded Bergson as the "most characteristic" philosopher of his age, second in importance only to James, summarizes his contribution as follows:

> Bergson introduced into philosophy the organic conceptions of physiological science. He has most completely moved away from the static materialism of the seventeenth century. His protests against spatialization is a protest against taking the Newtonian conception of nature as being anything except a high abstraction. His so-called anti-intellectualism should be construed in this sense. In some respects he recurs to Descartes; but the recurrence is accompanied with an instinctive grasp of modern biology.[21]

What Bergson did, in short, was to animate the universe. He conceived of the world as a single organism, continuously evolving, and containing within it innumerable small organisms, each sharing in the life principle of the whole, the *élan vital*. Historically, the evolution of the life force had proceeded through successively higher biological forms ending in man with the manifestation of the consciousness. Bergson thus disposed of the mechanistic-organic dualism of his German predecessors by extending biological organization to an ultimate metaphysical principle. Coleridge's fervent effort to believe that Nature in some way shared "the life that is within us" at last found metaphysical footing in the external world.

Equally important, as Professor Whitehead remarks, was Bergson's negative achievement—his attack upon the concept of a static reality. Here he returned to the arguments of the Eleatic school—to Zeno's paradoxes— and used them to attack the reality of the space-time continuum, specifically Kant's *a priori* space-time conditions. Kant himself had allowed that these conditions prevented the mind's access to whatever reality might lie behind the phenomenal world of objects. This was the point upon which Bergson capitalized. If time and space stood between mind and reality, then space and spatialized time should be regarded as the falsifying interpretation of intellect. By transcending this spatialization, the mind would be able to know reality in terms of a "pure" time continuum, of experiencing what Bergson called "real duration." Both matter and mind reveal themselves from this viewpoint as perpetual flux or "becomingness," of which the life principle, the *élan vital,* supplies the unifying bond, "the very stuff of reality."

> Matter or mind, reality has appeared to us as a perpetual becoming. It makes itself or it unmakes itself, but it is never something made. Such is the intuition that we have of mind when we draw aside the veil which is interposed between our consciousness and ourselves. This, also, is what our intellect and senses themselves would show us of matter if they could obtain a direct and disinterested idea of it.[22]

Bergson's philosophy is essentially mystical, and its mystical implications will be examined at some length in a later chapter. What is relevant here is his treatment of the problem of knowledge. As one might predict, Bergson found the mind's fullest experience of real duration lay in the act of self-consciousness.

Let us seek, in the depths of our experience, the point where we feel ourselves most intimately within our own life. It is into pure duration that we then plunge back, a duration in which the past, always moving on, is swelling unceasingly with a present that is absolutely new.... We must, by a strong recoil of our personality on itself, gather up our past which is slipping away, in order to thrust it, compact and undivided, into a present which it will create by entering. Rare indeed are the moments when we are self-possessed to this extent: it is then that our actions are truly free. And even at these moments we do not completely possess ourselves. Our feeling of duration, I should say the actual coinciding of ourself with itself, admits of degrees. But the more the feeling is deep and the coincidence complete, the more the life in which it replaces us absorbs intellectuality by transcending it.[23]

One should notice how many of the familiar themes of the modern idealist tradition are interwoven in this passage: the grounding of reality in self-consciousness, the emphasis upon immediacy, freedom, radical creativity, the transcendence of the Understanding, and the coincidence of subject and object accompanied by deep feeling.

Bergson's faculty for this self-creative moment is intuition or the Intensive Manifold. Its function in respect to the external world is similar to its internal function. It is capable of a perceptual act so intense that it assimilates change immediately, piercing the spatial mold of ordinary perception. This peculiar power is possible by virtue of the mind's original unity with the vital impetus of all external reality, a unity which enables it by an act of "sympathetic projection" to see things from the "inside," as Bergson puts it, rather than from the outside. By such successive contacts with the external source of creative energy, consciousness replenishes its own creative impetus. As its energy is expended, however, it is gradually confined by the static conceptions of the intellect, so that the process must be constantly repeated.

It may seem like a long voyage from the Coleridgean imagination to Bergson's Intensive Manifold, but the distance, as T. E. Hulme among others realized, is surprisingly short. Through T. E. Hulme, Bergson became one of the intellectual sponsors of the Imagist movement, and Hulme had no difficulty in seeing that Bergson's Intensive Manifold was really a modernized version of the "organic" imagination. He concludes his description of its perceptual operation:

The point to notice here is that at the beginning of this act, at this moment of tension, all the separate parts which before and after were separated out, were gathered up together in this act of intuition. They didn't exist side by side in the mind as they would have done in any intellectual representation. In Coleridge's phrase, they were fused together in the central heat of the imagination.[24]

Bergson seemingly offered the artist what he had, since Descartes, most needed: an organic world, radically creative and indeterminate. But more important, he made the artist supreme; he vindicated the Coleridgean imagination as the key to reality. He gave science and scientific rationalism no more than they deserved: the lie. For modern idealism he held out new hope of escape from its solipsistic predicament. In place of the religious faith of the Germany Idealists there was the *élan vital*. In place of spectral appearances there was immediacy. In place of the alienated human consciousness there was biological good-fellowship. As Professor Whitehead concluded, Bergson had "put the mind back into nature."[25]

So it appeared. When the brilliance of Bergson's attack upon the enemies of art had ceased to dazzle, the *élan vital* looked to more sober minds like pantheism in search of its Godhead. Irwin Edman remarks in his foreword to *Creative Evolution:*

> Bergson's philosophy was once hailed as a new thing in the world. Its elements are very old; its mysticism is as old as Plotinus, to whom Bergson acknowledged himself as indebted. His *élan vital* goes back a long way too: ultimately to the Dionysiac mysteries and, in the modern world, to Schopenhauer. Its romanticism goes back to Schelling, Fichte and Rousseau.[26]

Equally disturbing was the question of what actually had been gained by Bergson's theory of knowledge. Neither the spatial molds of perception nor the static abstractions of intellect correctly interpreted reality. The mind touched external reality only in a fleeting intuitive moment, a moment that could be immediately experienced but that was by definition inexpressible. This was an odd basis for a new theory of knowledge.[27] Bergson works around the difficulty by reminding the reader that his epistemology is keyed to an evolutionary future, that it requires "developing also another faculty," which will be able to "complete the intellect and its knowledge of matter by accustoming it to install itself within the moving."[28] But there is still the question of what is to be gained by such a faculty, and here Bergson, admitting that its knowledge would be "practically useless," depends simply upon that seemingly irresistible lure of so much modern philosophy— the "real." The promise afforded by his intuitive faculty is that "if it succeeds, it is reality itself that it will hold in a firm and final embrace."[29] What that embrace will be like seems very similar to the pantheist's self-annihilating immersion in the All, a theme Bergson approaches upon occasion. But what is of more interest is that the alternative is, for him, the solipsistic predicament. Unless you are willing to "thrust intelligence outside itself by an act of will," he warns, "you are inside your own thought; you cannot get out of it."[30] As other philosophers pointed out, Santayana among them, this prospect of self-transcendence contained a serious difficulty. In order to know otherness there must be consciousness of otherness *as* otherness, but in Bergson's system there was no otherness, there was merely immediate identification with the vast spiritual current from which human consciousness had somehow become separated. Bergson's reality, when the mystical moment had cleared, held only the image of Narcissus.

None of these difficulties appear in the interpretation of Bergson provided by T. E. Hulme, who by minimizing the mystical sources of the philosophy, managed to extract an aesthetic conducive to stylistic reforms. What Hulme and the Imagists found in Bergson—those who cared about such matters—was a new philosophical justification for the cult of immediacy. The intensity of perception and descriptive condensation cultivated in Imagist poetry are the legitimate offspring of Bergson's Intensive Manifold. He made it possible for the poet to burn with a gemlike flame and yet escape the mechanistic psychology in which impressionism and associationism were rooted. It could be said that he had had the last word in Coleridge's quarrel with Hartley. If in practice Imagism and impressionism at times seemed precariously close, they were nevertheless metaphysical worlds apart.

For Stevens, as one might expect, Bergsonian philosophy meant considerably more than a message of stylistic reform. It afforded a variation upon the second of his proposed approaches to truth—truth through reality. If the modern poet had no use for the German transcendentalists, except as he remarks on one occasion, "to keep up the window in which the cord is broken,"[31] Bergson offered a more acceptable alternative. In point of fact, the choice of realities behind ordinary perception appears at times to be remarkably wide.

> There is inherent in the words the *revelation of reality* a suggestion that there is a reality of or within or beneath the surface of reality. There are many such realities through which poets constantly pass to and fro, without noticing the imaginary lines that divide one from the other.[32]

The reality of the Bergsonian flux remained, however, one of the preferred choices. Like Hulme, Stevens usually tries to minimize the mystical core of the philosophy. His major reliance is upon the theory of radical novelty with a distinctively Bergsonian stress upon the necessity of intense and constantly renewed perceptions to replace the stultifying experience of the past. The mystical overtones of the *élan vital* are nevertheless perceptible in both the poetry and the prose. Usually these are accompanied by Stevens' characteristic elusiveness, his habit of exploring ideas primarily for their psychological effect. In one essay, for example, he refers to Bergson's account of the mystical experience of saints, comparing the experience to the elation which accompanies the poet's activity.

> To describe it by exaggerating it, he [the poet] shares the transformation, not to say apotheosis, accomplished by the poem. It must be this experience that makes him think

of poetry as possibly a phase of metaphysics; and it must be this experience that teases him with that sense of the possibility of a remote, a mystical *vis* or *noeud* to which reference has already been made.[33]

Bergson, in the earlier reference was discussing religious aspiration, which is not, Stevens continues, what he has in mind at all. It is merely that the mystic's experience is similar to the poet's experience of the imagination's "power to possess the moment it perceives." Precisely what Stevens does have in mind would be difficult to say, for his explanation is typical of his talent for intellectual sleight of hand—what Mr. Blackmur once called his "hocus-pocus."

> This sense of liberation may be examined specifically in relation to the experience of writing a poem that completely accomplishes the purpose of the poet. Bergson has in mind religious aspiration. The poet who experiences what was once called inspiration experiences both aspiration and inspiration. But that is not a difference, for it is clear that Bergson intended to include in aspiration not only desire, but the fulfillment of desire, not only the petition but the harmonious decree.... If then when we speak of justification we mean a kind of justice of which we had not known and on which we had not counted; if when we experience a sense of purification, we can think of the establishing of a self, it is certain that the experience of the poet is of no less a degree than the experience of the mystic....[34]

What gives this passage its curious involutions is the *élan vital* that now you see and now you don't. The terms "liberation," "exodus," "purification," "harmonious decree," are simply ascribed to a state of mind for which there can be no explanation. The state of mind may be subjectively real of course, and for an idealist unable to counter the subjectivist direction of his logic, this may have to suffice.

For the most part, Stevens' most obvious reliance upon Bergson is in his stress upon change and upon the poet's ability to express the novelty of the moment. The theory that novelty manifests the self-creative principle of mind was a commonplace in the idealist tradition long before Bergson. Bergson's distinctive contribution to this tradition is the identification of change with reality itself. The identification invests novelty with indiscriminate value. Change so long as it is change becomes an expression of the *élan vital's* triumph over a debilitating stasis of intellect that at every moment threatens it. Describing its struggle for novelty, Bergson writes:

> Even in its most perfect works, though it seems to have triumphed over external resistances and also over its own, it is at the mercy of the materiality which it has had to assume.... Our freedom, in the very movements by which it is affirmed, creates the growing habits that will stifle it if it fails to renew itself by a constant effort: it is dogged by automatism.

And so on to the conclusion:

By success must be understood, so far as the living being is concerned, an aptitude to develop in the most diverse environments, through the greatest possible variety of obstacles, so as to cover the widest possible extent of ground.[35]

Stevens, writing this time in 1951, in the last essay of *The Necessary Angel,* moves to a level of generality in which the intellectual background provided by Bergson is virtually lost, only the indiscriminate cultivation of novelty remaining.

Men feel that the imagination is the next greatest power to faith: the reigning prince. Consequently their interest in the imagination and its work is to be regarded not as a phase of humanism but as a vital self-assertion in a world in which nothing but the self remains, if that remains.... The extension of the mind beyond the range of the mind, the projection of reality beyond reality, the determination to cover the ground, whatever it may be, the determination not to be confined, the recapture of excitement and intensity of interest, the enlargement of the spirit at every time, in every way, these are the unities, the relations, to be summarized as paramount now.[36]

The passage could have been written by Bergson, but Bergson is not referred to, nor is the reader provided with any comprehensible motive for this excursion into an almost ecstatic rhetoric. One has merely the key phrases of Bergson's equally ecstatic message to the modern artist: that the intuitive faculty of the artist is most capable of the "vital self-assertion" which transcends the "range of the mind," escaping the molds in which the intellect is "confined" and achieving by its self-creative energy the "enlargement of the spirit."[37] A few pages later, however, Paul Klee's remark, echoing Bergson, that the artist must place himself "where the organic center of all movement in time and space—which he calls the mind or heart of creation—determines every function" is conceded to be "a bit of sacerdotal jargon."[38] No more enlightening is a still later reference to what is now called Bergson's most "poetic" contribution to philosophy: "In the case of Bergson, we have a poetry of language, which made William James complain of its incessant euphony. But we also have the *élan vital.*"[39]

The best the critic can hope to do with such uncertain evidence is to bear in mind that Bergson's approach to the problem of knowledge, especially as it affects the artist, was attractive to Stevens. In so far as he adopts a similar approach in his own poetry, a familiarity with Bergson, as will be shown, clarifies much that is obscure or at least subject to misinterpretation.

With William James and George Santayana, Bergson's philosophical innovations were taken into American tradition, the tradition of Harvard at the turn of the century. Stevens was an undergraduate at Harvard from 1897 to 1900, and as a New Englander for most of his later years, he appears to have retained his intellectual ties with the university. The only modern philosophers to whom he alludes with obvious respect are Bergson and the three most celebrated Harvard professors of philosophy after 1900, James, Santayana, and Whitehead.

At the turn of the century the Harvard department of philosophy was dominated by two rival factions. Under Josiah Royce, who was at Harvard from 1882 to 1913, Harvard became the center of the resurgence of German transcendentalism known as Neo-Hegelianism or Absolute Idealism.[40] Santayana at the time was a distinguished young disciple of Royce. The opposing faction was led by an iconoclast named William James, Professor in Philosophy from 1880 to 1907.

James's rise to prominence signalized in intellectual camps the death of the genteel tradition and the triumph of a new American spirit, "pragmatism." James himself, of course, belonged to that displaced "genteel" generation—along with his brother Henry, Edith Wharton, and Henry Adams. It was the generation which, as Stevens said, was "instinct with the fatal"; and William James was certainly a member of that "intellectual minority" who "began to convince us that the Victorians had left nothing behind."[41] Yet this is a judgment in retrospect that does little justice to James's efforts within a particular historical context. Like so many of his contemporaries, James recorded in his early correspondence and notebooks his personal struggle with skepticism and the painfully self-conscious regimen by which he recovered from a period of religious melancholia verging upon insanity. The experience clearly marked his later philosophical career with its sustained attack upon Roycean idealism. The elements of Royce's school which he found most reprehensible were those which for him epitomized the complacent intellectual American culture at the turn of the century, a culture which he found too effete to resist the encroachments of materialism and skepticism.

In "The Will to Believe," James elaborated upon what had once been for himself and for a good many others the skeptical minimum: "the sustaining of a thought *because I choose to.*" It was probably in that phrase as much as in his pragmatic method that James lived up to the title of "spokesman for the whole age that passed with the Great War."[42] "The Will to Believe," however, was an effort to give that phrase philosophical justification, to defend religious belief as a purely volitional act, a response of "our passional nature" in gratifying our psychological needs. For this, James was willing to affront the orthodox and to depend for his bargaining power upon skepticism itself: "There is but one indefectibly certain truth, and that is the truth that pyrrhonistic scepticism itself leaves standing— the truth that the present phenomenon of consciousness exists."[43] Argued from this ground—the uncertain validity of all human knowledge—the assent to a "religious hypothesis" seemed to James a justifiable risk, provided it is regarded *as* a risk and not as assent to any absolute truth. Thus giving Pascal's wager a good pragmatic twist, James urges the adoption of his own solution, "my willingness to run the risk of acting as if my passional need of taking the world religiously might be prophetic and right."[44] Such was James's compromise with the skeptical adherents of modern empiricism, and the argument has had endless reverberations — in the "as if" philosophies which Krutch laments in *The Modern Temper,* in the recourse to psychologies of credibility, in Santayana's *Scepticism and Animal Faith,* in Wallace Stevens' contention that belief in poetry requires sticking to "the nicer knowledge of / Belief, that what it believes in is not true."[45] The habit of mind is familiar enough. That we can believe provided we do not, that what is true is true by virtue of being false, that skepticism shall be the firm rock of faith — it all must have seemed like contemptible nonsense to a mind firm in its convictions. So it appeared, certainly, to many of James's more pious contemporaries. And so it appeared to Henry Adams. But the corrosive effect of skepticism upon that distinguished mind is all too sadly apparent to students of American literature. One has only to read the correspondence between Henry Adams and William James in their late years to recognize that a desperate optimism may be better than none, or as James preferred to put it, "For my own part, I have also a horror of being duped, but I can believe that worse things may happen to man in this world."[46]

What is more relevant here is that Stevens and James both sound at times the tragic rhetoric of a common intellectual legacy. James, for example, writing in his notebooks of his recovery from religious despair, emphasizes his total dependency upon volition. After learning to sustain a thought by choice, he writes, he came to the second step of his recovery:

> ...I will go a step further with my will, not only act with it but believe as well; believe in my individual reality and creative power. My belief, to be sure, can't be optimistic — but I will posit life (the real, the good) in the self-governing resistance of the ego to the world.[47]

This is not, to be sure, a unique attitude toward human affairs, but those who are committed to the view of Stevens as a "comic spirit" or as an exquisitely refined hedonist need to be reminded that there is an intellectual tradition involved. Stevens' defense of poetry was that it was an assertion of self "in a world in which nothing but the self remains," and that the imagination represented a "resistance to reality" which has "something to do with our self-preservation."

To return: James's ascendency over the Roycean school was greatly indebted to Bergson. In one of his Harvard lectures he acknowledges that he could never have freed himself from the "unintelligible intellectualism" of contemporary idealism "if I had not been influenced by a comparatively young and very original French writer, Professor Henri Bergson. Reading his works is what has made me bold."[48]

What James had learned from Bergson is evident in the way he attacked the fundamental postulate of the Absolute Idealists, their concept of the One, the Whole, or Spiritual Unity as the ultimate reality or ground of all existence. James argued what Coleridge had surmised, that the idealist was committed by his epistemology to an absolute or metaphysical idealism. He had to posit a reality behind appearances as an escape from solipsism, and whether he called that reality mind or matter could make no difference; in either case its intelligibility depended upon its being contained by a divine intelligence, the Whole which contained all particularity in one eternal unity. If all things had to be part of this divine Whole, then reality could be nothing less than the Whole, a "block universe." Particularity was a meaningless temporal illusion, for particulars could not alter the perfect unity that had already been posited as the ground of their existence. Change, perception, creativity, were part of a meaningless superficial flux beneath which lay an unremitting identity, an all pervasive sameness.[49] More important, James urged, were the moral implications of Royce's "so-called transcendental idealism of the Anglo-Hegelian school." For James, the Whole was an abstraction so vast as to be meaningless; one could neither know it in its entirety nor alter it in its particularity; it was, in fact, a pantheistic concept incompatible with Protestant morality and a theistic god.

> It is pantheistic, and undoubtedly it has already blunted the edge of the traditional theism in protestantism at large.... The absolute mind which they offer us, the mind that makes the universe by thinking it, might for aught they show us to the contrary have made any one of a million other universes just as well as this. You can deduce no single actual particular notion of it. It is compatible with any state of things being true here below.[50]

On this point James aligned himself with the empiricists, agreeing with writers like Morrison Swift that the "tender-minded" Bostonian intellectual of Roycean persuasion was like a sleepwalker. Lost in the "monumental vacuity" of his religious All, he could see no reality in temporal particulars.

> "Religion," says Mr. Swift, "is like a sleep-walker to whom actual things are blank." And such, tho possibly less tensely charged with feeling, is the verdict of every seriously inquiring amateur in philosophy to-day who turns to the philosophy-professors for the wherewithal to satisfy the fullness of his nature's needs. Empiricist writers give him a materialism, rationalists give him something religious, but to that religion "actual things are blank."[51]

Thus Bergson's attack upon static materialism was followed by James's attack upon static idealism. The pragmatic bias of James's argument is of course distinctively James's. Both philosophers emphasized the necessity of a universe in which real change, metaphysical change, was possible. For James, this did not mean that change or becoming was the sole reality. Metaphysical change meant for him a justification of particularity, a refusal to deprive particulars of any functional efficacy in the universal scheme and hence to discount them as metaphysically irrelevant.

The epistemological question was more difficult, but as James said, Bergson had made him bold. The boldness lay in his reassertion of a realist position. The argument is intricate in detail but in its main outlines it is astonishingly simple. Absolute idealism was, he argued, fatally monistic. Its monism was the inevitable result of defining matter and mind as "independent" heterogeneous elements and then assuming that what was "independent" could be in no way related. The assumption resulted in an epistemological cleavage which required that a third term be called in to reconcile the original two. But with everything divided into matter or mind, the third term would always be one of the original two, namely mind. The third term, itself, would then have to be related by calling on a fourth term, the fourth would require a fifth, and so on through an infinite series which could be arrested only by positing an absolute mind capable of relating all by containing all. The only way to avoid this reasoning, James maintained, was to begin with a single, neutral concept of reality. He called it, after Bergson, "pure experience." "Pure experience" referred to the immediately given content of the sensible world, called as you please—"a bald *that,* a datum, fact, phenomenon, content, or whatever other neutral or ambiguous term you prefer to apply."[52] Beginning with this neutral reality, one can regard it as functioning in two different ways, or in two different contexts. Subjectively it enters into consciousness as perceptual knowledge; objectively it enters into external existence as a physical object. Conceived in this manner, "pure experience" can be regarded as the point of intersection between two lines, the one extending into the mind and the other into the external world. The important matter for James is that the lines can and do intersect, so that the reality of perceptual knowledge can be verified at the point of intersection. One might, for example, remember the features of an acquaintance vaguely or to some extent incorrectly, but the reality of such knowledge can be verified when the acquaintance is again encountered in experience.

Such, in barest outline, was James's solution to the epistemological dualism which was forcing the Roycean school into increasingly esoteric and oversubtle intellectualism.[53] The solution formed the basis of James's experiential philosophy of "radical empiricism." Nominalistic, relativistic, and utilitarian—James's world was not, as Mr. Ransom would say, the best of all possible worlds. It was clearly a compromise. But it restored the physical world; it elevated reason by elevating what had long been conceded to be its proper domain, the practical; and in place of religious belief it left not certainty, but hope—and the willingness on the part of Christian gentlemen "to act *as if* the invisible world which our religious needs suggest were real."[54]

What James adapted, in greatly altered form, from Bergson was the doctrine of pure experience and the anti-intellectualism which seemed a healthy contrast to the endless theorizings of the Harvard idealists. He wrote of Bergson:

> He directs our hopes away from them [rationalistic philosophies] and toward the despised sensible flux. *What he reaches by their means is thus only a new practical attitude.* But he restores, against the vetoes of intellectualist philosophy, our naturally cordial relations with sensible experience and common sense. This service is surely only practical; but it is a service for which we may be almost immeasurably grateful. To trust our senses with good philosophic conscience!—who ever conferred on us so valuable a freedom before?[55]

No one who has followed the arduous path from Kant to Royce can fail to feel something of the force of this appeal, but few could have predicted that Bergson's *élan vital,* winged from Dionysian rites and Plotinian mysticism, should arrive bearing the needed admonition "to trust our senses with a good philosophic conscience." A great temperamental and philosophical chasm is ignored with James' seemingly innocent reference to what is "only practical." Bergson had little use for the merely practical, and James had less use for the *élan vital.* For James there was no unifying center, just as there was no unifying Whole. Experience reports a world of multiplicity, not unity, the many not the One. Particulars may form related systems, but each system is discrete—overlapping, contradicting, abutting, but never resolving into a single coherent Whole. The only trustworthy cementing medium was experience. From there on, one played by the ear of conscience, or what one hoped was a conscience. And here, James was open to such responses from intellectual quarters as T. S. Eliot's wry observation that "the great weakness of Pragmatism is that it ends by being of no *use* to anybody."[56]

The final figure in this rather remarkable Harvard period is George Santayana. Santayana's relation to the idealist tradition is unique. Although he began his career at Harvard as a disciple of Royce, his religious skepticism was incompatible with Royce's philosophy, and he found himself increasingly drawn into the pragmatic camp. His autobiography contains an amusing account of how, as his publications began to please Royce less, they began to please James more. His two most famous books on aesthetics, however, *The Sense of Beauty* (1896) and *Interpretations of Poetry and Religion* (1900) are more amenable to the tradition of Royce, the first elaborating a psychophysical basis for what is essentially the Kantian aesthetic, the second affirming Matthew Arnold's hope that the fictions of poetry would salvage what religion had lost. James called the latter "the perfection of rottenness." Santayana later explained:

> ...what arrested his attention was my aestheticism, that seemed to find the highest satisfaction in essences or ideals, apart from their eventual realisation in matters of fact...what he called rottenness was my apparent assumption that in the direction of religion and morals imagination was all, and there was nothing objective. Mine, he also said, was the most anti-realistic book he had ever read. I reported this saying to Royce, who observed, "That is just the side of it I agree with."[57]

Santayana had some cause to resent James's criticism. He had merely proposed that in place of belief in "Platonic Ideas and the deities and dogmas of religion" poetry offered ideals which could be enjoyed without belief because "they were fictions inspired by the moral imagination, and they expressed unsatisfied demands or implicit standards native to the human mind."[58] It was, after all, James who proposed to regard religion as a need of his "passional nature" upon which he was willing to take a risk. Santayana had accepted the need; he merely declined the risk.

In his subsequent career, Santayana divorced himself from Royce to become a vehement opponent of modern idealism. Interestingly, one of his most effective attacks was aimed at the new Bergsonian idealism. Of Bergson, "the most circumspect and best equipped thinker of this often scatterbrained school," he wrote:

> Truth, according to M. Bergson, is given only in intuitions which prolong experience just as it occurs, in its full immediacy....
>
> With this we seem to have reached the extreme of concentration and self-expansion, the perfect identity and involution of everything in oneself. And such indeed is the inevitable goal of the malicious theory of knowledge to which this school is comitted.... Solipsism has always been the evident implication of idealism.[59]

Santayana's own philosophy presents a unique combination of the ideas which have been discussed here with reference to Bergson and James. He claimed to be a materialist and naturalist, following James in reverting to a modified epistemological realism. On the other hand it is not hard to see in his evolutionary account of human progress through the "realms of being" the working out of the *élan vital*.[60] It is an account of the phases of human progress conceived as a naturalistic advance from matter to the ultimate realm of "spirit," a realm in which is achieved the highest human aspiration, the contemplation of "essences." The theory of "essences" is the most distinctive feature of his philosophy, and it represents, as Santayana himself acknowledged, his most radical departure from the tradition of Royce and modern idealism generally. The departure lay in a simple and most ingenious move: the separation of essence from existence. After Coleridge's "images" created out of the poet's own mind, Croce's intuited "forms," and Bergson's intuitive moment of the Intensive Manifold, comes the novel formula of Santayana's nonexistent "essences." Scorning the transcendental reliance upon an invisible noumenal world as a "romantic dream" suitable for "the mystic and the madman," Santayana proposed that all one needed to transcend material reality was sufficient "as if" detachment. His essences belong to what might be described simply as a hypothetical realm of infinite possibilities. The theory was widely misunderstood, perhaps because, as Santayana eventually explained, it was for philosophical minds "too simple." It is best to retain Santayana's later definition in all its simplicity: "An essence is anything definite capable of appearing or being thought of."[61] A few critics had supposed that his essences were really Platonic ideas, a supposition that overlooked their most important characteristic — nonexistence. It also overlooked that essences extend to anything that can be recognized or "thought of" as distinct from anything else. Unchanging and self-identical, an essence is any *this* which can be distinguished from any *that,* whether an appearance, an idea, or the wildest fancy. And finally, it overlooked the fact that Santayana regards the primary "field" or locus of essences to be the phenomenal world. Every object in the physical world reflects an essence — that is, an essence that is there, provided we assume that it is not. As he explains, "An essence is what anything turns into in our eyes when we do not believe in it."[62]

It is important to see why this kind of intellectual gamesmanship (for so it may well appear) should be necessary. Why should anyone posit a nonexistent realm and then discuss it, ecstatically and at book length, as though it existed? And why should anyone propose as the supreme human experience the contemplation of nonexistents which are rewarding not *in spite* of their nonexistence but because of it. The answer is fairly simple. Santayana is a materialist on one level and an idealist on another, and the only thing that can survive both levels at once is something that, metaphysically, never was. So at least was Santayana's understanding of the matter, as is evident in his rejection of James's solution to the epistemological problem. James's concept of a neutral term which could absorb the subject-object antithesis, was for Santayana a logical solution only, without metaphysical reality:

> We cannot say that neutral entities exist by themselves, so that, in James's example, the leaping fire in the hearth is one fact, merely *called* material or mental by virtue of

simultaneous relations in two different directions, in one path physical and in the other biographical.... The pictorial fire is no longer in the hearth at all, as James wished to believe; it is *only* in the *brain,* the fire being inhabited by other, nonhuman, neutral entities, existing only in that physical medium. So transformed and corrected I gladly accept the theory, except that my neutral entities are essences only.... I cannot conceive truly neutral entities *composing* either mind or matter.... [63] (Santayana's italics)

Lest the reader, an understandably weary one at this point, assume that he has merely come back to Coleridge's original predicament, it may be appropriate to recall again the historical context. This, Santayana himself does in responding to a European transcendentalist who preferred to regard him as a misguided "representative of the New World" who had strayed from the idealist tradition:

He forgets that I and many of the older American professors were pupils of Royce and students of Bradley and were brought up—thank God, not exclusively—on Kant and Hegel; and he forgets Emerson. There was little need of reminding the New World of transcendentalism. As for me my Catholic background and Latin mind placed me in conscious and sometimes violent contrast with Old Boston [transcendental], and also with the new America that has grown up for the most part after my day [pragmatic].... [64]

For Santayana, idealism had had its day and James was in the ascendency. The lesson that James had taught was not to be forgotten. Transcendentalism had ended in the "solipsism of the present moment"; it was "a blind alley; and its blindness proved the incompatibility of idealism with any claim to knowledge...." [65] But James had in his own way opened a new route to skepticism. We must "trust our senses," but as James readily admitted, the sensible world does not suffice, and for Santayana the only remaining epistemological step was the step into nonexistence or a fictional world:

With such trustworthy human knowledge [empirical knowledge] I have always been perfectly content, discontented as I may have been with the realities that it reports.... The use of philosophy, and in particular of the discrimination of essence, is to distil the wine out of those trodden grapes, in order that in whatever kind of world we may be living, we may live freely in the spirit. The relief that I find, when in the presence of facts I can discern essences, does not come, as in religious faith, through trust in any higher facts. It comes through liberation from anxiety, from the need of faith, and from the very problem of knowledge. [66]

One has in Santayana the perfect inversion of real and unreal that was described in an earlier chapter as the historically evident trend of idealist thought. What is interesting is that the inversion is now the work of an avowed realist and that it is justified as an effort to rescue the trustworthiness of human knowledge from the hands of idealists. If I make essences real, Santayana argues, I am committed to the idealist trap, and I must deny as unreal what is the only "trustworthy" human knowledge, sensible reality. Moreover, without religious faith I cannot even posit the reality of the idealist's mental world. The obvious compromise was to keep the sensible world as real, but without spiritual value; and to maintain the idealist world as the unreal, but of the highest spiritual value.

Thus Santayana chose to resolve the epistemological deadlock by resorting to a "nonexistent" neutral term. His neutral term, however, can be regarded like James's term in two distinct ways. As animals, we may by an instinctive "act of faith" in reality, accept sense phenomena as an accurate representation of the physical world of objects. As spirits, on the other hand, we deny the physical reality, perceiving only the disembodied appearance, just as one might look at a painting behind which there is nothing. The pictorial quality which the latter viewpoint gives to perception has been observed by others, but for Santayana the transformation from physical reality to appearance, which he explains as a "trick of the mind," somehow evokes the mysterious:

> An essence is an "idea," but an idea lifted out of its immersion in existing objects and in existing feelings; so that when considered in itself and recognized as pure essence its very clarity seems to strip both objects and feelings of their familiar lights: reality becomes mysterious and appearance becomes unreal; an intolerable thought to pictorial realists and pictorial idealists. But no analysis can threaten the reality of appearances *as* appearances: that is just the reality that the theory of essence proclaims, and places in its proper logical sphere. In denying that appearances are existences or powers, this theory merely banishes superstition and idolatry. Essences are not ghosts that someone says he has seen in the dark: they are precisely that which is clearest and most indubbitably present in the brightest light. They are, in any "idea," all that can be observed, retained, recalled, or communicated....
>
> My theory ought to be intelligible to poets and artists who have not bothered with modern philosophy, a radically subjective and sophistical thing. For there is a natural transition between focussing attention and perceiving that what thereby comes to light is an essence and not a fact. This transition gives the artist his liberty. He may yield to inspiration. There will be enough relevance to the world in his originality, if this originality springs from his deeper self, which is a living part of that world, existing only in constant contact with the rest.[67]

Several points here are worth stressing. The first is that appearances *as appearances* involve no epistemological problem, so long as one does not assert their existence either in themselves or as representatives of existing objects. As James had said, if they are treated merely as phenomena of consciousness, they are the one certainty that even "pyrrhonistic scepticism itself leaves standing." Second, when an appearance is recognized as immaterial, a transference has been made from sense perception to "spirit" perception (in effect, from materialism to idealism). The resulting clarity of the appearance, because *unfamiliar,* assumes an air of ineffability. Santayana's terms vary, but whether characterized by "clarity," "transparence," or "luminosity," the peculiar alteration is sufficient to make an essence "mysterious," "inspiring," and appropriately "spiritual." In this ineffable *difference* the artist finds his liberty—though why this should be so when the difference is merely psychological, is somewhat puzzling. In any event, the realization of an essence is the signal that the artist may "yield to inspiration" and trust to his "deeper self." At this point Santayana seems to put the validity of the artist's inspiration on a radically empirical basis. The artist has withdrawn from the world of matter, action, knowledge and value, into a subjective realm of "the ideal or moral excitation which that world arouses," but since he is himself still a part of nature, his subjective experience will be "relevant."

Once Santayana's theory of essences is grasped, it has, in comparison to the Kantian tradition, certain obvious advantages. With only a slight manipulation of the epistemological scheme, one can be for practical purposes a realist, for spiritual purposes an idealist; and as an idealist, neither Kant's noumenal world nor Royce's Universal Mind are requisite. The problems of the Bergsonian flux are avoided also, since an essence is merely whatever identifiable form the flow of matter happens to assume at any given moment. Since an essence does not inhere or subsist in matter, it is independent of material change. Like an abstraction, it has the stability of a contemplated object; it can be "detached" both from self and matter. It is not limited to immediate experience, nor does it have to be identified with self. In these respects Santayana's essences are an improvement over the Bergsonian immersion in the immediate and the transcendental penetration of reality. But in addition to the dubious attraction of nonexistent "fictions" (the word does not trouble Santayana), there is the problem of how one is to make one's way in a realm of infinite possibilities. One is given a realm of spiritual aspiration but of aspiration toward no end; complete freedom, but no principle of selection. In the world of essences no values inhere, in the world of spirit no obligations. One is afloat in a sea of infinite possibilities, where to sink or to swim are equally meaningless alternatives. The world of spirit is, for Santayana, a world of "post-rational detachment," where neither emotion nor thought are efficacious. It represents, in fact, the full fruition of the skepticism and aestheticism so characteristic of its author. It is notable that "disillusionment" is a word closely associated with spiritual aspiration. Spirituality comes easily, for instance, to men "thoroughly disillusioned about the course of nature and the decrees of fate."[68] Disillusionment is, in fact, an aid in the perception of essences because

...in a disillusioned analytic mind attention intently fixed on the given, far from inducing belief, induces definition of the given, and suspension of all belief; for now what in animal life was a mere incident in action has become absorption in intuition, and belief in existence has turned into contemplation of essence. I happen to be able to do this trick and to enjoy doing it;...[69]

It will be noticed in this passage that what was a "mere incident" on the plane of animal existence is somehow more enjoyable when by a trick of mind one ceases to believe in it. Among the philosophical critics who do not share Santayana's preference for the trick, Irving Edman has summarized more emphatically some of the implications already mentioned.

He describes spirituality, as he defines it, as difficult for most men, but the most sublime ambition open to man. In just what does its sublimity consist, however?..... To survey essences, the indelible self-identifying character of forms, not their use or beauty or delight, but simply for the tautological pleasure of identifying them—why is that sublime?....

Spirituality may be sublime, but this sublimity is somewhere beyond humanity. For it is characterized, on the one hand by detachment, a detachment so complete that it recognizes neither any special source nor any special object. "In the spiritual life," he writes, "there is nothing obligatory." It beholds all essences or any essence with equal interest, or, more precisely, with equal lack of interest. Spirit has no commitments, no allegiances, no preferences, no scale of values. It has no associations and is a member of no society.... The detachment which is the acme of liberation turns out to be not the detachment of a saint worshipping a god, but of an esthete playing with images, with a waking dream, with all the joys and griefs of illusion.[70]

Santayana's ultimate position, Edman concludes, is not humanism but posthumanism, and the sublime deliverance it offers is "the consolation of the poet's Nirvana." For a poet like Stevens, willing to settle for a "supremely acceptable fiction," that objection might well appear beside the point. Stevens could scarcely have found a philosopher more compatible with his own temperament—aristocratic, aesthetic, romantic, skeptical. His profound admiration for Santayana is explicit, both in the prose passage already cited, in which Santayana is the examplar of "the function of the imagination," and in the poem "To an Old Philosopher in Rome." Other passages suggest a more specific interest in the theory of essences. There is, for instance, a description of paintings in a modern art exhibit which turns upon the peculiar clarity of appearances divested of their physical reality.

A woman lying in a hammock was transformed into a complex of planes and tones, radiant, vaporous, exact. A tea-pot and a cup or two took their places in a reality composed wholly of things unreal. These works were *deliciae* of the spirit as distinguished from *delectationes* of the senses and this was so because one found in them the labor of calculation, the appetite for perfection.[71]

In addition to the same luminous unreality which Santayana ascribes to essences — "radiant, vaporous, exact" — there is a specific reference to the transference from sense to spirit, along with the implicit identification of unreality with spiritual aspiration. These themes reappear throughout Stevens' later prose. In one passage art is described as a process by which "reality changes from substance to subtlety";[72] in another the unfamiliar clarity of artistic perception initiates the transference from reality to an imagined unreality:

> It is as if a man who lived indoors should go outdoors on a day of sympathetic weather. His realization of the weather would exceed that of man who lives outdoors. It might, in fact, *be intense enough to convert the real world about him into an imagined world.* In short, a sense of reality keen enough to be in excess of the normal sense of reality creates a reality of its own. Here what matters is that the intensification of the sense of reality creates a resemblance: that reality of its own is a reality.[73] (italics added)

The problem of selection from infinite possibilities, of some standard of relevance between real and unreal worlds, of the meaning of spiritual aspiration without end or definable values, remains for Stevens as it does for Santayana. On one occasion the perception of the self-identity of objects is justified precisely as Professor Edman found it to be justified for Santayana — "simply for the tautological pleasure of identifying them."

> To know facts as facts in the ordinary way has, indeed, no particular power or worth. But a quickening of our awareness of the irrevocability by which a thing is what it is, has such power, and it is, I believe, the very soul of art.... What I desire to stress is that there is a unity rooted in the individuality of objects and discovered in a different way from the apprehension of rational connections.[74]

The nature of that unity, and the particular "power or worth" involved are not explained.

These are the terms, then, with which Stevens' long dalliance with the idealist tradition apparently ends. It would be misleading to suggest that Santayana's influence was a final or definitive one. As with Bergson, he represents one alternative among many, but it is an alternative which has more in common with the direction taken in Stevens' later prose than any afforded by figures discussed earlier.

Since the purpose of this chapter has been to provide a philosophical context which aids in the interpretation of individual poems, Stevens' poem on Santayana furnishes an appropriate conclusion. The poem is overly long for full quotation; the relevant passages are the following:

To An Old Philosopher In Rome

On the threshold of heaven, the figures in the street
Become the figures of heaven, the majestic movement

Of men growing small in the distances of space,
Singing, with smaller and still smaller sound,
Unintelligible absolution and an end—

The threshold, Rome, and that more merciful Rome
Beyond, the two alike in the make of the mind.
It is as if in a human dignity
Two parallels become one, a perspective, of which
Men are part both in the inch and in the mile.

How easily the blown banners change to wings...
Things dark on the horizons of perception,
Become accompaniments of fortune, but
Of the fortune of the spirit, beyond the eye,
Not of its sphere, and yet not far beyond,

The human end in the spirit's greatest reach,
The extreme of the known in the presence of the extreme
Of the unknown. The newsboys' muttering
Becomes another murmuring; the smell
Of medicine, a fragrantness not to be spoiled...

The bed, the books, the chair, the moving nuns,
The candle as it evades the sight, these are
The sources of happiness in the shape of Rome,
A shape within the ancient circles of shapes,
And these beneath the shadow of a shape

In a confusion on bed and books, a portent
On a chair, a moving transparence on the nuns,
A light on the candle tearing against the wick
To join a hovering excellence, to escape
From fire and be part only of that of which

Fire is the symbol: the celestial possible.
Speak to your pillow as if it was yourself.
Be orator but with an accurate tongue
And without eloquence, O, half-asleep,
Of the pity that is the memorial of this room,

So that we feel, in this illumined large,
The veritable small, so that each of us
Beholds himself in you, and hears his voice
In yours, master and commiserable man,
Intent on your particles of nether-do,

    . . . .

It is a kind of total grandeur at the end,
With every visible thing enlarged and yet
No more than a bed, a chair and moving nuns,
The immensest theatre, the pillared porch,
The book and candle in your ambered room,

> Total grandeur of a total edifice,
> Chosen by an inquisitor of structures
> For himself. He stops upon this threshold,
> As if the design of all his words takes form
> And frame from thinking and is realized.[75]

It might be difficult to persuade an innocent reader, confronted by so many reassuring elements of a traditional Christian rhetoric, that this poem is a tribute by an atheist poet to an atheist philosopher. But such are the known biographical facts, and they are supported in this instance by an additional consideration. Not only is a Christian reading of the poem unfeasible line by line, but it would destroy the point of the poem — which depends upon a rather exact knowledge of Santayana's contribution to the problem of knowledge.

The poem describes Santayana meditating in the seclusion of the Catholic nursing home to which he retired in his last years. The first stanza seemingly introduces a vision by a dying philosopher about to enter a Christian heaven, an interpretation enforced by the Roman setting. The human figures he contemplates, however, are simultaneous occupants of the sensible world and heaven. Their dual existence is explained in the second stanza. The philosopher's point of vision is a "threshold" common to two worlds, sensible Rome and an ideal or imagined Rome, and their apparent identity is a mental construction, they are "alike in the make of the mind." In the ninth line the dualism of the real and imagined world is implicitly resolved by a reference to Santayana's theory of essences. The concept of parallel lines "become one" is a figure Santayana himself uses in explaining his epistemology. In James's scheme, it will be recalled, the identity of objective and subjective worlds was conceived figuratively as the point at which two diverging lines, subjective and objective, intersect. Santayana, objecting that the point of intersection or identity could not be metaphysically real, chose to regard the apparent identity as the result of a peculiar perceptual act by which a sensible appearance was transformed into an immaterial essence. In this conception, the figure of momentarily superposed parallels was more appropriate since it permitted the absolute distinction he regarded as basic between essence, a permanent form, and existence, a temporal flux.

> But nothing can ever make existence and essence continuous, as nothing can ever make architecture continuous with music; *like parallels* such orders of being can never flow into one another. But they may be conjoined or superimposed; they may *be simultaneous dimensions of the same world*....[76]

This distinction may have limited fascination for students of literature, but it was an important philosophical maneuver which evoked considerable attention from Santayana's professional colleagues, and it is worth noticing that Stevens renders it precisely. The perception involved is identified as a peculiarly "human perspective," echoing Santayana's theory that to perceive essences was a uniquely human act as opposed to an animal function, an act by which man transcended his animal existence for the moral life of "spirit." The last line of the stanza gives a curious ambivalence to the perspective described. On the sensible level the contemplated figures naturally grow smaller as they move away into the distance. From a fixed perspective they would appear inch-sized ("in the inch") at the same time they appeared a mile distant ("in the mile"). The apparent meaning, however, is that by substituting for the reality of particular man the more imaginative perspective of man as essence, one enters the realm of possible essences where collective man may be idealized into a more grandiose vision. The latter reading is more in keeping with Santayana's understanding and is reinforced by a later contrast, in stanza eight, between the "illumined large" and the "veritable small." The third stanza describes the ameliorative changes which take place in the world of essences. The central notion is one already examined in the prose of both Santayana and Stevens: certain aspects of appearance which are undiscerned in ordinary sense perception ("dark on the horizons of perception") are suddenly made vivid in the fortuitous clarity of essences. Lines eleven and twelve specify that a transformation from sense to spirit has occurred. Essences are now the "fortune of the spirit," closely related to sense perception, but now belonging to the sphere of possibilities "beyond the eye." In the fourth stanza, the first two and a half lines identify the non-Christian context. Human aspiration is an end itself and consists in the imaginative "reach" from a given sense particular, "the known," to the ultimately possible essence, the "extreme of the unknown." The examples which follow depict the idealizing possibilities presented by the physical details of the philosopher's cloistered environment. One should notice how in the sixth stanza these details assume the luminous and mysterious unreality so fascinating to both Santayana and Stevens. A mere physical detail becomes a "portent," a "transparence," a "symbol" of human aspiration. The first line of the seventh stanza defines the aspirant's realm as the realm of infinite possibilities, the "celestial possible," a phrase which might again mislead the Christian interpreter. In the eighth stanza, Santayana's meditation upon his "particles of nether-do" is probably a reference to the status of "nonexistence" he assigns to essences, although it may refer simply to his preoccupation with the seemingly trivial forms of physical particulars. The reference to the "veritable small," is again a reference to such details regarded as sensible objects, the "real."

The concluding two stanzas recapitulate the previous themes. The idealized world of the philosopher's meditation is acknowledged to have no objective reality beyond the visibly given — "no more than a bed, a chair and moving nuns." Stevens picks up in this stanza, incidentally, a favorite figure of Santayana, who refers often to reality as a "grand theatre" for the exchange of essences. The concluding sentence brings the poem, unusual for its elevated rhetoric and abandonment to superlative, back to the skeptical ground of an "as if" commitment.

"To an Old Philosopher in Rome" is one of Stevens' most admired poems. It is a finished example of his skill, certainly, in the handling of rhetoric and detail, and the subject is one which enables him to combine his characteristic themes — the epistemology of the poet's fictional world and the self-ameliorative possibilities of the human spirit — in an unusually moving manner. Much of the poem's effect, however, depends upon vague associations with the Christian tradition which it disowns. The poem has a tradition of its own, however, and the analysis here is intended to demonstrate not merely that the two traditions are easily confused, but that the terms necessary for their distinction are sometimes dependent upon a more precise knowledge of the relevant philosophical background than has been supposed. The significance of the poem does not derive simply from Stevens' adaptation of Santayana's theory of essences, although a familiarity with that theory in its more technical aspects is obviously useful. Its significance depends rather upon a grasp of the relation between Santayana's theory and the epistemological problems which are the focus of Stevens' poetry over some forty years.

5

The Early Poetry

The preceding chapters have outlined the philosophical dimensions of Stevens' major theme—the problem he preferred to call the relation of reality and imagination. They have considered the historical sources of the problem as it is reflected in Coleridge and its aesthetic philosophical development among such modern figures as Croce, I. A. Richards, Bergson, James, and Santayana. The evidence cited of Stevens' involvement with this tradition has been confined, except for his poem on Santayana, to his prose. This has given the prose unmerited importance, but the exclusion of the poetry has seemed advisable for several reasons. No one familiar with the literature on Stevens can fail to be unsettled by the range of interpretation his poetry has elicited. The poetry is difficult. Much of it is conceptually vague, if not obscure. As a number of critics have pointed out, the obscurity derives largely from Stevens' distaste for direct statement, his habit of garbing ideas in metaphor, fable, anecdote and leaving the reader with a minimum of interpretive clues. In the long expository poems, those giving the fullest account of his aesthetic theories, metaphor is combined with abstract statement, but the argument is intentionally fragmented. Without considerable reconstruction, the fragments can mean almost anything. Another difficulty is the vocabulary, which has the character of a private shorthand to the uninitiated, even though its basic symbolism is traditional. Finally, there is the matter of attitude which, in the early poetry especially, is all too often uncertain. Here the ambiguity follows naturally enough from the difficulties already mentioned, but it is heightened by Stevens' use of three closely related stylistic mannerisms: understatement, irony, and the whimsical treatment of serious content. In a poet as elusive as Stevens, the meaning of a poem is often dependent upon the reader's ability to distinguish among such tenuous stylistic shadings.

The best illustration of these interpretative problems is provided by Stevens' own interpretation of one of his poems. Here is the poem, "Les Plus Belles Pages":

> The milkman came in the moonlight and the moonlight
> Was less than moonlight. Nothing exists by itself.
> The moonlight seemed to.
>   Two people, three horses, an ox
> And the sun, the waves together in the sea.
>
> The moonlight and Aquinas seemed to. He spoke,
> Kept speaking, of God. I changed the word to man.
> The automation, in logic self-contained,
> Existed by itself. Or did the saint survive?
> Did several spirits assume a single shape?
>
> Theology after breakfast sticks to the eyes.[1]

And here is Stevens' commentary on it:

> Apparently the poem means that the conjunction of milkman and moonlight is the equivalent of the conjunction of logician and saint. What it really means is that the inter-relation between things is what makes them fecund. Interaction is the source of poetry. Sex is an illustration. But the principle is not confined to the illustration. The milkman and the moonlight are an illustration. The two people, the three horses, etc., are illustrations. The principle finds its best illustration in the interaction of our faculties or of our thoughts and emotions. Aquinas is a classic example: a figure of great modern interest, whose special force seems to come from the interaction of his prodigious love of God. The idea that his theology, as such, is involved is dismissed in the last line. That the example is not of scholarly choice is indicated by the title. But the title also means that *les plus belles pages* are those in which things do not stand alone, but are operative as the result of interaction, interrelation. This is an idea of some consequence, not a casual improvisation. The inter-relation between reality and the imagination is the basis of the character of literature. The inter-relation between reality and the emotions is the basis of the vitality of literature, between reality and thought, the basis of its power.[2]

The reader steeped in Stevens' poetry might find nothing remarkable in this explanation, but it is a convenient demonstration, both in respect to theme and mannerisms, of the familiarity required. One begins with the knowledge that the bulk of the poetry represents variations upon a single theme: that satisfying art (or satisfying human experience) depends upon the interaction between reality and imagination. Beyond that, one needs to know such details as the following: (1) French culture is associated for Stevens with aesthetic or imaginative values, and the appropriation of French phrases indicates an assertion of aesthetic value as opposed to intellectual value. (2) The moon is Stevens' consistent symbol for imagination, as the sun is his symbol for reality. (3) God is the product of the imagination, whereas any uninspiring detail of the quotidian is likely to represent the drabness of reality. (Here the context is the determining factor, however.) (4) Reason and logic are associated pejoratively with determinism, mechanism, automatism. (5) Stevens' "illustrations" of the interactions between things are frequently confined to the naming of more than one particular, the interaction simply being asserted or implied—as in "Two people, three horses," etc. Given this much information, however, the poet's attitude toward Aquinas remains, without his prose explanation, ambiguous. The questions in the final lines are raised only to be dismissed by the ironic concluding line, the point of which might well escape any literate reader who is unaccustomed to distinguishing the "saint" from the "theologian."

In view of the interpretative difficulties which this poem illustrates, it is not surprising that much of the poetry has not been adequately explained. The procedure of this study has been, therefore, to exclude the poetry from a supporting role in its major thesis, relying upon the prose as the least disputable evidence. In turning now to the poetry, a more tentative approach should be permissible. Most of the interpretations offered here are in some respect novel. The two long poems to be considered are noted for their obscurity. They are not the best of Stevens' poems, but they are keys to the rest. The first, "The Comedian as the Letter C," is representative of the early poetry—*Harmonium* and *Ideas of Order*. It has been discussed so often that one is reluctant to belabor it further, but it provides evidence of Stevens' early interest in contemporary philosophy and, in particular, of a relation to William James that has not been pointed out. The final chapter will be concerned with a poem fairly representative of the poetry after 1940, "Notes Toward a Supreme Fiction." This is one of Stevens' most famous and most obscure poems. Little has been done with the interpretive problems it presents. It is therefore a good poem with which to illustrate how much of Stevens' obscurity is illuminated by the relevant philosophical background.

Harmonium and William James

Stevens' first volume of poems, *Harmonium,* reflects the philosophical explorations of a modernist poet, divorced from his intellectual tradition and in search of a position capable of sustaining a new aesthetic. It seems probable that the most important influence in these explorations was William James. The relationship is largely a matter of viewpoint, of Stevens' approach to various philosophical alternatives, and as such it is impossible to document convincingly. It is possible, however, to show the striking coincidence in their ideas generally. Since the intellectual context of *Harmonium* is still largely neglected in preference for the long established stress upon its hedonistic and solipsistic elements, the similarities between

Stevens and James are worth investigation. At least the similarities place *Harmonium* in a somewhat different light, and in some cases, I am convinced they clarify individual poems and reveal an intention that has been overlooked.

The major themes of *Harmonium* are (1) the loss of Christian faith and the collapse of traditional values, (2) the implications of the opposed philosophical positions of idealism and materialism, and (3) the specifically aesthetic implications of the former subjects.

It is well known that "Sunday Morning," usually regarded as Stevens' finest early poem, asserts the loss of Christian faith and argues for a naturalistic religion of man and nature. In defending a purely human ideal of divinity, Stevens treats classical and Christian religions as antecedent myths in which the original separation of human and divine was followed by their union in the human figure of Christ.

> Jove in the clouds had his inhuman birth.
> No mother suckled him, no sweet land gave
> Large-mannered motions to his mythy mind.
> He moved among us, as a muttering king
> Magnificent, would move among his hinds,
> Until our blood, commingling, virginal,
> With heaven, brought such requital to desire
> The very hinds discerned it, in a star. (p. 68)

The reference to Jove has produced some disagreement in the interpretation of this passage. In a poem which deals explicitly with the loss of Christian faith, it suggested to early critics that Stevens was advocating a return to pagan ritual. It is now generally recognized that Stevens uses classical and Christian appellations of divinity interchangeably. "Phoebus," "Triton," "Vulcan," "Jove," "God" may refer alike simply to the concept of an omnipotent being. Thus in a late essay dealing with the modern disbelief in gods, "both ancient and modern," he uses Jove as a representative figure, noting that he is merely one of various images the mind has formed of God.

> When we think of Jove...we take him for granted as the symbol of omnipotence, the ruler of mankind....All the noble images of all the gods have been profound and most of them have been forgotten.[3]

In "Sunday Morning" Jove is symbolic of an ancient concept of omnipotence divorced from humanity. He was not born of a human mother; he is an abstracted monarch who is as independent of his physical world as he is indifferent to its inferior inhabitants. It is thus unlikely that the "commingling" of human and divine refers to Jove's terrestrial philandering. The reference is rather to the humanizing of omnipotence in the union of "heaven" with "virginal" blood. The terms are notably devoid of sexual connotation and it is much more probable that the reference is to the virgin birth. In Christ, man conceived of a God who, unlike Jove, was capable of sharing in human emotions and the enjoyments of his "sweet land." Certainly this is strongly suggested by the appearance of the star which, if it is the star of Bethlehem, brings requital to the human desire to share in divinity. It is made manifest to the "very hinds" who were unworthy of Jove's concern. Moreover, this interpretation is more in keeping with the rest of the poem, which argues for the acceptance of Christ's mortality as the last stage of religious faith and urges that divinity must now be recognized in its remaining "human" embodiment, man himself. In respect to this general argument, the Jove stanza is structurally united to the rest of the poem if it is read as here interpreted. In the preceding stanza, the woman protagonist of the poem is told that "divinity must live within herself." The Jove stanza develops this argument by reviewing the humanizing evolution of religious belief. Following the appearance of the star, Stevens continues the humanizing process by transforming the blood of Christ to human blood and a heavenly paradise to an earthly one.

> Shall our blood fail? Or shall it come to be
> The blood of paradise? And shall the earth
> Seem all of paradise that we shall know?
> The sky will be much friendlier then than now,
> A part of labor and a part of pain,
> And next in glory to enduring love,
> Not this dividing and indifferent blue. (p. 68)

In the next stanza classical and Christian myths of immortality are combined in the same fashion:

> There is not any haunt of prophecy,
> Nor any old chimera of the grave,
> Neither the golden underground, nor isle
> Melodious, where spirits gat them home,
> Nor visionary south, nor cloudy palm
> Remote on heaven's hill, that has endured
> As April's green endures.... (p. 68)

Stevens has a habit of summarizing traditions in this highly abbreviated fashion. In "The Comedian as the Letter C," for example, the same method is used to summarize past traditions in poetry. Finally, the implied relation between Jove and Christ can be documented by a much later poem, "Esthetique du Mal," which attributes the loss of religious belief to the "overhuman" conception of Christ:

> ...now both heaven and hell
> Are one, and here, O terra infidel.
>
> The fault lies with an over-human god,
> Who by sympathy has made himself a man
> And is not to be distinguished....
>
> A too, too human god, self-pity's kin
> And uncourageous genesis.... (p. 315)

Christ is a god motivated by sympathy, not a god regally indifferent to the desires of his "hinds." Here too, however, the birth of Christ proves fatal because a god who assumes flesh assumes, in Stevens' view, the fate of flesh; and so, as "Sunday Morning" argues,

> "The tomb in Palestine
> Is not the porch of spirits lingering.
> It is the grave of Jesus, where he lay." (p. 70)

In failing to recognize this argument, writers like Louis Martz regard Stevens's admiration for "the specifically human," as a late development in his career which represents the abandonment of his earlier hedonism for a humanistic position. This is to misrepresent both periods. The nobility of man is a continuous theme and one concomitant with his original rejection of Christian belief. Moreover the conception of Stevens as a hedonist turned humanist overlooks the fact that his supposed humanism is based, from *Harmonium* on, upon the naturalistic evolution of man from nature. The concern in *Harmonium* for the sensual beauties of a temporal world is less a reflection of pagan sensuality than of the prevailing philosophical spirit of the period. Intellectual New England had already heard from William James that the triumph of pragmatism meant a revolution comparable, as James put it, to the protestant reformation. It meant a rejection of the intellectual complacency of religious idealism. It promised a shift of interest from the idealist's vision of God, "an *erkenntnisstheoretische Ich,*" to the more vital preoccupations of the temporal world.

> The real vital question for us all is, What is this world going to be? What is life to make of itself? The centre of gravity of philosophy must therefore alter its place. The earth of things, long thrown into shadow by the glories of the upper ether, must resume its rights.[4]

Such is Stevens's message to the woman of "Sunday Morning" who is found amid the "complacencies of the peignoir" on Sunday rather than in church. She "dreams a little" of the Crucifixion, but her vision merely transforms the vivid reality about her into a procession of the dead wending to "silent Palestine" in quest of immortality.

> The pungent oranges and bright, green wings
> Seem things in some procession of the dead....

And so she is urged to give up her lifeless concept of divinity which "can come / Only in silent shadows and in dreams" for the temporal world of "things to be cherished like the thought of heaven."

In defense of this theme, Stevens takes up James's attack upon the Absolute Idealist's conception of God. The poem is entitled "Negation."

> Hi! The creator too is blind,
> Struggling toward his harmonious whole,
> Rejecting intermediate parts,
> Horrors and falsities and wrongs;
> Incapable master of all force,
> Too vague idealist, overwhelmed
> By an afflatus that persists.
> For this, then, we endure brief lives,
> The evanescent symmetries
> From that meticulous potter's thumb. (pp. 97–98)

This is not, for reasons that will be made clear presently, the traditional God of Christian theology. This is the God of modern idealism, the unifying All who sustains in his eternal thought the perfect unity of his creation. He is represented as a "too vague idealist," because for him the particulars of reality in their temporal existence are meaningless. He rejects them as "intermediate parts." As James explains the idealist's God:

> Ordinary monistic idealism leaves everything *intermediary* out. It recognizes only the extremes, as if, after the first rude face of the phenomenal world in all its particularity, nothing but the supreme in all its perfection could be found.[5] (italics added)

The poem argues that human suffering is thus resolved in the omniscient vision of perfection which perceives man only as a contributing part of the whole, the "evanescent symmetries" of an eternal abstraction. Such a diety, who permits evil for the sake of his aesthetic enjoyment, is rejected as an inhuman object of worship.

The inhuman character of the Absolute Idealists' conception of God was also James's favorite point of attack. Of their vision of the Absolute in its perfect unity, he observes:

> They give it a particular nature. It is perfect, finished. If there is want there, there also is the satisfaction provided.... In this world crimes and horrors are regrettable. In that

totalized world regret obtains not, for "the existence of ill in the temporal order is the very condition of the perfection of the eternal order."[6]

Such a vision of absolute teleological unity is, for James, a product of a vicious rationalism which commits mankind to an inhuman God by generalizing away that existence of evil.

> We see indeed that certain evils minister to ulterior goods, that the bitter makes the cocktail better, and that a bit of danger or hardship puts us agreeably to our trumps. We can vaguely generalize this into the doctrine that all the evil in the universe is but instrumental to its greater perfection. But the scale of the evil actually in sight defies all human tolerance; and transcendental idealism, in the pages of a Bradley or a Royce, brings us no farther than the book of Job did — God's ways are not our ways, so let us put our hand upon our mouth. A God who can relish such superfluities of horror is no God for human beings to appeal to. His animal spirits are too high. In other words the "Absolute" with his one purpose is not the man-like God of common people.[7]

James's argument is strikingly like the argument of "Negation," even with respect to terminology. James complains that the God of the prevailing idealism is indifferent to the "horrors and crimes" of his creation; Stevens complains that he must neglect the "horrors and falsities and wrongs" of his creation. The idealists, for James, are content to "vaguely generalize" away the reality of evil; Stevens characterizes the idealists' God as a "too vague idealist." James argues that such a God must be able to "relish such superfluities of horror"; Stevens contends that he is "overwhelmed by an afflatus that persists." Most important, both men express moral revulsion for a God who can regard human suffering merely as the necessary instrument for his aesthetic enjoyment of his perfect harmony.

The agreement here helps to explain the contrasting attitudes of "Negation" and "Lunar Paraphrase." In the latter, Stevens expresses nostalgia for what he regards as the unavailable Catholic tradition of the past, a "golden illusion" in which the intimacy of God and man was symbolized in the "humanly near" figures of Christ and Mary.

> When the body of Jesus hangs in a pallor,
> Humanly near, and the figure of Mary,
> Touched on by hoar-frost, shrinks in a shelter
> Made by the leaves...
>   a golden illusion
> Brings back an earlier season of quiet
> And quieting dreams in the sleepers in darkness —
>
> The moon is the mother of pathos and pity. (p. 107)

That Mary is momentarily sheltered from the "hoar-frost" is not an insignificant detail. "Hoar-frost" is one of Stevens' numerous winter symbols which like "snow," "ice," "January" and similar terms indicates that which has become frigid, lifeless, devoid of meaning or of imaginative value. So Mary, who has been touched by the frost, now appears to be sheltered and part of a returning illusion of an earlier time. In contrast to this nostalgic vision, the bitterness of "Negation" is directed against the degradation of that tradition in the prevailing idealism of American culture. What had replaced the sympathetic figures of Christ and Mary was a philosophical conception, an inhuman God who, as James relentlessly argued, was no longer "the man-like god of common people" but a meaningless abstraction.

This distinction runs throughout *Harmonium,* and it illuminates the treatment of rationalism and idealism in poems which are nonreligious in theme, as well as those which are specifically concerned with Christian belief. One more example may illustrate the importance of the distinction for Stevens, as well as the relevance of James.

"The Bird with the Coppery Keen Claws" is another satire upon a philosophical conception of God. This time the conception is developed metaphorically, however, and, as is common in Stevens, the metaphorical treatment makes for interpretative difficulties.

> Above the forest of the parakeets,
> A parakeet of parakeets prevails,
> A pip of life amid a mort of tails.
>
> (The rudiments of tropics are around,
> Aloe of ivory, pear of rusty rind.)
> His lids are white because his eyes are blind.
>
> He is not paradise of parakeets,
> Of his gold ether, golden alguazil,
> Except because he broods there and is still.
>
> Panache upon panache, his tails deploy
> Upward and outward, in green-vented forms,
> His tip a drop of water full of storms.
>
> But though the turbulent tinges undulate
> As his pure intellect applies its laws,
> He moves not on his coppery, keen claws.
>
> He munches a dry shell while he exerts
> His will, yet never ceases, perfect cock,
> To flare, in the sun-pallor of his rock. (p. 82)

The general meaning of the poem presents no great difficulty. The "parakeet of parakeets," the "perfect cock" of pure intelligence, is God; and the satiric point of the poem emerges from the historical contrast in stanza three. God is no longer the glorified policeman of a heavenly paradise—

"of his gold ether, golden alguazil." In place of the traditional Christian God, is a god reduced to the function of an ineffectual parakeet governing a more rudimentary paradise, the temporal world. But whether he represents the modern idealist's God or the God reduced by science to the creator of physical laws is ambiguous. Many of the details point to the latter interpretation. God's power is now limited to the performance of a necessary intellectual function, sustaining as a pure mind the laws of his creation. The drop of water apparently represents his abstract conception of creation, upon which he now statically "broods," investing it with the appearance of change, "of storms," by willing the application of his laws. Since he is no longer the moral magistrate of paradise, these laws are presumably physical laws, which might lead one to suppose that the subject of satire is the scientistic conception of God as a kind of divine physicist whose presence accounts for the physical order of the universe. In this light, he would be the God of a materialistic universe and not, as in "Negation," the "incapable master of all force" struggling to harmonize the moral chaos of his creation. Several details of the poem do not yield convincingly to such an interpretation, however. The figure of God as an effete parakeet is in itself sufficiently bizarre, but the concern with the bird's plumage in lines three, ten, and eleven is troubling. The attention given to their methodical arrangement suggests that the "mort of tails" represents more than useless plumage. The reference to physical particulars which compose the "rudiments" of the tropics is also uncertain in meaning. The white eyelids and metallic claws connote the monstrously grotesque and vicious, yet these suggestions seem in excess of any apparent justification. They are more in accord with the moral revulsion expressed in "Negation." All of this points to the possibility that here, too, the idealists' God is the subject of attack. James strengthens the possibility by using the same bizarre figure to illustrate how the idealists' God becomes an "absolute bird."

> We see that no smallest raindrop can come into being without the whole shower, no single feather without a whole bird, neck, crop, beak and tail, coming into being simultaneously: so we unhesitatingly lay down the law that no part of anything can be except so far as the whole also is. And then, since everything whatever is part of the whole universe, and since (if we are idealists) nothing, whether part or whole, exists except for a witness, we proceed to the conclusion that the unmitigated absolute as witness of the whole is the one sole ground of being of every partial fact, the fact of our own existence included. We think of ourselves as being only a few of the feathers, so to speak, which help to constitute that absolute bird. Extending the analogy of certain wholes, of which we have familiar experience, to the whole of wholes, we easily become absolute idealists.[8]

This is a perfectly feasible gloss for the most obscure details of the poem. One particular of the natural world, a raindrop, implies for an idealist the conceptual existence of the whole, the "whole shower." In the poem a drop of water becomes God's conceptual whole "full of storms." One bird implies an absolute bird who must be the "whole of wholes"—or in the poem, the "parakeet of parakeets." Since the bird supplies the all-containing intelligence, called by James "the sole ground of being," men in their particularity are meaningless appendages of that single intelligence—"a few of the feathers." For Stevens, God is the only life, "a pip of life," amid "a mort of tails." The "mort of tails" would be equivalent to the ineffectual "brief lives" in "Negation" in this case, and their methodical arrangement would correspond to God's vision of their "evanescent symmetries" in that poem. James explains that for the idealist nothing can exist unless God is present as "witness of the whole," and Stevens explains that God is now God only because "he broods there and is still."

In criticizing this absolute bird, James elaborates upon the same objections implicit in Stevens' satire. The bird who is blind to the "rudiments" of the tropics is blind because the rudiments are parts, sensible particulars such as the color of the lily and the pear. These are merely the rudiments of what the bird sees, the conceptual whole. Thus James explains, "The bird-metaphor is physical, but we see on reflection that in the physical world there is no real compounding. 'Wholes' are not realities there, parts only are realities."

A second objection is the relation between God's mind and finite minds. An Absolute which unifies all finite minds in a single unity is, according to James, indistinguishable from the sum of those minds. A God who is thus limited to thinking the sum of his parts has no independent existence. He cannot know his own mind since the experience of omniscience would be different from finite experience, but the idealists' Absolute is defined simply as the totality of finite minds. It is in short a pantheistic god. An independent God, the theistic God of orthodox Christianity, is incompatible, James concludes, with idealism.

> So the feather-and-bird analogy won't work unless you make the absolute into a distinct sort of mental agent with a vision produced in it by our several minds analogous to the "bird" vision which the feathers, beak, etc., produce *in* those same minds. The "whole," which is *its* experience, would then be its unifying reaction on our experiences, and not those very experiences self-combined. Such a view as this would go with theism, for the theistic God is a separate being; but it would not go with pantheistic idealism, the very essence of which is to insist that we are literally *parts* of God, and he only ourselves in our totality—the word "ourselves" here standing of course for all the universe's finite facts.[9]

This distinction between a pantheistic and the more orthodox theistic God may well provide the philosophical intention behind the third stanza of the poem. God is no longer the independent inhabitant of a gold ether because he is no longer free to assume the moral authority of a "golden alguazil." Such independence and authority would require, as James says, a theistic god who is free to *react* upon human experience, rather than a God who simply sustains it by thinking it.

The point is not deducible from the poem itself. For that matter, there is no way to demonstrate that Stevens ever encountered James's bird metaphor. All that is certain is that similar metaphors are used for similar purposes, the criticism of an idealist conception of God as pure intellect — that, and the fact that Stevens was beyond question familiar with James's philosophy.

Other poems in *Harmonium* attack the belief in immortality in less intellectual terms, and usually without distinguishing between periods of Christian faith. Such poems usually stress the argument of "Sunday Morning," that Christian otherworldliness neglects the realities of temporal life for an illusory paradise. One of the bitterest versions of the theme is "Cortege for Rosenbloom," in which funeral mourners are pictured transporting the dead Rosenbloom to his heavenly abode. The mourners are described as childish misanthropes who commit men to a life lived in hope of an empty illusion.

> They are bearing his body into the sky.
>
> It is the infants of misanthropes
> And the infants of nothingness
> That tread
> The wooden ascents
> Of the ascending dead. (p. 80)

The militant atheism of this poem contrasts significantly with the attitude in "The Palace of the Babies," in which immortality is again ridiculed as the comforting illusion of infantile minds, but as in "Lunar Paraphrase," the Catholic context provokes longing for the religious ideal.

> The disbeliever walked the moonlit place,
> Outside the gates of hammered serafin,
> Observing the moon-blotches on the walls.
>
> . . . .
>
> The walker in the moonlight walked alone,
> And in his heart his disbelief lay cold.
> His broad-brimmed hat came close upon his eyes. (p. 77)

The moonlight, from which the protagonist is protected by his hat, symbolically identifies religious belief as a product of the imagination. But while the Church is an institution for babies who are "drawn close by dreams of fledgling wing," the protagonist who stands outside its gates feels his exclusion as a "harsh torment." This Laforguian blending of sentiment and irony, longing and disbelief, has long been recognized to be as characteristic of the early Stevens as of the early Eliot. The practice is explained in a little poem candidly entitled "Explanation," in which the contrast between the drabness of a Protestant culture and the vivid spirituality of an earlier Catholic culture is at the same time a statement of the inability of the modern poet to recover the ideals of the past.

> Ach, Mutter,
> This old, black dress,
> I have been embroidering
> French flowers on it.
>
> Not by way of romance,
> Here is nothing of the ideal,
> Nein,
> Nein.
>
> It would have been different,
> Liebchen,
> If I had imagined myself,
> In an orange gown,
> Drifting through space,
> Like a figure on the church-wall. (pp. 72–73)

The German girl, whose black dress symbolizes the impoverishment of her Protestant culture, assures her mother that a little French embroidery does not consitute romantic aspiration. Her mother explains that such aspiration would have been natural had she inherited the more imaginative religious ideals of that culture. The point of the poem is provided in one of Stevens' last essays when he remarks that the problem of the modern poet is that he "shares the disbelief of his time," and therefore "he does not turn to Paris or Rome for relief from the monotony of reality."[10]

Similarly, the identification of German culture with Protestantism and a debased religious idealism can be illustrated by reference to later poems. It is most explicit in a passage from "The Greenest Continent" in which the German phrasing is pointedly used to contrast a dead Protestant tradition with an earlier European tradition, not specifically identified as Catholic.

> The heaven of Europe is empty, like a Schloss
> Abandoned because of taxes...
>   it ceased to exist, became
> A Schloss, an empty Schlossbibliothek...

> There was a heaven once,
> But not that Salzburg of the skies. It was
> The spirit's episcopate, hallowed and high,
> To which the spirit ascended.... (*O. P.*, p. 53)

The loss of religious faith was a common concern among poets of Stevens' generation, of course. In *Harmonium,* however, Stevens' treatment of the subject bears closest resemblance to James' philosophical attack upon the Anglo-American resurgence of German idealism. It is not surprising that *Harmonium* also reflects James' stress upon the contemporary schism between a "tender-minded" idealism and a "tough-minded" empiricism. James naturally maintained that neither alternative was feasible. He wanted to confront his audience with a dilemma which only the philosophy of experience could resolve, and the dilemma as he describes it provides an excellent introduction to the concerns of Stevens' early poetry.

> You want a system that will combine both things, the scientific loyalty to facts and willingness to take account of them, the spirit of adaptation and accommodation, in short, but also the old confidence in human values and the resultant spontaneity, whether of the religious or romantic type. And this is then your dilemma: you find the two parts of your *quaesitum* hopelessly separated. You find empiricism with inhumanism and irreligion; or else you find a rationalistic philosophy that keeps out of all definite touch with concrete facts and joys and sorrows.[11]

This is, in sum, the problem which *Harmonium* explores: on the one hand, a rationalistic idealism incapable of sustaining either religious or romantic ideals; on the other an empiricism that had become hopelessly materialistic and devoid of human meaning. Together the alternatives provide the terrifying vision of "The Snowman," a man of snow confronting a world composed of the "Nothing that is not there and the nothing that is."

All too often the philosophical motive behind such poems is a matter of uncertain inference. But on occasion the details of a poem are strikingly clarified by James's and Stevens's common approach to a subject. Such is the case of "Metaphors of a Magnifico," a poem dealing with the venerable subject of the One and the Many.

> Twenty men crossing a bridge,
> Into a village,
> Are twenty men crossing twenty bridges,
> Into twenty villages,
> Or one man
> Crossing a single bridge into a village.
>
> This is old song
> That will not declare itself...

Twenty men crossing a bridge,
Into a village,
Are
Twenty men crossing a bridge
Into a village.

That will not declare itself
Yet is certain as meaning...

The boots of the men clump
On the boards of the bridge.
The first white wall of the village
Rises through fruit-trees.

Of what was it I was thinking?
So the meaning escapes.

The first white wall of the village...
The fruit-trees.... (p. 19)

The purpose behind the transposed numerical relations in the first stanza may be self-evident, but James provides a useful parallel if one is in doubt. The ultimate identity of the One and the Many was a central doctrine of Absolute Idealism and one that James was at pains to discredit. His chief argument was that since the idealist considered all plurality to be grounded ultimately in the unity of the One, any specified plurality — seven, thirty, five hundred — was actually a symbol of precisely the same ultimate number, the One. So interpreted, the doctrine seemed to James a meaningless number game in which any number could be substituted for any other with the assurance that metaphysically any number could have only the reality of the One. Moreover, if the One and the Many were thus interchangeable terms, the idealist's preference for the One was wholly arbitrary, a superstition to be mocked as "number-worship."

> "The world is one!" — the formula may become a sort of number-worship. "Three" and "seven" have, it is true, been reckoned sacred numbers; but, abstractly taken, why is "one" more excellent than "forty-three," or than "two million and ten"? In this first vague conviction of the world's unity, there is so little to take hold of that we hardly know what we mean by it.[12]

Whether or not this was a wholly fair representation of the idealist position, it was part of James's more fundamental and telling contention that the abstractions of the modern idealists were so far removed from experience that they could grant no metaphysical relevance to the particulars of life. "It is as if," James goes on, "the actual peculiarities of the world that is were entirely irrelevant to the content of truth. But they cannot be irrelevant; and the philosophy of the future must imitate the sciences in taking them more and more elaborately into account."[13] Thus James urged his students that the dismissal of the One and an acceptance of the Many, of a "pluralistic universe," was the first step in his program for recovery from a "bankrupt" intellectual tradition.

> The return to life can't come about by talking. It is an *act;* to make you return to life. . . . I must *point,* point to the mere *that* of life, and you by inner sympathy must fill out the *what* for yourselves. The minds of some of you, I know, will absolutely refuse to do so, refuse to think in non-conceptualized terms. I myself absolutely refused to do so for years together, even after I knew that the denial of manyness-in-oneness by intellectualism must be false. . . . But I hoped ever for a revised intellectualist way around the difficulty, and it was only after reading Bergson that I saw that to continue using the intellectualist method was itself the fault. I saw that philosophy had been on a false scent ever since the days of Socrates and Plato, that an intellectual answer to the intellectualist's difficulties will never come, and that the real way out of them, far from consisting in the discovery of such an answer, consists in simply closing one's ears to the question. When conceptualism summons life to justify itself in conceptual terms, it is like a challenge addressed in a foreign language to someone who is absorbed in his own business; it is irrelevant to him altogether—he may let it lie unnoticed.[14]

In passages such as this, one sees how deeply the anti-intellectualism of Bergson bit into American culture. One may gather, too, something of the intellectual inheritance behind Stevens' remark that the end of philosophy is despair and that "for all the reasons stated by William James, and for many more, we do not want to be metaphysicians."[15] It is a new breed of philosopher who deals with the problem of the One and the Many by advising his audience to "let it lie unnoticed."

To return, Stevens' treatment of the same subject in "Metaphors of a Magnifico" follows the Jamesian formula. As usual the title is significant. "Magnifico" is one of Stevens' many ironic terms for presumptuous intellectualism.[16] The Magnifico's "metaphors" are evidently the particulars of the scene, which he treats as interchangeable equivalents of the One. In lines seven and eight the reduction of twenty particulars to the universal One is found to be an incomprehensible "old song"—just as James found it to be an error pursued since Plato. From this point on, the Magnifico adopts the corrective attitudes urged by James. He recognizes that while the existence of particularity is not explicable, the fact of its existence is nonetheless certain. Thus the enumeration of particulars as actually given in experience "will not declare itself / Yet is certain as meaning." This notion is similar to James's observation that to point to the "that" is not to supply the "what," but the pointing nevertheless signifies a return to the non-conceptualized realities of life. Having settled for the meaning which is certain, the speaker begins to concentrate more fully upon the details of the scene. As he does so, a curious shift of perspective takes place; the viewpoint of the observer becomes the viewpoint of the participants in the action. The first wall of the village "rises" into view, as it would for the men actually entering the village. Having gained this viewpoint, the speaker realizes that the conceptual problem has become irrelevant. He dismisses it altogether, and returns to his concentration upon the details of the marchers' progress into the village. He has, as James put it, become "absorbed in his own business"; and thus absolved of fruitless conceptualizing, he can let the problem lie.

The ridicule of philosophical speculation, of abstraction and rationalism is made in these terms throughout *Harmonium*. "Anecdote of Canna" introduces a symbolic treatment of the theme which is characteristic, that of representing abstract thought as a dreamworld for sleepers as opposed to the awareness of particulars enjoyed by the awake observer.

> Huge are the canna in the dreams of
> X, the mighty thought, the mighty man.
> They fill the terrace of his capitol.
>
> His thought sleeps not. Yet thought that wakes
> In sleep may never meet another thought
> Or thing.... (p. 55)

A more interesting development of this symbolism occurs in "Disillusionment at Ten O'Clock."

> The houses are haunted
> By white night-gowns.
> None are green,
> Or purple with green rings,
> Or green with yellow rings,
> Or yellow with blue rings.
> None of them are strange,
> With socks of lace
> And beaded ceintures.
> People are not going
> To dream of baboons and periwinkles.
> Only, here and there, an old sailor,
> Drunk and asleep in his boots,
> Catches tigers
> In red weather. (p. 66)

The poem is often cited by critics who stress the nonsensical or eccentric elements of Stevens' style, but the eccentricity is less interesting than the point of the poem, which concerns the vapid spirituality or intellectualism (the two are difficult to distinguish) of respectable American society. The citizens of that society are represented as ghosts, haunting their houses in "white night-gowns." "Whiteness" and "ghosts" are Stevens' usual symbols for those given to wholly unreal conceptions, to lifeless abstractions.[17] As inhabitants of a common world of abstractions, the citizens are undifferentiated from each other by any attributes of physical reality, and since they are complacently satisfied with their empty abstractions, they have nothing to dream (i.e. think) about. Only the disreputable outcast of this refined culture, the drunken old sailor who sleeps in his boots, is able to conceive of "catching tigers in red weather." Red is commonly recognized as a basic term in Stevens' color symbolism, signifying objective or physical reality as opposed to blue, signifying imagined or subjective reality. The evident point of the poem is that conventional society has abandoned reality for a dead tradition, whereas the old sailor remains, even in the subjective realm of his own thoughts, devoted to the satisfactions of a physical reality. It will be recalled that this interpretation of American culture was also James'. He had, in fact, made the point in a similar fashion by declaring that the prevailing New England Idealism had produced a society of "sleep-walkers" for whom "actual things are blank."

It may be sheer coincidence, but one worth noting, that one of James's most important essays, included in *Pragmatism,* is entitled "On Catching Tigers in India." The essay deals with James' view of the relation between conceptual knowledge and external reality. Since the subject is one that would certainly have interested Stevens, the significance of James' tiger is intriguing. James begins by explaining that conceptual knowledge may be abstract or particular: "the tigers now in India, for example, or the scholastic system of philosophy are known only representatively or symbolically." His interest is in the particular, the tiger in India, and of the epistemological problem of its conceptual existence.

> Suppose, to fix our ideas, that we take first a case of conceptual knowledge; and let it be our knowledge of the tigers in India, as we sit here. Exactly what do we *mean* by saying that we here know the tigers? . . . . Most men would answer that what we mean by knowing the tigers is having them, however absent in body, become in some way present to our thought; or that our knowledge of them is known as presence of our thought of them. A great mystery is usually made of this peculiar presence in absence; and the scholastic philosophy, which is only common sense grown pedantic, would explain it as a peculiar kind of existence, called *intentional inexistence,* of the tigers in our mind. At the very least, people would say that what we mean by knowing the tigers is mentally *pointing* towards them as we sit here.
>
> But now what do we mean by *pointing,* in such a case as this? . . .
>
> To this question I shall have to give a very prosaic answer — one that traverses the prepossessions not only of common sense and scholasticism, but also those of nearly all the epistemological writers whom I have ever read. The answer, made brief, is this: The pointing of our thought to the tigers is known simply and solely as a procession of mental associates and motor consequences that follow on the thought, and that would

lead harmoniously, if followed out, into some ideal or real context, or even into the immediate presence, of the tigers. It is known as our rejection of a jaguar, if that beast were shown us as a tiger; as our assent to a genuine tiger if so shown.... It is even known, if we take the tigers very seriously, as actions of ours which may terminate in directly intuited tigers, as they would if we took a voyage to India for the purpose of tiger-hunting and brought back a lot of skins of the striped rascals which we have laid low.[18]

The interesting feature of this discussion is the reference to images of absent experience, of the possibility of "presence in absence." If Stevens did have James's tiger in mind, the bizarre details of the poem might have the same point. The things the people are not going to dream of, for instance, are bizarre precisely because they are not things within the realm of their actual experience; to think of them would be to imagine them as absent presences. On the other hand, the old sailor's tiger is also an absent presence, but one he can conceive of as actually caught in reality, just as James insists that the presence of a mental tiger has a verifiable reality since it could lead to the capture of an actual tiger. The feasibility of such an interpretation is strengthened by the fact that other poems of this period already show Stevens' interest in the epistemological problem of the relation between conceptual and perceptual knowledge.

One of the earliest examples, which merely introduces the theme, is the little poem, "The Indigo Glass in the Grass."

> Which is real—
> This bottle of indigo glass in the grass,
> Or the bench with the pot of geraniums, the stained
>   mattress and the washed overalls drying in
>   the sun?
> Which of these truly contains the world?
> Neither one, nor the two together.[19]

While this is not a remarkable poem, it is one of the earliest in which Stevens introduces the imagination-reality dualism, and along with it, his characteristic symbols. The indigo glass, which reappears in later poems as a blue mirror, or simply as blue, refers to a subjective or imaginative reality; the uninspiring particulars—the geraniums, mattress and overalls—refer to objective reality. The conclusion that neither viewpoint is satisfactory is one that *Harmonium* explores repeatedly in terms of the cleavage between the real and the ideal.

In "Homunculus et la Belle Étoile" the emotional need of human ideals is distinguished from the rationalistic idealism of philosophers. The poet's ideal is symbolized by a star, "la Belle Étoile," the French phrasing implying as usual an aesthetic or emotional value as opposed to an intellectual one. The ideal is defined simply as the "ultimate Plato" and is treated as frankly romantic.

> In the sea, Biscayne, there prinks
> The young emerald, evening star,
> Good light for drunkards, poets, widows
> And ladies soon to be married. (p. 25)

Like religious ideals, its validity is measured in terms of the emotional response it elicits, and it is therefore incompatible with the dispassionate rationalism of philosophers.

> It is better that, as scholars,
> They should think hard in the dark cuffs
> Of voluminous cloaks,
> And shave their heads and bodies. (p. 26)

The theme is again one that James was fond of elaborating upon, that "ideals taken by themselves give no reality." And of course for James, too, the conspicuous example of vapid idealism is the rationalist scholar. "And your college professor, with a starched shirt and spectacles, would if a stock of ideals were all alone by itself enough to render a life significant, be the most absolutely and deeply significant of men."[20]

Other poems, such as "Stars at Tallapoosa" and "Anecdote of the Prince of Peacocks" assert the incompatibility of the ideal and the real without qualification. In the former, the idealist's world is the wholly conceptual world of abstractions which admit no perceptual reality, in which the eye becomes "an eye that studies its black lid." The "Anecdote of the Prince of Peacocks" is apparently a reworking of this theme in terms of the romantic predicament. Birds ordinarily represent poets in Stevens, and the peacock, traditionally associated with pride and regal splendor, would indicate the poet of grandiose conception. (By contrast, the "inchling" poet who limits himself to his individual experience is represented by a bantam in "Bantams in Pinewoods.") The Prince of Peacocks would thus represent, in Stevens' terms, the extreme romantic. The Prince is depicted as a sleepwalker, wandering in the moonlight, and absorbed in the "milky blue" of his dreams—all details symbolizing the unreal, conceptual world of the imagination. In the midst of his dream, the Prince encounters a figure called Berserk, who is "sun-colored," "awake" and "sleepless"—all details characteristic of the empirical observer, or realist. Berserk informs the Prince that not even dreamers can escape the "trap" he has set. The poem ends with the lament of the disillusioned romantic, unable to escape the unyielding pediment of reality.

I knew from this
That the blue ground
Was full of blocks
And blocking steel.
I knew the dread
Of the bushy plain,
And the beauty
Of the moonlight
Falling there,
Falling
As sleep falls
In the innocent air. (p. 58)

The same problem is set forth in various guises. The idealization of love in "The Ordinary Women," is interesting not only as a preface to the best of the early love poems, "Le Monocle de Mon Oncle," but as an early version of Stevens' theory of the cyclical history of the imagination. The poem is a whimsical account of the development and destruction of romantic love. The aspirations of "ordinary women" lead to the spiritualized ideal of courtly love. But the chastity of the courtly ideal is wholly imaginative, and they replace it by the Christian idealization of marriage, reading from the stars the Christian version.

As they leaned and looked
From the window-sills at the alphabets,
At beta b and gamma g
To study
The canting curlicues

Of heaven and of the heavenly script.
And there they read of marriage-bed. (p. 11)

The next stage brings the transformation from the spiritual to the sensual ideal of beauty and they adopt the elaborate coiffures and ornate fans associated with eighteenth-century court life. Finally even this idealization becomes unreal, and the women turn from the "poverty" of idealized love to the unadorned reality from which they came.

While the parallels are not significant, it is worth noting here again the similarity of approach between Stevens and James. The appeal of contemporary idealism was, according to James, the monistic desire for the "supreme in all its perfection." But such ideals, being unrealizable, argued for a "native poverty" of mind which could be supplanted only by a return to the needs of man's passional nature, and its temporal satisfactions.

May not satisfaction with the rationalistic absolute as the alpha and omega, and the treatment of it in all its abstraction as an adequate religious object, argue a certain native poverty of mental demand? Things reveal themselves soonest to those who most passionately want them, for our need sharpens our wit. To a mind content with little, the much in the universe must always remain hid.[21]

It is of incidental interest that Stevens customarily uses the Greek alphabet as James does to symbolize abstract ideals. Thus in "The Ordinary Women" the "beta" and "gamma" indicate a secondary rather than the initial phase of a developing idealism. More important is that James supplies the terms of attack upon a traditional idealism which Stevens exploits in his rejection of both romantic and religious ideals. The satiric treatment of romantic love in "The Ordinary Women" depends upon the implicit theme that ideals, whether religious or romantic, have been successively abandoned as they failed to fulfill the emotional needs of an increasingly humanized tradition. In short, the treatment of love in this poem parallels the treatment of religious myth in "Sunday Morning."

In contrast to the repeated exposure of the imaginary ideals of the past, are those poems devoted to the opposite extreme, a reality limited to objective observation. In "Le Monocle de Mon Oncle" the alternatives become the terms of dramatic conflict. The traditional idealized conceptions of love are juxtaposed with a modern context in which the transcience of physical beauty, mortality, and sexual motivations are the realities against which the past must compete. The monocular vision of the protagonist does not indicate, as is usually assumed, his aristocratic background; it indicates his inability to focus simultaneously upon starkly opposed alternatives, and hence to resolve them. "The Emperor of Ice Cream" represents the abandonment of idealism and the acceptance of the ultimate degradation of a culture without illusion. Stevens' attitude is not expressed, but it is implicit in the naturalistic details of a working-class wake. The meaningless embroidery of "Explanation" reappears upon the shrouding sheet of the corpse, once more suggesting the pathetic emblem of a tradition deprived of an ennobling ideal. It is intended as an assessment of a culture which as James put it was incapable of "raising more than ice-cream soda water to the brute animal of man."[22] The pessimistic rendering of this culture becomes the explicit assessment of the objectivist approach in "Gubbinal":

> That strange flower, the sun,
> Is just what you say.
> Have it your way.
>
> The world is ugly,
> And the people are sad. (p. 85)

These poems, then, define the terms of the conflict which the longest and most ambitious poem of the volume, "The Comedian as the Letter C," is intended to resolve. A number of shorter poems anticipate the resolution, but since the "Comedian" brings together the variety of positions represented in *Harmonium,* it is the most useful gloss for the entire volume.

"The Comedian as the Letter C" is a blank verse narrative in six sections recounting a sea voyage taken by the protagonist, Crispin. The voyage is generally understood to be a symbolic account of Stevens' early poetic development. Mr. J. V. Cunningham has summarized the accepted interpretation of the voyage in observing that it reflects Stevens' "quest of a new intelligence" following his "rejection of his society as banal and trite."[23] Like most interpreters of the poem, Mr. Cunningham neglects the geographical symbolism of the voyage. He writes, "The hero of the poem makes a sea voyage to a strange and exotic country, in this case Yucatan, and back to his own land." Stevens is known to have taken such a trip during this early period, but Crispin's voyage does not accord with autobiographical fact. His voyage is not the holiday excursion of a New England lawyer. It begins in Bordeaux, France, and ends in the Carolinas. It is plainly described as a "westward voyage" in which Crispin crosses the Atlantic in search of a "still new continent" where he hopes to establish a colony. In terms of literary convention, the poem's prototype may be, as Mr. Cunningham believes, Wordsworth's "Prelude." The prototype of the voyage itself, however, is the historical crossing of the American colonists from the old world to the new, from the civilized culture of Europe to the primitive settlements of the American wilderness. Moreover, the voyage spans more than continents. Crispin is a figure of timeless identity, encompassing the intellectual growth of Western civilization. His name derives from the role of the comic-valet, a stock character of French comedy. William Van O'Conner has suggested that he is modeled upon the Crispin of *Le Legataire universel* (1708) of Jean-Francois Regnard.[24] But Crispin is older than the eighteenth century. He begins as an "ancient Crispin," a "knave" and "thane," who, emerging from his medieval sources, is shaped by the history of European culture and brought finally into the contemporary world where he must come to terms with his modern identity. In his historical role he is European, in his modern role he is American, and the exchange of identities occurs in the symbolic Atlantic crossing.

The historical phase of the voyage is concluded in section I, which bears the misleading title "The World Without Imagination." The title reflects Stevens' habit of dividing the world into perceptual and conceptual parts and expressing the opposition as reality and imagination. In this usage imagination does not mean the poetic faculty, but the conceptual mind in general. Opposed to sensible reality, the conceptual world represents the "unreal," and hence imaginary.

The world without imagination is not the world in which the voyage begins, but the new world at which Crispin arrives as the first section concludes. The poem opens in a world that is, for Stevens, all too imaginary, the world of medieval philosophy. The proposition which Crispin is to test in the first phase of his voyage is the scholastic definition of man: man is in essence a rational animal who by virtue of his rationality occupies a privileged position in the scale of being. Stevens parodies the scholastic definition by mocking the Latin phrasing of its dialectic and its reliance upon classical sources:

> Nota: man is the intelligence of his soil,
> The sovereign ghost. As such, the Socrates
> Of snails, musician of pears, principium
> And lex. Sed quaeritur: is this same wig
> Of things, this nincompated pedagogue,
> Preceptor to the sea? Crispin at sea
> Created, in his day, a touch of doubt. (p. 27)

At sea, Crispin discovers that his rational authority is limited to the world of physical particulars. He has "An eye of land, of simple salad-beds/ Of honest quilts." But the sea, which by contrast apparently represents the unknown, the vast mystery of creation, is inpenetrable to reason. The threading waves form "inscrutable hair in an inscrutable world." Crispin's return to land is cut off, however, by a storm that arises. He encounters "That century of wind in a single puff," and is blown out to sea, severed forever from his "lost terrestial." The century is apparently the nineteenth century since it destroys the traditional myths of man and God and brings Crispin, divested of his illusions, to confront the problems of the modern poet in a new world. So it is that the dying God whom Crispin encounters in the storm is dissolving in "verboseness" — surely a reference to speculative thought — and is no longer a vital part of his creation.

> Could Crispin stem verboseness in the sea,
> The old age of a watery realist,
> Triton, dissolved in shifting diaphanes
> Of blue and green? A wordy, watery age
> That whispered to the sun's compassion, made
> A convocation, nightly, of the sea-stars,
> And on the clopping foot-ways of the moon
> Lay grovelling. Triton incomplicate with that
> Which made him Triton, nothing left of him,
> Except in faint, memorial gesturings,... (pp. 28-29)

The description of the age repeats the symbolism of such poems as "Homunculus et La Belle Étoile" and "The Stars at Tallapoosa," and its usage here to depict an age reduced to "grovelling" in the fruitless supplication of imaginary ideals certainly suggests Stevens' usual view of romantic idealism.

The supplication of the moon is a characteristic indication in Stevens of the last phase of Christian culture.[25] Further evidence of the period intended is Crispin's statement that at this phase of the voyage "The valet in the tempest was annulled," an explicit reference to his eighteenth-century role. It should also be recalled that France, like Rome, symbolizes in *Harmonium* the superior vitality of an earlier Catholic tradition and that Crispin departs from France armed with his scholastic training, only to find nothing left of his earlier concept of God except "in faint, memorial gesturings." The reference to God dissolving in verboseness might also be compared to Stevens' account of his generation at the turn of the century, a generation convinced by an "intellectual minority" that "the Victorians had left nothing behind."[26]

Just as the nineteenth century dissolves Triton, it dissolves Crispin by destroying the medieval concept of man; but with the destruction of God he also loses his role in creation as a comic valet. The significance of the valet role is again a reflection of Stevens' agreement with the philosophical attack by James and others upon the concept of teleological unity. The argument that God's eternal plan divested man of any significant role in creation, making him merely the temporal instrument of divine will, a part of a "universal block," recurs throughout the later poetry. In "The Man with the Blue Guitar," for example, Stevens rejects a former "generation's dream," calling it "the only dream they knew,/ Time in its final block, not time to come." "The Latest Freed Man" celebrates his escape from "the old descriptions of the world," to a freedom in which, without doctrinal interpretation, "the ant of the self changed to an ox." Crispin, discovering that he is no longer a comic servant, an observer rather than a participant in creation, refers back to the medieval treatises which had defined him in that role. He finds that he is now the "merest minuscule" of what he had been. He is no longer, that is, an abstract definition but a discrete individual, a single letter of medieval cursive script, the letter "c" of the poem's title. Just as his medieval identity as man is "washed away by magnitude," his conglomerate identity as poet, the identity afforded him by his old world tradition, is also lost.

> What counted was mythology of self,
> Blotched out beyond unblotching. Crispin,
> The lutanist of fleas, the knave, the thane,
> The ribboned stick, the bellowing breeches, cloak
> Of China, cap of Spain, imperative haw
> Of hum, inquisitorial botanist,
> And general lexicographer of mute
> And maidenly greenhorns, now beheld himself,
> A skinny sailor peering in the sea-glass. (p. 28)

This display of fantastic eloquence is intended to summarize the historical development of the poet's role, much as classical and Christian religious traditions are summarized in "Sunday Morning." The "lutanist of fleas," suggests the wandering minstrel, the medieval troubadour. As the "ribboned stick and bellowing breeches" he was the jester or fool of Shakespearian tradition, bearing the traditional symbol of his profession, the jester's "ribboned stick." He next develops into an "imperative haw of hum"; that is, he adopts the role of pretentious moralizing, a tradition which would be associated, for Stevens, with neoclassic poetry. The reference to the Chinese cloak and Spanish cap, suggesting a presumption to the role of universal spokesman, may well be a parody of what modern critics occasionally cite as the supreme example of eighteenth-century pomposity— Johnson's wordy beginning to "The Vanity of Human Wishes":

> Let observation, with extensive view,
> Survey mankind from China to Peru.

This is, of course, one of the most famous moralizing poems of the neoclassic period; it begins with an "imperative"; and it assumes a universal application to "mankind" from China to Peru. Johnson is, moreover, just the type of poet Stevens would select for parody, and for just the reasons given. In fact, he makes his position on Johnson plain in a passage deleted from "Owl's Clover" and reprinted by Morse in *Opus Posthumous:*

> The civil fiction, the calico idea,
> The Johnsonian composition, abstract man,
> Are all evasions like a repeated phrase
> Which, by its repetition, comes to bear
> A meaning without a meaning. (*O. P.,* p. 65)

It is a pretty good guess that the pompous moralizer wearing a Chinese cloak and a Spanish cap has assumed that fictitious abstraction of "Johnsonian composition."

The final reference to the botanist and "lexicographer of mute and maidenly greenhorns" is possibly intended to suggest the subsequent development of the Romantic poet's role as the interpreter of nature and spokesman of the common man. The poet who supplies words for "mute and maidenly greenhorns" sounds remarkably like Gray, dedicating himself to speak for mute, inglorious Miltons. One cannot be certain in such matters, but it is obvious that Stevens is mocking the historical role of the poet, which supplied for Crispin that "mythology of self, blotched out beyond unblotching"; and it is also evident that the poet who progresses from a lutanist of fleas to a biologist and lexicographer for the inarticulate has undergone an historical evolution. Moreover, since Crispin is presumably somewhere in the nineteenth century undergoing the loss of religious faith, his retrospective view of his traditional role would naturally bring him up to the late eighteenth and early nineteenth-century tradition. To be sure, the parody here is, unlike the opening parody of scholastic dialectic, overly subtle. As R. P. Blackmur, J. V. Cunningham and others have observed, however, Stevens' excursions into apparent nonsense have a way of yielding an intelligible meaning if one makes a determined effort.[27]

Having lost his civilization, his God, his human identity and his poetic tradition, Crispin considers his plight. He has nothing left except "some starker, barer self/ In a starker, barer world." He can make nothing of the sea because it bears no resemblance to the Christian world of his past. It is a world

> in which the sun
> Was not the sun because it never shone
> With bland complaisance on pale parasols,
> Beetled, in chapels, on the chaste bouquets. (p. 29)

With no illusion left he sees creation as it really is, "the veritable ding an sich, at last," only to discover that he is alone in an inhuman and meaningless solitude. Save for the dying god, "negligible Triton," he finds no trace of his human identity about him. He concludes that he is hopelessly cut off from all his past, even his former self.

> Severance
> Was clear. The last distortion of romance
> Forsook the insatiable egotist. The sea
> Severs not only lands but also selves.
> Here was no help before reality. (p. 30)

With the destruction of his last illusion, the storm ends and Crispin concludes the first phase of his voyage by entering a new world, a world "without imagination."

The symbolism of this first section does much to explain the anti-intellectualism and the distaste for philosophy which accompanies the loss of religious faith in *Harmonium*. It explains also what was to remain for Stevens the crucial experience upon which both his skepticism and aestheticiam were based. In his last years, he wrote movingly of that experience in terms that provide a useful summary of Crispin's discovery.

To see the gods dispelled in mid-air and dissolve like clouds is one of the great human experiences. It is not as if they had gone over the horizon to disappear for a time; nor as if they had been overcome by other gods of greater power and profounder knowledge.

It is simply that they came to nothing. Since we have always shared all things with them and have always had a part of their strength, and, certainly, all of their knowledge, we shared likewise this experience of annihilation. It was their annihilation, not ours, and yet it left us feeling that in a measure, we, too, had been annihilated. It left us feeling dispossessed and alone in a solitude.... What was most extraordinary is that they left no momentoes [sic.] behind, no thrones, no mystic rings, no texts either of soil or of the soul. It was as if they had never inhabited the earth. At the same time, no man ever muttered a petition in his heart for the restoration of those unreal shapes. There was always in every man the increasingly human self, which instead of remaining the observer, the non-participant, the delinquent, became constantly more and more all there was or so it seemed; and whether it was so or merely seemed so still left it for him to resolve life and the world in his own terms.[28]

Just so, Crispin finds himself sharing the annihilation of Triton, left alone in a solitude that contains no mementos of the past, no longer committed to the role of the comic-valet—"the observer, the non-participant, the delinquent"—and forced to resolve life in his own terms. He enters the new world with a Shakespearean flare:

> The drenching of stale lives no more fell down.
> What was this gaudy, gusty panoply?
> Out of what swift destruction did it spring?
> It was caparison of wind and cloud
> And something given to make whole among
> The ruses that were shattered by the large. (p. 30)

The second section of the poem, "Concerning the Thunderstorms of Yucatan," represents two stages in Crispin's recovery. Upon arrival in Yucatan, Crispin finds that the poets there are still devoted to the nightingale of romantic tradition:

> In Yucatan, the Maya sonneteers
> Of the Caribbean amphitheatre,
> In spite of hawk and falcon, green toucan
> And jay, still to the night-bird made their plea.... (p. 30)[29]

But the romantic is a commonplace and Crispin is "Too destitute to find/ In any commonplace the sought-for aid" (p. 30). He seeks out the "green barbarism" of the tropics with a twofold intention: to rid himself of his "stale intelligence" by immersion in new and vivid perceptual experience, and to find some ultimate truth, some underlying reality, which will reestablish his relation to the world. He seeks "aggrandizement," sensing that he will discover in the tropics

> an elemental fate,
> And elemental potencies and pangs,
> And beautiful barenesses as yet unseen.... (p. 31)

The experiment is successful. The vividness of the primitive landscape refreshes his senses; he finds "a new reality in parrot-squawks" (p. 32), but this is a mere "trifle" compared to the mystical experience which occurs in a tropical thunderstorm. The significance of the storm is puzzling, and since it seems to be crucial to Crispin's development — and Stevens' — it is helpful to consider thematic elements of the experience as they recur in other poems. Although the thunderstorm occurs in Yucatan, its source seems to lie in the East; it comes from the "mountainess ridges, purple balustrades" lying "west of Mexico." The reference suggests that the thunder evokes both a tropical primitivism, or worship of the "elemental" creative forces of nature, and Eastern mysticism. Two other poems in *Harmonium* suggest a mystical experience in both locales. In "Tea at the Palaz of Hoon," the speaker adopts the guise of Hoon, an Eastern potentate who, "dressed in purple," descends from the sky into "the western day" and mentally re-creates his new world. (Purple, which appears also in the "purple balus-trades" beyond Yucatan, is Stevens' usual symbol for the imagination at its conceptual extreme, divorced wholly from reality.) In "The Cuban Doctor," however, the primative, tropical origins of a mystical storm appear without Eastern connotation. The doctor of the title has fled his tropical world in order, he says, "to escape the Indian"; but he finds that even in arid country "the Indian struck/ Out of his cloud and from his sky." Like the doctor, Crispin tries to escape the mystical storm by reclaim-ing his membership in Western civilization. He realizes that Yucatan repre-sents the extremity of the "Atlantic coign," beyond which he cannot ven-ture, and he seeks the refuge of Christian society by retreating to a cathedral.

> Crispin, here, took flight.
> An annotator has his scruples, too.
> He knelt in the cathedral with the rest.
> This connoisseur of elemental fate,
> Aware of exquisite thought. (p. 32)

The "exquisite thought" which comes in the wake of the storm is an awareness of his participation in divinity, in the creative force of the nat-ural world. This is the specifically human divinity which the woman of "Sunday Morning" is told must be recognized "within herself" to replace her Christian faith, and which leads in that poem to a vision of a secular religion in which the sun will be worshipped as the creative source of man and nature — "not as a god but as a god might be." For Crispin the creative source appears in the form of a fecundating thunder storm:

> This was the span
> Of force, the quintessential fact, the note
> Of Vulcan, that a valet seeks to own,
> The thing that makes him envious in phrase. (p. 33)

One might notice how Stevens here picks up the relationship between Jove and his hinds in "Sunday Morning," in the form of Vulcan and a valet, and also how he simply shifts from Triton of the sea-crossing to a more appropriate symbol of divinity. Perhaps the best explanation of the storm's significance is provided by a later poem which retains the symbolism of the exiled European seeking restoration in the tropics but omits any reference to Eastern mysticism. In the section entitled "Description of a Platonic Person" in "The Pure Good of Theory" the Platonic person of the title is a man exiled from the Christian community of Europe. He seeks out Brazil in order to "nourish the emaciated Romantic with dreams of her avoirdupois." Like Crispin he comes "out of solitude," and though he is convalescing from his European experience, he chooses to remain near the western extremity of the Atlantic, "on the west wall of the sea." His malady is vaguely defined as one concerning his "sense of happiness":

> Was it that—a sense and beyond intelligence?
> Could the future rest on a sense and be beyond
> Intelligence? On what does the present rest?
>
> This platonic person discovered a soul in the world
> And studied it in his holiday hotel.
> He was a Jew from Europe or might have been. (p. 331)

This unhappy idealist resembles Crispin. His discovery of a "soul in the world," meaning the discovery of a new human self, is not explained. In other poems, however, it is associated with Eastern mysticism. In some respects the voice of the thunder indicates a spiritual rejuventation similar to that which Eliot in "The Wasteland" symbolizes by the use of an Indian myth from the Upanishads in the section "What the Thunder Said." For Stevens, however, the voice of thunder is not the revelation of a supernatural being but simply of his own being—mystical in that it is an inexpressible intuition. In "Extracts from Addresses to the Academy of Fine Ideas," he refers to the thunder king as a symbol for the collective thought of modern man ideally united to his environment and thus transfigured

> . . . into a dark-blue king, un roi tonnerre,
> Whose merely being was his valiance,
> Panjandrum and central heart and mind of minds— (p. 254)

In "Life on a Battleship," the creative power of the natural world is symbolized by the Key West jungle which is, in turn identified with an Eastern "tropical whole."

> But one lives to think of this growing, this pushing life,
> The vine, at the roots, this vine of Key West, splurging,

> Coming from the East, forcing itself to the West,
> The jungle of tropical part and tropical whole. (*O. P.,* 80)

In "Articifical Populations" the poet who seeks, like Crispin and the possible Jew from Europe, a cure for his spiritual illness finds it at the point where

> ...the Orient and the Occident embrace
> To form that weather's appropriate people
> The rosy men and the women of the rose,
> Astute in being what they are made to be.
>
> This artificial population is like
> A healing-point in the sickness of the mind.... (*O. P.,* 112)

Finally, there is the curious little prose fable, "A Ceremony" which Morse includes among the posthumous collection and dates 1940. The fable concerns three emigrant brothers who leave Holland, Stevens' ancestral home, to settle respectively in Ceylon, Brazil, and New Netherland. Only the brother who settles in the New World, and thus retains his ties with Western tradition, survives the experiment successfully. The moral is the simple one that sends Crispin out of the storm and into the cathedral: "...the appeal to tradition is not an appeal that can be made to barbarians, whether elephants or otherwise, since it is predicated on something that is held in common honor."[30]

This repeated association of southern tropics and the Orient is intended to convey the potential range of experience available to the Western poet, the "emaciated romantic," outside his own culture.

Thus Hoon, who enters the Western world in the trance of an Indian mystic, symbolizes the discovery, at the extreme of solipsistic idealism, of the creative power of the mind.

> Out of my mind the golden ointment rained,
> And my ears made the blowing hymns they heard.
> I was myself the compass of that sea:
>
> I was the world in which I walked, and what I saw
> Or heard or felt came not but from myself;
> And there I found myself more truly and more strange. (p. 65)

Hoon, it will be noticed, is now "the compass of that sea" which destroyed Crispin when he attempted to navigate it as a rational animal of Christian tradition. The significance of Hoon is explained further in a poem from a subsequent volume, "Sad Strains of a Gay Waltz." The poet accepts the loss of tradition and the emergence of "the epic of disbelief" in more pessimistic terms here. His pessimism is increased by his recognition that Hoon symbolizes a solipsistic escape which is no longer available.

> Too many waltzes have ended. And then
> There's that mountain-minded Hoon,
> For whom desire was never that of the waltz.
>
> Who found all form and order in solitude,
> For whom the shapes were never the figures of men.
> Now, for him, his forms have vanished. (p. 121)

In a still later poem, "The Sail of Ulysses," it is the transmuted figure of Hoon who becomes the "true creator."

> This is the true creator, the waver
> Waving purpling wands, the thinker
> Thinking gold thoughts in a golden mind,
> Loftily jingled, radiant.... (*O. P.,* 100)

In this case also, the true creator has received a mystical "divination," of his own creative power, his participation in a worldly divinity which is

> ...something illogically received,
> A divination, a letting down
> From loftiness, misgivings dazzlingly
> Resolved in dazzling discovery.
> There is no map of paradise.
> The great Omnium descends on us
> As a free race. (*O. P.,* 101–2)

In a later revision of this poem, the final two lines are justified in philosophical terms by the monistic identification of mind and being which harkens back to Berkeley's *esse est percippi:*

> ...since knowing
> And being are one—the right to know
> Is equal to the right to be.
> The great Omnium descends on me,
> Like an absolute out of this eloquence. (*O. P.,* 106)

These are later expressions of Crispin's Yucatan experience, but they show a consistent development of the symbolism which centers in the two *Harmonium* poems, the "Comedian" and "Tea at the Palaz of Hoon." Crispin's discovery of a new "self" in a mystical storm coming from the "mountainous ridges" and "purple balustrades" of the East is equivalent to the figure of the "mountain-minded Hoon" who "descends the western day" dressed in purple and isolated in a self-created conceptual world. So, too, the later references to a mystical "divination," which is a "letting down from loftiness" to the spiritual potential of men, are anticipated in Crispin's mystical experience. He receives a "self" that was not available in the "crusty town" of Bordeaux, but by refusing to journey farther west he retreats from the mystical source of the storm:

> His mind was free
> And more than free, elate, intent, profound
> And studious of a self possessing him,
> That was not in him in the crusty town
> From which he sailed. Beyond him, westward, lay
> The mountainous ridges, purple balustrades,
> In which the thunder, lapsing in its clap,
> Let down gigantic quavers of its voice,
> For Crispin to vociferate again. (p. 33)

With this stage of spiritual recovery, the Yucatan section ends and Crispin turns toward Carolina and the establishment of his colony.

The Yucatan section is the least satisfactory of the poem. The narrative structure breaks down under the welter of sensory detail in a world "too jucily opulent." Havana, announced earlier as part of the itinerary, fails to materialize. Possibly it lodges the cathedral to which Crispin takes flight, but one is not told. The significance of the mystical storm is altogether obscure and must be reconstructed from other poems. It is interesting to notice, incidentally, how Crispin's mystical "span of force" anticipates Stevens' later admiration of Bergson's *élan vital,* also closely associated with the primitive. It is also worth remarking that in the figure of Hoon Stevens initiates the solipsistic dilemma traced in preceding chapters. The pose of the mystic reveals to him that the mystic's experience is an illusion. Yet illusion is self-creation, and creation is man's share of divinity.

In the third section, "Approaching Carolina," Crispin considers his traditional notions about North America. He had regarded it as a land of "legendary moonlight," given over to the most visionary romanticism of the past. It is a land of "polar-purple," Stevens' usual symbolism for a frozen, lifeless and wholly unreal conceptual world, the work of the imagination at its decadent extreme. It is thus described in Stevens' usual combination of winter and moon symbols.

> America was always north to him,
> A northern west or western north, but north,
> And thereby polar, polar-purple, chilled
> And lank, rising and slumping from a sea
> Of hardy foam, receding flatly, spread

In endless ledges, glittering, submerged
And cold in a boreal mistiness of the moon. (p. 34)

Approaching land, Crispin reflects that this new continent could hardly afford him that new vision of reality which he has been seeking, the "sequestered bride" he had originally sensed in Yucatan. The marriage metaphor introduced at this point should be kept in mind since it is of importance later in the poem. The bride Crispin now declares he is seeking is the motive for his voyage, since she is to furnish

The liaison, the blissful liaison,
Between himself and his environment,
Which was, and is, chief motive, first delight,
For him, and not for him alone.[31]

In spite of his fears that America will not furnish the bride he seeks, but merely the same romantic "indulgences" of his past tradition, Crispin moves inland by water. He finds that with his perceptions restored by the tropics, he is capable of a realism undistorted by imagination—"The moonlight fiction disappeared." Nor does he require the exotically sensual, as he did in Yucatan. Arriving in spring, he rejects the beauties of the season because they are not the "sequestered bride," but a "gemmy marionette to him that sought/ A sinewy nakedness." As the ship docks, he is exhilarated by the raw sensations of the harbor scene.

He inhaled the rancid rosin, burly smells
Of dampened lumber, emanations blown
From warehouse doors, the gustiness of ropes,
Decays of sacks, and all the arrant stinks
That helped him round his rude aesthetic out.
He savored rankness like a sensualist.
He marked the marshy ground around the dock,
The crawling railroad spur, the rotten fence,
Curriculum for the marvelous sophomore.
It purified. It made him see how much
Of what he saw he never saw at all. (p. 36)

The third and final phase of Crispin's voyage concludes with his discovery that such perceptual realism is the "one integrity" still possible for the poet in "a world so falsified."

Section IV, entitled "The Idea of a Colony," forms an interlude in the narrative that prepares for the concluding two sections. Because of its obscurity the importance of this section has not been recognized. Superficially, it presents a continuation of Crispin's self-mocking account of his quest. It presents at the same time, however, Stevens's assessment of the modernist movements in American poetry and of his own participation in them.

The section begins with Crispin, committed now to a scrupulous realism, setting up his program for a new "colony" of American poets. He begins by inverting the original proposition of his old world tradition. In place of the scholastic definition of man as the rational intelligence of his world, he establishes a naturalistic definition, once more asserting his total rejection of the past.

> Nota: his soil is man's intelligence.
> That's better. That's worth crossing seas to find.
> Crispin in one laconic phrase laid bare
> His cloudy drift and planned a colony.
> Exit the mental moonlight, exit lex,
> Rex and principium, exit the whole
> Shebang. Exeunt omnes. (pp. 36–37)

Crispin's "cloudy drift" is his development as a visionary modernist poet, determined to make a "new intelligence prevail." In summarizing this development, he recalls how his earliest poems represented (in typical modernist fashion) a rejection of his literary tradition. He began by writing "prose" poetry in which he celebrated "rankest trivia," inverted conventional values, and disdained to use "the appointed power" of traditional poets. Having established his severance from the past, however, he found himself equally dissatisfied by his recourse to the primitive and semi-mystical experiences of his Yucatan period. These, too, he determines to reject.

> He made a singular collation. Thus:
> The natives of the rain are rainy men.
> Although they paint effulgent, azure lakes,
> And April hillsides wooded white and pink,
> Their azure has a cloudy edge....
>
> On what strange froth does the gross Indian dote,
> What Eden sapling gum, what honeyed gore,
> What pulpy dram distilled of innocence,
> That streaking gold should speak in him
> Or bask within his images and words? (pp. 37–38)

These excursions into primitive and alien cultures are, Crispin decides, a romantic evasion of his own environment. As a converted realist he decides he must apply his principles, "abhorring Turk as Esquimau" for a truly American regionalism. Hence he forms his idea of his American colony which he envisions as an "island hemisphere" in which all poets will be spokesmen of their respective locales.

> The man in Georgia waking among pines
> Should be pine-spokesman

And in the southern hemisphere as well, poets should abandon primitivism for a realistic portrayal of their environment.

> Sepulchral señors, bibbling pale mescal,
> Oblivious to the Aztec almanacs,
> Should make the intricate Sierra scan. (p. 38)

At this stage, Crispin is reflecting Stevens' divorce from one phase of the modernist movement — from that group which, following Pound, sought a renaissance in American letters through foreign, exotic, and, especially, primitive sources. The regionalism of Crispin's colony represents Stevens' subsequent alliance with the opposing modernist faction — with poets like Sandburg, Frost, and Williams, who espoused a distinctively American poetry confined to native sources. This alternative, too, proves to be unsatisfactory, and Crispin abandons his plan, mocking the regionalists' vision of hemispheric reform and mocking himself as "Progenitor of such extensive scope." The reformist program, he concludes, is merely the "monotonous babbling" of new romantic visionaries:

> These bland excursions into time to come
> Related in romance to backward flights,
> However prodigal, however proud,
> Contained in their afflatus the reproach
> That first drove Crispin to his wandering. (p. 39)

The "reproach" which Crispin cannot abide is the attempt to force the individual poet into a conventional or prescribed role. Stevens' detachment from modernist movements has already been discussed in regard to the early essay "On the Irrational Element in Poetry." To recall, in that essay he dismisses the Imagist school as needlessly restrictive, preferring to allow the poet the freedom to experience whatever he "happens to experience." Crispin here expresses the same aversion to the prescriptions that would be imposed upon an American colony of regionalist poets. He abandons his plan on the grounds that he cannot distort or restrict his experience "With fictive flourishes that preordained/ His passion's permit...." He concludes, as Stevens concludes in the essay mentioned, that he prefers an impartial commitment to chance experience.

> Such trash
> Might help the blind, not him, serenely sly.
> It irked beyond his patience. Hence it was,

Preferring text to gloss, he humbly served
Grotesque apprenticeship to chance event,
A clown, perhaps, but an aspiring clown. (p. 39)

"The Idea of a Colony," then, brings the earlier autobiographical sections of the poem together by summarizing Crispin's parallel development in terms of the literary events of the period: first, the rejection of tradition; second, a recourse to primitive and foreign sources; third, an alignment with the new American regionalism; and finally an abandonment of these stages for the poet's individual experience. Primarily, however, "The Idea of a Colony" is devoted to the third stage, and like the earlier stages, it is linked to shorter poems throughout the volume. Poems such as "Ploughing on Sunday," "In the Carolinas," and "Life is Motion" are obvious illustrations of Stevens' complicity in the regionalist program. It is notable that such poems are among the least distinguished of the volume. They appropriate a variety of American locales and celebrate the wedding-to-the-soil credo, but they are little more than perfunctory statements of the theme. If they give the impression of half-hearted exercises in a current fashion, the explanation may well lie in Crispin's discovery that the scrupulous realism of the regionalist program was unsuited to his temperament and "irked beyond his patience." The same conclusion underlies one of the most amusing poems of the volume, 'The Revolutionists Stop for Orangeade." In this poem, Stevens satirically records his flagging devotion to realist principles by adopting the pose of a disaffected footsoldier who has become weary of his leader's revolutionary zeal. He exhorts his captain to suspend operations long enough to permit his troops, who have been made to "sing standing in the sun," a little refreshment. (The "orangeade" of the title signifies an American form of refreshment, just as "tea" in "Tea at the Palaz of Hoon" signifies an Eastern form.) In this case the refreshment suggested is in keeping with Crispin's preference for "Grotesque apprenticeship to chance event." The poet asks for the freedom to adopt whatever pose he pleases: to turn to the primitive ("Sing a song of serpent-kin"); to play the self-mocking comedian ("Sing in clownish boots"); to deal in the eccentric or exotic as an escape from reality, "the real that wrenches." The poem provides, in short, a fairly explicit statement of the theme of Crispin's "Idea of a Colony." It identifies a realist program with a "revolution" in American poetry and indicates Stevens' eventual dissatisfaction with the movement.

The final two sections represent the resolution of Crispin's quest. They describe how Crispin, having abandoned his colonial aspirations, finds contentment in his personal experience. He chooses to dwell in the land as a hermit, and in time builds a cabin, marries, and acquires four daughters.

For some reason the notion persists among interpreters that these events signify the failure of Crispin's quest and his consequent abandonment of poetry. Actually, these final sections represent the successful resolution of the quest, in so far as Crispin is concerned, and a renewed dedication to his role of poet.

The fifth section, "A Nice Shady Home," begins with the announcement of what is to be the determining event in Crispin's development. In his previous roles of speculative sailor, perceptual "annotator," and aspiring literary colonizer, Crispin had been a theorizer of experience. He now accepts the conclusion of the previous section and "abandons gloss for text."

> Crispin as hermit, pure and capable,
> dwelt in the land. (p. 40)

He discovers that he is no longer the "prickling realist" of the earlier sections, who in rebellion against the falsifications of tradition had assumed the mocking pose of the poet-clown,

> Choosing his element from droll confect
> Of was and is and shall or ought to be.... (p. 40)[32]

And as he lives in the land, he finds that his colonizing aspirations dwindle from continental proportions to an acceptance of his immediate surroundings.

> Crispin dwelt in the land and dwelling there
> Slid from his continent by slow recess
> To things within his actual eye, alert
> To the difficulty of rebellious thought
> When the sky is blue. (p. 40)

Accepting life on these terms, Crispin comes gradually to the realization that the sensible world is the one irreducible element of experience, the one permanent and certain truth he has been seeking. This recognition is anticipated earlier in the poem at the conclusion of Section III, and its repetition here has led to some misunderstanding. It is repeated here in somewhat different terms and as an explanation of Crispin's divorce from reformist movements. The true realist, he explains, does not require a "matinal continent"; he needs only the reality of his immediate experience.

> The words of things entangle and confuse.
> The plum survives its poems. It may hang
> In the sunshine placidly, colored by ground

> Obliquities of those who pass beneath,
> Harlequined and mazily dewed and mauved
> In bloom. Yet it survives in its own form,
> Beyond these changes, good, fat, guzzly fruit.
> So Crispin hasped on the surviving form,
> For him, of shall or ought to be in is. (p. 41)

The first two sentences of this passage have been repeatedly cited as evidence that Crispin's quest ends in defeat and that he abandons his art or continues to practice it half-heartedly for inexplicable reasons. But Crispin is merely elaborating here upon his earlier decision to "abandon gloss for text." He does so because, as he now explains, whatever subjective falsification words or the "ground obliquities" of human perspective may contribute, the reality of the external world survives, a part of the present as much as of any visionary future. He does not require, in short, a matinal continent, purified of European tradition, upon which to build a new American culture.

Such an interpretation of this passage requires no great ingenuity, and the theme is explicit in other early poems. The "surviving form" of the plum has the same status as the "April green" which survives all religious belief in "Sunday Morning," and as "Susanna's beauty" which survives in the flesh though not in the mind in "Peter Quince at the Clavier."

The meaning of Crispin's discovery is crucial to the lines which immediately follow and which again suggest the abandonment of poetry.

> Was he to bray this in profoundest brass
> Arointing his dreams with fugal requiems?
> Was he to company vastest things defunct
> With a blubber of tom-toms harrowing the sky?
> Scrawl a tragedian's testament? Prolong
> His active force in an inactive dirge,
> Which, let the tall musicians call and call,
> Should merely call him dead? Pronounce amen
> Through choirs infolded to the outmost clouds?
> Because he built a cabin who once planned
> Loquacious columns by the ructive sea?
> Because he turned to salad-beds again?
> Jovial Crispin, in calamitous crape?
> Should he lay by the personal and make
> Of his own fate an instance of all fate? (p. 41)

The key to this passage is Crispin's decision to build his humble, private cabin rather than pursue his dream of building the edifice, the "loquacious columns," of a new world culture. The rest of the passage explains, again somewhat repetitiously, why he has abandoned the successive stages of modernist reform through which he passed. He cannot imitate the great poets of the past, the "tall musicians," since the past is dead and his role would be limited to mourning its death in tragic dirges. Nor is he willing any longer to celebrate the loss of tradition with a purifying primitivism, a "blubber of tom-toms." And, finally, he will not assume a reformist role, disregarding the "personal," the individuality of poets, in order to see them conform to his example. Ironically, he finds that he is back where he began at the beginning of his voyage, at the commonplace reality of his own "salad-beds."

At this point Crispin builds his cabin and marries. The significance of the wife is unfortunately ambiguous since she is both a symbolic figure and a literal wife. She is not the "sequestered bride" which Crispin had sought in an earlier section, but a human figure, "a blonde to tip the silver" and preside over his table. Her symbolic function is suggested by the mysterious "duenna" who brings her. The duenna is the spirit who appears in other poems and who is personified by foreign titles. In "O Florida, Venereal Soil," for example, she is a "donna," who remains a "virgin of boorish births," but may bring to a lover the gift of a satisfying physical reality:

> Donna, donna, dark,
> Stooping in indigo gown
> And cloudy constellations,
> Conceal yourself or disclose
> Fewest things to the lover—
> A hand that bears a thick-leaved fruit,
> A pungent bloom against your shade. (p. 48)

The same figure appears in other poems where she figures simply as the traditional Coleridgean imagination, the faculty empowered to bridge the metaphysically unbridgeable, to achieve the "reconcilliation of opposites," of mind and reality, which Crispin has been seeking. So it is that the "prismy blonde" whom she brings was formerly the "sequestered bride" of his quest, but now, within the context of personal experience, she provides his "blissful liaison" with reality. The same blonde appears in other poems, for example, in "Depression Before Spring":

> The hair of my blonde
> Is dazzling,
> As the spittle of cows
> Threading the wind. (p. 63)

The symbolic wedding of the poet and his blonde does not in this case occur because the reconciling spirit, the spring "queen," does not appear.

In "The Apostrophe to Vincentine" the contrast between Crispin's "sequestered bride" and his human bride is further explained. The poet imagines his mate as a "heavenly Vincentine" and as a nude who dwells somewhere between earth and sky. To his surprise, he finds her in "a group/ Of human others," and in his meeting with her he is reconciled with his physical world.

> Monotonous earth I saw become
> Illimitable spheres of you.... (p. 54)

Similarly, in a later poem, "The Sense of the Sleight-of-Hand Man," Crispin's "prismy blonde" becomes the "pearly spouse" of sensual reality, providing the liaison which Crispin seeks.

> It may be that the ignorant man, alone,
> Has any chance to mate his life with life
> That is the sensual, pearly spouse, the life
> That is fluent in even the wintriest bronze. (p. 222)

Crispin's wife, then, is both literal and symbolic. The ambiguity arises from the peculiar strain of the relationship. She must function as a literal wife in order to signify her physical reality, yet her physical reality is itself symbolical. In later poems the marriage figure is used consistently for the synthesis of opposites, usually of poet and reality. Stevens does not try as he does here, however, to realize the metaphor on a literal level. Here, he is forced to stress her literal existence in order to distinguish her from the phantom bride of Crispin's earlier quest.

The rest of the section celebrates the consequences of the marriage, the poet's liaison with his own quotidian and the recovery of his poetic vitality. The common notion that Crispin abandons poetry for marriage and family apparently arises from the misreading of a passage which follows the consummation of the marriage, a passage in which Crispin is purportedly "sapped by the quotidian."[33]

> Good star, how that to be
> Annealed them in their cabin ribaldries!
> Yet the quotidian saps philosophers
> And men like Crispin like them in intent,
> If not in will, to track the knaves of thought. (p. 42)

It will be noticed that the quotidian saps men *like* Crispin who continue the philosophical pursuit of ultimate truths. But Crispin has abandoned that quest. Like Candide, he is content to cultivate his own garden—"Like

Candide,/ Yeoman and grub"—on the assumption that "For realist what is, is what should be." So it is that a few lines later he finds that the quotidian has had the opposite effect upon him:

> ...the quotidian
> Like this, saps like the sun, true fortuner.
> For all it takes it gives a humped return
> Exchequering from piebald fiscs unkeyed. (p. 43)

The quotidian "saps like the sun," that is, as the sun restores the sap of a tree, it restores him to life. It unlocks his true wealth, the nature of which is the subject of the final section.

The poem's conclusion, entitled "And Daughters with Curls," begins with a self-mocking "grand-pronunciamento" concerning the birth of Crispin's enigmatic four daughters:

> The chits came for his jigging, bluet-eyed,
> Hands without touch yet touching poignantly,
> Leaving no room upon his cloudy knee,
> Prophetic joint, for its diviner young. (p. 43)

The "diviner young" refers back to Crispin's colonizing phase when he was the visionary reformer aspiring

> To colonize his polar planterdom
> And jig his chits upon a cloudy knee. (p. 40)

In contrast, the daughters who now appear are less divine, but they are "true daughters both of Crispin and his clay" (p. 44). This does not mean that they are literal daughters, but that they come of legitimate parentage, from the wedding of the poet with reality. A similar contrast between the visionary and the real is provided by the colonizer, who in section IV was "progenitor of such extensive scope," and the now humbled settler, whose progeny are the offspring of his own land:

> All this with many mulctings of the man,
> Effective colonizer sharply stopped
> In the door-yard by his own capacious bloom. (p. 44)

The identity of these blooming daughters has remained the most difficult enigma of the poem. They are clearly symbolic, having "Hands without touch, yet touching poignantly" and being "Infants yet eminently old." The theory that they represent the four seasons is certainly untenable. When "jigged" upon the poet's knee, they sing in unison, becoming his "four blithe instruments." It is safe to assume, as several critics have, that they represent the commingling elements of the poet's creative process—four styles or the four creative stages through which Crispin has passed. The real problem is that of distinguishing one daughter from another and here one must work from the recurrent symbolism of other early poems. The relevant symbolism is provided by the passage in which the daughters are described in their youth and in their eventual maturity.

> First Crispin smiled upon
> His goldenest demoiselle, inhabitant,
> She seemed, of a country of the capuchins,
> So delicately blushed, so humbly eyed,
> Attentive to a coronal of things
> Secret and singular. Second, upon
> A second similar counterpart, a maid
> Most sisterly to the first, not yet awake
> Excepting to the motherly footstep, but
> Marvelling sometimes at the shaken sleep.
> Then third, a thing still flaxen in the light,
> A creeper under jaunty leaves. And fourth,
> Mere blusteriness that gewgaws jollified,
> All din and gobble, blasphemously pink.
> A few years more and the vermeil capuchin
> Gave to the cabin, lordlier than it was,
> The dulcet omen fit for such a house.
> The second sister dallying was shy
> To fetch the one full-pinioned one himself
> Out of her botches, hot embosomer.
> The third one gaping at the orioles
> Lettered herself demurely as became
> A pearly poetess, peaked for rhapsody.
> The fourth, pent now, a digit curious. (p. 45)

The capuchin habits of the first daughter identify her as the child of introspection and reflection. Stevens' use of similar religious titles to designate spiritual preoccupation—"rabbi" and "monk" are most common—is generally recognized. She is his "goldenest demoiselle," the French term designating as usual the spiritually or aesthetically satisfying. "Golden" is Stevens' color symbol for the same meaning. In "The Paltry Nude Starts on a Spring Voyage" the poet's ideal muse is described as a "paltry nude," divested of the traditional grandeur of Boticelli's Venus, but fated for similar perfection when she becomes "the goldener nude/ Of a later day" (p. 6). Similar usage is illustrated by the "gold ether" of the "Golden alguazil" in "The Bird With the Coppery Keen Claws," by the "golden illusion" in "Lunar Paraphrase," and the "golden ointment" in "Tea at the Palaz of Hoon." The meaning is explicit in the comment in "Adagia," "The gold dome of things is the perfected spirit." (*O. P.,* 168) The daughter's attention to the "coronal of things" has like associations. In "To the One of Fictive Music" the "pale head" of the divine muse is banded with jewels; in "O Florida, Venereal Soil" she wears a jeweled tiara. The first daughter is thus the voice of the ultimate poet — introspective, spiritual, idealistic. In maturing to a "vermeil capuchin" she undergoes the reddening process that is Stevens' usual indication of proper maturation through the realization of actual experience. The meditative protagonist of "Le Monocle de Mon Oncle," for example, develops from a theorizing "dark rabbi" to a "rose rabbi" seeking the explanation of love in terms of his own experience. Similarly, in the later "Notes Toward a Supreme Fiction," the poet — again represented as an aspiring colonist — seeks a realizable ideal, an ideal which is "pink/ If seen rightly and yet a possible red." The "vermeil capuchin," then, seems to symbolize the fully realized ideal, the ultimate fruition of the poet's aspirations.

The second daughter, the counterpart of the first, is not yet fully awake and therefore unable to produce the full-fledged bird of poetry. Birds of course are traditionally symbolic of poets and poetry, and Stevens is noted for his exploitation of the symbol by using all variety of birds to symbolize types of poetry. Since the usage here is vague, the best recourse is to another poem of *Harmonium* which combines the bird figure with the symbolic dreamer who has not yet wakened to reality. This occurs in a passage in "Hymn from a Watermelon Pavilion."

> You dweller in the dark cabin,
> To whom the watermelon is always purple,
> Whose garden is wind and moon,
>
> Of the two dreams, night and day,
> What lover, what dreamer, would choose
> The one obscured by sleep?
>
> Here is the plantain by your door
> And the best cock of red feather
> That crew before the clocks. (pp. 88–89)

The governing symbolism, "dark," "cabin" and "sleep," has been sufficiently explained. The sleeper here is the poet still committed to the vapid romanticism of the past. In his garden of "wind and moon," symbols of the romantic, he sees reality only as the romantic idealist — "always purple." If he wakes to reality, however, he may find that his best voice is the voice of reality or actual experience, symbolized here by the red feathers of the cock. So, too, the second sister is still "obscured by sleep" and must be awakened before she can produce from her "botches" a "full-pinioned one," a bird fully endowed for poetic flight. Yet in spite of her failings, she is the idealistic dreamer, the romanticist of the past, and is therefore the "most sisterly counterpart" of the superior daughter, the idealist of the present.

The third child is the child of awakened perception, a duplication of Crispin's awakening perception during his Yucatan phase. She "letters" herself on the sensory perceptions necessary for the poet. Like her sisters she develops from humble, uncertain beginnings to the exotic extreme, from creeping underleaves to "gaping at orioles,"—just as Crispin finds "a new reality in parrot squawks." The importance of this range is indicated in a later poem in which the commonplace crow and the tropical oriole symbolize the possible range of perceptual vitality.

> From oriole to crow, note the decline
> In music. Crow is realist. But, then,
> Oriole, also, may be realist. (p. 154)

The final sister is scarcely commensurate in value with the others. She has a facility in the trivial, in childish noise ("all din and gobble"), and she reflects an inordinate preference for reality, being "blasphemously pink" at birth rather than "delicately blushed" like her ideal sister. With the maturation of her superior sisters, her childish antics are significantly curbed, she becomes a "pent" and eccentric figure, a "curious digit." Crispin has already explained her origin by numerous references to the clownish antics of his earliest period when he was content to celebrate "rankest trivia" and blasphemously outrage conventional standards.

> Hence the reverberations in the words
> Of his first central hymns, the celebrants
> Of rankest trivia, tests of the strength
> Of his aesthetic, his philosophy,
> The more invidious, the more desired:
> The flourist asking aid from cabbages,
> The rich man going bare, the paladin
> Afraid, the blind man as astronomer,
> The appointed power unwielded from disdain. (p. 37)

Stevens' dissatisfaction with this phase is indicated not only by Crispin's later refusal to "accompany vastest things defunct," but by the fact that a number of poems in this vein were omitted from *Harmonium* and left for Morse to reprint in *Opus Posthumous*. *Harmonium* has its blasphemous representatives, notably the poem on Saint Ursula (p. 21) and "A High-Toned Old Christian Woman"; and a number of critics have noted the element of sacrilegious parody in "Sunday Morning." The pose of the rebellious modern exposing the follies of his peers is, as Crispin here acknowledges, a childish commotion unworthy of the mature poet. Few who have looked over the rejected pieces in *Opus Posthumous* would be inclined to argue. One such piece, however, is of interest because it seems to present the originals of Crispin's four daughters. The poem, "Piano Practice at the Academy of the Holy Angels," describes how five convent girls react during piano practice to the traditional music they are required to play. The first four girls are early versions of Crispin's daughters. The last girl, "Crispine," became the Comedian himself.

> The time will come for these children, seated before their long
>   black instruments, to strike the themes of love —
> All of them, darkened by time, moved by they know not what,
>   amending the airs they play to fulfill themselves;
> Seated before these shining forms, like the duskiest glass,
>   reflecting the piebald of roses or what you will.
> Blanche, the blonde, whose eyes are not wholly straight, in a
>   room of lustres, shed by turquoise falling,
> Whose heart will murmur with the music that will be a voice
>   for her, speaking the dreaded change of speech;
> And Rosa, the muslin dreamer of satin and cowry-kin, disdaining
>   the empty keys; and the young infanta,
> Jocunda, who will arrange the roses and rearrange, letting the
>   leaves lie on the water-like lacquer;
> And that confident one, Marie, the wearer of cheap stones, who
>   will have grown still and restless;
> And Crispine, the blade, reddened by some touch, demanding
>   the most from the phrases
> Of the well-thumbed, infinite pages of her masters, who will
>   seem old to her, requiting less and less her feeling:
> In the days when the mood of love will be swarming for solace
>   and sink deeply into the thin stuff of being,
> And these long, black instruments will be so little to them that
>   will be needing so much, seeking so much in their music. (*O. P.,* 21-22.)

Blonde Blanche prefigures Crispin's goldenest daughter. She suffers, like that "humbly eyed" daughter, a degree of visual handicap, but she, too, is the introspective one, capable of bringing an outmoded music into accord with her own emotional needs even though such transformation requires that she hear "the dreaded change of speech," that is, the painful conversion from the idealism of the past. The "lustres" of "turquoise" is another symbolic indication of the presence of subjective ideals. The second girl, Rosa, is not capable of this accomplishment. Like Crispin's second daughter, she is the impoverished romantic dreamer, content to compensate for her unsatisfactory muslin by romantically imagining herself glamorous and exotic. The important point is that she prefers to dream rather than play her instrument. For the same reason, Crispin's second daughter must be "shaken" from her sleep and pursuaded to produce the "full-pinioned one." Stevens sums up his attitude toward both these dreamers when he remarks in "Adagia," "There must be some wing on which to fly." Jocunda, the third girl, is the child of perceptual reality, like Crispin's third daughter; but she differs from her later counterpart in a significant way. She is content merely to "arrange" and "rearrange" the same familiar perceptual content. She has no perceptual curiosity; the leaves do not interest her. When she reappears as one of Crispin's vitalized offspring, she begins developing her perceptual awareness by inspecting those neglected leaves, the trivial but unnoticed aspect of Jocunda's conventionalized perceptions. In similar terms Crispin explains that perceptual stage in his development when he sought not the rose but the leaf, and so became "The florist asking aid from cabbages" (p. 37). Among the poems of *Harmonium* the same theme is developed in the poem on Saint Ursula. Ursula, having made a conventional offering of "roses/ Frail as April snow," makes in secret a second offering of "radishes and flowers." God prefers the second gift because he has become bored by the conventional and "in His garden sought/ New leaf and shadowy tinct" (p. 21).

Finally, there is Marie, who foreshadows the last of Crispin's daughters and is, like her, all too obscurely drawn. She has been the least troubled by the inadequacies of conventional music, because she is the least aspiring. She has been "confident" and content with "cheap stones," a phrase which has meaning only if one is aware that precious stones are symbolic for Stevens of ultimate ideals. His habit of adorning his ideal muse with a jewelled crown has been mentioned. Similarly, an emerald is explicitly defined as signifying "the ultimate Plato" and the "tranquilizing" jewel in "Homunculus et La Belle Étoile." Marie's cheap stones, then, indicate that she has been easily satisfied by conventional or commonplace ideals. But even she is now aware of her discontent and, having ceased to play, is "restless" for change. She is, in short, ready to be transformed into the least of Crispin's daughters, the noisy celebrator of "rankest trivia," but temporarily valuable since she is actively rebelling against conventional music with her own "din and gobble."

Crispine is not defined by a specific character trait except that she, like the later Crispin, is a "blade." She alone has been "reddened," or awakened to reality, and is alive to the inadequacies of her traditional masters. Her playing is active, a "demanding" for satisfaction that will lead her eventually to abandon the past and thus become the transformed Crispin in quest of a new tradition. And Crispin in turn will transform these unhappy musicians, confined as the title indicates to the Christian tradition and boring rehearsals of the past, to "four blithe instruments/ Of differing struts." These new instruments are the substitute for the "long, black instruments" which the Catholic girls must in time abandon.

Crispin's four daughters, then, reprsent the four stages through which he has passed (in which he produced the four types of poems represented in *Harmonium*) and the components of his own creative faculties, which individually formed "strident" voices, but which he now hears coming "to accord" upon his lap.

With the daughters thus understood, the remainder of "The Comedian" presents few problems. Continuing their description, Crispin comes to an important discovery. In spite of his children's virtues, he admits that they are "four mirrors blue/ That should be silver" (p. 45); that is, they do not reflect the world purely, but only as colored by the imagination, the subjectivity, of the poet. A parallel admission occurs in "Landscape with Boat."

> He brushed away the thunder, then the clouds,
> Then the colossal illusion of heaven. Yet still
> The sky was blue. He wanted imperceptible air.
> He wanted to see. He wanted the eye to see
> And not be touched by blue. He wanted to know,
> A naked man who regarded himself in the glass
> Of air, who looked for the world beneath the blue,
> Without blue, without any turquoise tint or phase,
> Any azure under-side or after-color. Nabob
> Of bones, he rejected, he denied, to arrive
> At the neutral centre, the ominous element,
> The single-colored, colorless primitive (pp. 241–42)

It is interesting to see in this later poem the emerging concern for the epistemological essence of the problem. Here, too, Stevens concludes as Crispin does that one never arrives at the "neutral center," that the mind reflects reality only through the distorting blue glass of its own subjectivity. One might recall the passage from Flaubert that was cited in an earlier chapter—the one in which the devil tempts Saint Anthony by explaining that things reach us only through the intermediary of the spirit, which like a convex glass distorts and deludes. Thus the blue mirrors presented by Crispin's daughters become the problem central to the later poetry. Here, they afford Crispin with the self-mocking conclusion to his tale, the recognition that his long struggle to escape the romantic illusions of the past had led him in the end to the acceptance of his own illusions. The world cannot be "daubed out/ Of its ancient purple," and Crispin accepts it on these terms as the "same insoluble lump," the same old combination of fact and fiction, reality and imagination.

> Crispin concocted doctrine from the rout.
> The world, a turnip once so readily plucked,
> Sacked up and carried overseas, daubed out
> Of its ancient purple, pruned to the fertile main,
> And sown again by the stiffest realist,
> Came reproduced by purple, family font,
> The same insoluble lump. The fatalist
> Stepped in and dropped the chuckling down his craw,
> Without grace or grumble. (p. 45)

So it is that Crispin admits that his tale may appear to end "fadedly" in view of his once grand ambitions, or it may appear to be an optimistic "glosing" of a familiar problem; but if it proves nothing,

> . . . what can all this matter since
> The relation comes, benignly, to its end?
> So may the relation of each man be
> clipped. (p. 46)

The final line is somewhat ambiguous, but apparently means that just as Crispin has brought his quest to a harmless conclusion by accepting his own experience, he would have others do the same.

"The Comedian" serves not only as the necessary guide through the conflicting styles and themes of *Harmonium;* it proposes a resolution of the basic conflict emerging from the poems of the volume. I have proposed that the cleavage between conceptual and perceptual worlds which furnishes the essential dialectic of *Harmonium* reflects the influence of William James, who exaggerated the disparity between modern materialism and idealism and attacked both in terms that are strikingly similar to Stevens's approach. Whether or not the evidence is convincing on this point, there is no question that Crispin's resolution of the problem amounts to an acceptance of James's pragmatic faith in experience. Just as, for James, the epistemological problem was solved by the uniting of subject and object in actual experience, the union of real and ideal was the product of experience. That union entailed a rejection of intellectual solutions for an active commitment to the actual world of one's private experience. Like Stevens, James frequently uses the marriage figure to express the mysterious reconciliatory power of experience:

> The significance of a human life for communicable and publicly recognizable purposes is thus the offspring of a marriage of two different parents, either of whom alone is barren. . . . significance in life does seem to be its character of *progress,* or that strange union of reality with ideal novelty which continues from one moment to another to be present.

In 1899, while Stevens was a Harvard student, James published two essays developing this theme as a lay sermon on the good life, "On a Certain Blindness in Human Beings" and "What makes a Life Significant."[34] The union of real and ideal as James explains, entails a rejection of intellectualistic approaches for an active commitment to the actual world of individual experience. Thus the first step in the recovery of life's ideals was the abandonment of the complacent intellectualism of American culture:

> Life is always worth living, if one have...responsive sensibilities. But we of the highly educated classes (so called) have most of us got far away from Nature.... We are stuffed with abstract conceptions, and glib with verbalities and verbosities....[35]

This is equivalent to Crispin's discovery during the sea crossing that he cannot stem the "verboseness" of "a wordy watery age," and his later recognition that whereas the "quotidian saps philosophers," the quotidian accepted as actual experience awakens his true wealth. For recovery from a society of "overeducated pessimists" James recommends the refreshment of a primitive society since the primitive savage best exemplifies what the intellectual has lost, "that intense interest that life can assume when brought down to the non-thinking level, the level of pure sensorial perception."

> The remedy under such conditions is to descend to a more profound and primitive level.... The savages and children of nature, to whom we deem ourselves so much superior, certainly are alive where we are often dead, along these lines.[36]

In illustration, James cites W. H. Hudson's account of his spiritual recovery from intellectual pessimism through a vacation excursion into the Patagonian wilderness (*Idle Days in Patagonia*). The passage describes how the author, after extended communion with nature, achieves the primitive level of sensory vigilance in which nature restores him in traditional Rousseauistic fashion:

> I had undoubtedly *gone back;* and that state of intense watchfulness or alertness, rather, with suspension of the higher intellectual faculties, represented the mental state of the pure savage. He thinks little, reasons little, having a surer guide in his [mere sensory perceptions]. He is in perfect harmony with nature....
>
> (The interpolation is James'.)[37]

In this state, Hudson experiences "a strong feeling of elation" indicating that an inexpressible "something had come between me and my intellect." The moral of this account, James concludes, is that one discovers an "inner secret" in the mysterious sensual life that is unavailable in more civilized culture. It is such experiences which make the "holidays of life...its most vitally significant portions."

James' explanation is here again similar to Crispin's account of his Yucatan experience which is undertaken from the same motive:

> Crispin knew
> It was a flourishing tropic he required
> For his refreshment, an abundant zone,
> Prickly and obdurate, dense, harmonious.... (p. 35)

It is also the motive of the "emaciated Romantic" in "Description of a Platonic Person," who seeks a "holiday hotel" in the tropics. So, too, in both poems the tropics afford a mystical divination which proves to be inexpressible. Such primitivism is common enough in the romantic tradition, but it is worth noting that Crispin's interest in the "reality of parrot squawks" — sometimes cited as an example of his bizarre affectations — was a suitable adjunct to James' recommended tour for New England intellectuals.

Another parallel can be found in James' account of his own awakening to the reality of American life. The account involves two contrasting visions. The one, corresponding to Crispin's "ancient whim," is the product of "ancestral blindness" which sees America locked in the dead romanticism of the past. The other is, again like Crispin's discovery, a vision of its raw, "essential prose."

> I had been steeping myself in pure ancestral blindness, and looking at life with the eyes of a remote spectator.... I had failed to see it present and alive. I could only think of it as dead and embalmed, labelled and costumed, as it is in the pages of romance. And yet there it was before me in the daily lives of the laboring classes.... On freight-trains, on the decks of vessels, in cattle yards, and mines, on lumber rafts....
>
> As I awoke to all this unidealized heroic life around me, the scales seemed to fall from my eyes....[38]

The contrast between the vision of a remote spectator and the immediately experienced reality of the land is the same which Crispin makes. Only when he thinks of America at a distance, as a country remotely "always north," does it appear to him in the "polar-purple" of a lifeless romanticism:

> America was always north to him,
> A northern west or western north, but north,
> And thereby polar, polar-purple.... (p. 34)

The reality he finds there is the product of immediate perception and is explicitly contrasted to his "ancient" viewpoint.

> And thus he tossed
> Between a Carolina of old time,
> A little juvenile, an ancient whim,

> And the visible, circumspect presentment drawn
> From what he saw across his vessel's prow. (p. 35)

In both cases perception brings about the discovery of a new America. James sees it "unidealized"; Crispin sees its "essential prose" as the "moonlight fiction" disappears. James remarks that "the scales seemed to fall from my eyes"; Crispin remarks, "It made him see how much/ Of what he saw he never saw at all." There is, finally, a similarity also in the choice of naturalistic detail — James' "decks of vessels," "freight-trains," and "lumber rafts" reappearing in Crispin's "vessels' prow," "crawling railroad spur," and "burly smells/ Of dampened lumber."

While such similarities may be coincidence, they establish the point — that poet and philosopher are steering the same intellectual course in their recovery from an effete culture. To cite further examples, there is James's illustration that ideals are relative to individual experience and cannot be universalized:

> No one has insight into all the ideals. No one should presume to judge them off-hand. The pretension to dogmatize about them in each other is the root of most human injustices. . . .
>   Every Jack sees in his own particular Jill charms and perfections to the enchantment of which we stolid onlookers are stone-cold. And which has the superior view of the absolute truth, he or we? . . . . surely to Jack are the profounder truths revealed. . . . . For Jack realizes Jill concretely, and we do not. He struggles toward a union with her inner life. . . .[39]

The best illustration of this theme in *Harmonium* is the poem mentioned earlier, "Apostrophe to Vincentine." It will be recalled that in that poem, the poet seeks a heavenly muse but meets instead a "human" Vincentine. By union with her inner life, however, she is transformed into the ideal, the "heavenly Vincentine."

> And what I knew you felt
> Came then.
>   . . . .
> And that white animal, so lean,
> Turned Vincentine,
> Turned heavenly Vincentine. (p. 53)

Similarly, Crispin's union with a human bride, rather than a phantom "sequestered bride," leads to the realization of his personal ideals. As James advises, moreover, he realizes that ideals are relative and he refuses to "lay by the personal" in order to impose his experience on others.

> Should he lay by the personal and make
> Of his own fate an instance of all fate?

What is one man among so many men?
What are so many men in such a world?
Can one man think one thing and think it long?
Can one man be one thing and be it long?
The very man despising honest quilts
Lies quilted to his poll in his despite. (p. 41)

The doctrine of the relativity of truth which Crispin here enunciates is not a matter of coincidence. In a later poem Stevens clearly sets it in its proper philosophical setting—alongside James's argument that God's eternal and absolute truth denies the metaphysical reality of change, and his theory of a pluralistic universe in which particularity, the parts, are not reducible to a unified whole.

You...You said,
"There are many truths,
But they are not parts of a truth."
Then the tree, at night, began to change....

It was when I said,
"Words are not forms of a single word.
In the sum of the parts, there are only the parts.
The world must be measured by eye";

. . .

It was at that time, that the silence was largest
And longest, the night was roundest,
The fragrance of the autumn warmest,
Closest and strongest. (p. 203–4)

The point of the poem should be evident from the discussion of James in an earlier chapter: only when one has denied the abstract reality of the Absolute in its perfect unity, do the particulars of experience emerge in their full reality.

Finally, there is a significant illustration with which James introduces his discussion of the recovery of life's ideals. The figure develops around a cabin in North Carolina.

Let me take a personal example of the kind that befalls each one of us daily:—
Some years ago, while journeying the mountains of North Carolina, I passed by a large number of "coves," as they call them there, or heads of small valleys between the hills, which had been newly cleared and planted. The impression on my mind was one of unmitigated squalor. The settler had in every case cut down the more manageable trees, and left their charred stumps standing.... He had then built a log cabin....and there he dwelt with his wife and babes....[40]

The scene here is of course similar to the symbolism by which Crispin explains the resolution of his philosophical quest—the cabin in North Carolina, the settler, his wife and children, and the planted land. James' reaction to this scene is that the settler had divested himself of the achievements of his tradition, his "heritage and birthright," and that, "No modern person ought to be willing to live a day in such a state of rudimentariness and denudation." He learns upon inquiry, however, that the settler and his family have their own individual view of their quotidian, and from that view he derives the theme of his essay:

> But, when *they* looked on the hideous stumps, what they thought of was personal victory. The chips, the girdled trees, and the vile split rails spoke of honest sweat, persistent toil and final reward. The cabin was a warrant of safety for self and wife and babes. In short, the clearing, which to me was a mere ugly picture on the retina, was to them a symbol redolent with moral memories and sang a very paean of duty, struggle and success.
>
> I had been as blind to the peculiar ideality of their conditions as they certainly would also have been to the ideality of mine....
>
> Wherever a process of life communicates an eagerness to him who lives it, there the life becomes genuinely significant. Sometimes the eagerness is more knit up with the motor activities, sometimes with the perceptions, sometimes with the imagination, sometimes with reflective thought. But, wherever it is found, there is the zest, the tingle, the excitement of reality, and there *is* "importance" in the only real and positive sense in which importance ever anywhere can be.[41]

This is very much like Stevens' vision of Crispin's final success—a settler who has recovered his eagerness for life and his own peculiar ideality, and whose cabin is a "phylactery" for his children, an assurance of safety from the outside world. It should be noticed too how closely the four daughters in their eagerness for life—"Green crammers of the green fruits of the world" (p. 43)—resemble the four phases of life mentioned by James: the reflective, the imaginative, the perceptual, and the phase of mere activity.

In view of the more specifically philosophical parallels between James and Stevens which have been illustrated in the shorter poems of *Harmonium,* the resemblance between James's theory of the good life and Crispin's spiritual quest may well be more than coincidence. In any event, one may conclude that the poetry of *Harmonium* has more philosophical intention than has been supposed, and that if any modern philosopher can be said to have influenced Stevens at this period, William James is the most likely candidate.

6

Later Developments: The "Notes Toward a Supreme Fiction"

During the last fifteen years critical interest in Stevens has shifted to the later poetry, the poetry after, roughly, 1940. There is general agreement that the later volumes represent a significant change from the earlier period. They are said to show the emergence of a new style — or at least a development beyond the style of *Harmonium* — which becomes progressively serious, abstract, analytical and philosophical. The preoccupation with aesthetics has been recognized as an outgrowth of earlier themes and as an attempt, as Stevens once said, to make a theory of poetry into a "theory of life." Beyond this, while there has been much confusion at the interpretive level, only a few critics have failed to agree that the later poetry represents Stevens' highest achievement.

The most highly praised of the later poems is one of the longest works devoted to aesthetic theory, "Notes Toward a Supreme Fiction." The poem is widely accepted as Stevens' masterpiece, as his most important contribution to the theory of the imagination, and, by many, as the poem representing the ultimate resolution of his aesthetic problems. In view of its acknowledged importance, it seems a good choice with which to conclude this study, even though it is a relatively early example of the later Stevens. The poem was first published separately in 1943 and later included in *Transport to Summer* (1947). In 1947 it seemed a fitting conclusion to the work of a sixty-eight year old poet. It presented an exhaustive recapitulation of Stevens' familiar themes — the ideas that composed his theory of imagination — and it may be that its scope more than anything else contributed to its almost immediate acceptance as the triumphant resolution of his aesthetic problems. There are two considerations which by now should make that judgment suspect. The first is that Stevens continued to debate the same issues for over a decade following the poem's publication. The second is that while critical assessment normally presupposes an understanding of the work in question, the "Notes" is still an interpreter's nightmare.[1]

The reading that will be offered here indicates no significant change in Stevens' theories and no resolution of the overriding issues. To that extent it challenges the accepted critical view, but the focus is not primarily critical. The "Notes" presents enough problems at the interpretive level, and it should be sufficient here if the philosophical background examined in this study can be shown to reduce some of its obscurities.

The "Notes" is a blank verse poem written as a series of instructions to a novice poet addressed as "ephebe." It is divided into three sections, subtitled: I. "It Must Be Abstract," II. "It Must Change," and III. "It Must Give Pleasure." Each section is further divided into ten short poems of twenty-one lines. Usually the short poems have been regarded as a set of fragments or "notes" loosely grouped under the appropriate section heading like so many variations of a theme. The paraphrase offered here should show that the poem is more closely structured than has been supposed, that within each section the ten individual poems are sequentially related and comprise a rationally developed exposition of the section heading. Since many of these poems are ambiguous in isolation, a recognition of their sequential position is of considerable help.

Individually, the poems follow a fairly simple structural principle. A proposition is usually stated, often in the first line or two, and then developed metaphorically. For example, in Section I, poem iv, the first line states the proposition, "The first idea was not our own"; and poem x in the same section begins with the proposition, "The major abstraction is the idea of man." The difficulty lies in the metaphorical development, which may be intended as an illustration, a defense, a refutation, or a qualified acceptance of the proposition in question. The intention is largely a matter of inference and is all too easy to mistake when the poems are read in isolation, the customary practice. In recent years several such poems have been admired as moving examples of Stevens' deepest beliefs, when actually the theme in question is being refuted rather than defended.

The total poem is unfortunately too long for extensive quotation, and even a summary paraphrase must be greatly abbreviated. It is possible to show even in skeletal form, however, the development of the argument. The following paraphrase is offered on the assumption that it is, in the main, right. That it will not be corrected and superseded in its turn is unlikely, but in so far as it reconstructs the general argument of the three sections, it may correct a number of misconceptions about individual poems.

"It Must Be Abstract": (i) The novice poet should begin by learning to perceive a physical image of external reality, in this case the sun, without any intellectual distortion. This requires the viewpoint of an ignorant man who makes no assumptions about a divine creator of reality or about the nature of reality itself. (ii) The poet's fresh perception is the truth which he tries to express metaphorically because it fulfills a human need for renewed contact with reality, a contact lost by the conceptualizing mind. (iii) The poem which satisfies this need is emotionally exhilarating and awakens man's primitive sense of affinity with all being. (iv) The physical world preceded human consciousness; hence Cartesian dualism began with Adam and Eve, who initiated the effort to create a second, spiritual world in heaven. But heaven is empty air, and the poetry of heaven is pathetic rhetoric. (v) The heroic poet must rather attempt to assert his supremacy over his natural world, a supremacy which animals instinctively assert over their environment. This instinct is thwarted in the young poet who in his intellectual isolation feels inadequate to oppose external reality. (vi) The great poet has developed an imagination capable of combining the visible and invisible elements which compose his sense of reality. (vii) Without such a poet, men may be capable of fortuitous moments when they passively experience a feeling of harmony with the external world, moments which transcend the values of the intellect. (viii) The notion that the great poet speaks for the common man is a romantic illusion, because the poet is not the common man although he may inspire him. (ix) This does not mean that the great poet is the divinely inspired figure of romantic apotheosis. He is a possible man who has moved beyond reason, learning and tradition to find happiness in the reconciliation with his physical world. This is the ideal which every poet must strive to realize. (x) The ideal man is thus an abstraction which the great poet illustrates in himself. At the same time, the poet is part of that larger abstraction, the common man — an impoverished figure, searching the ruins of his past for values it no longer contains. The poet's obligation is to interpret his ideal of man for all such common men.

"It Must Change": (i) The religious mind of the past assumed a permanent spiritual order, thereby conceiving of temporal reality as the monotonous embodiment of abstract and static concepts, and ignoring the reality of change. (ii) The political mind tries to impose a permanent order upon reality by authority, unaware that reality cannot be fixed because it is composed of particulars existing in a time continuum. (iii) Not even the timeless world of art can contain a permanent order since the art of the past changes according to the changed conceptions of the age that judges it. (iv) Change can be explained as the interaction of opposites. In man change results from the interaction of imagination and reality, self and otherness — making imagination the artist's invaluable faculty. (v) The imagination makes life endurable by creating a possible ideal which man strives to embody in reality. (vi) The romantic poet distorted reality by converting everything into the monotonous spirituality of his own egocentric imagination. (vii) The romantic excesses have taught us that poetry must be based upon the actual world where men find accessible satisfactions in the fluctuations of thought and perception. (viii) But reality itself remains an alien, inflexible order before the merely passive mind; it can be truly possessed only by means of the fictions created from human thought and feeling. (ix) The poet strives to express this unique synthesis in words, an effort which requires a further synthesis between common language and the private speech of his imagination. (x) The poet is thus the student of a universal will to change, the volatile impetus which both mind and reality manifest in change. He studies the fluctuations of the sensible world as a mirror of the fluctuations of consciousness, endeavoring to capture the fresh transformations of both in language.

"It Must Give Pleasure": (i) It is easy for the poet to celebrate the common pleasures of life. It is possible to voice any range of experience, but the difficult art is to express one's unique and immediate perception. (ii) The effeminate romantic lives nostalgically, imposing upon present reality a lifeless, imaginative stereotype. (iii) A static imagination cannot resist reality. Moses' vision of God in a burning bush hardens with time to a vision of Medusa. Reality assumes an unchanging hue, an intolerable sameness which grows more hideous with time. The Greeks accounted for the variety and freshness of experience by the myth of Orpheus, who restored variety to life by the gift of the poetic imagination. (iv) A modern explanation is that reality is dependent upon the mind. Thus a modern myth might relate how a Captain (human intellect) married a native maiden (primitive instinct) and thereafter the two protected their earthly paradise from the ravages of time. (v) Christianity destroyed such marriages for a hypocritical asceticism. The ecclesiastic authority commits the faithful to an impoverished reality, praising their Christian resignation. (vi) The ecclesiastic himself aspires to the intellectual apprehension of god, but as with Satan of old, he finds that his imaginative flight cannot transcend the limits of his finite nature. He thereby learns to abandon the mutually exclusive dualism which satisfies neither mind nor body. (vii) The dualism is the consequence of man's evolution from an animal stage, where reality was ordered by instinct, to the intellectual stage, where it is ordered by reason. There must be a third, intuitive stage at which reality will be immediately apprehended without the distortions of mind. (viii) Otherwise the poet, caught in a hopeless dualism, does not know what to believe. There are times when a wholly imaginative experience suffices simply by being a satisfying emotional experience. There are other times when common reality suffices and imagination seems like the absurdest fairy tale. (ix) Both kinds of poetry may be enjoyable. Let the poet unmarried to reality (the "weedy wren") enjoy singing of the wholly unreal experience of angels; let the virile realist (the "cock robin") celebrate repetitiously the commonplace joys of ordinary men. (x) The narrator's only satisfaction, however, is in those fleeting moments of perceptual change when external reality and emotion are momently synthesized in the imagination. When this irrational distortion is ultimately accepted as rational, the poetic imagination may be accepted as the ultimate reality.

The poem concludes with an epilogue addressed, appropriately in 1942, to a soldier: The poet's war is a mental one between an ideal world and a real world, and this is a human war in which the physical warfare of the soldier is implicated. The soldier fights for a human ideal which the poet labors to articulate faithfully.

As a paraphrase of the "Notes" indicates, it contains nothing startlingly novel in so far as theories of poetry are concerned. What is distinctive, is the philosophical and specifically epistemological awareness with which the theories are elaborated. In the final section the problem emerges clearly in terms of the old conflict of *Harmonium* between philosophical materialism and idealism. The core of the problem, however, is in the most difficult section of the poem, "It Must Be Abstract." Several of the individual poems of this section require additional comment.

The first poem introduces a phrase which reappears throughout the section, the poet's "first idea" of reality. The definition is characteristically ambiguous.

> Begin, ephebe, by perceiving the idea
> Of this invention, this invented world,
> The inconceivable idea of sun,
>
> You must become an ignorant man again
> And see the sun again with an ignorant eye
> And see it clearly in the idea of it.
>
> . . . .
>
> There is a project for the sun. The sun
> Must bear no name, gold flourisher, but be
> In the difficulty of what it is to be. (pp. 380–81)

The omitted stanzas, which dismiss the possibility of a divine creator of the sun ("Phoebus is dead, ephebe. . . . .") are clear enough. The ambiguous statement is that of the first stanza, in which the novice poet is told to *perceive* an "inconceivable idea." Suggestions as to what this idea might be have ranged from a Platonic idea, to pure being, to Santayana's essences. The first two possibilities are traditionally regarded as conceivable rather than perceivable. Santayana's theory of essences is a possibility, but there is nothing in the passage which would distinguish Santayana's theory from, say, Bergson's theory of perception. The simplest explanation is that Stevens is merely stressing the opposition between perceptual and conceptual experience: sensible reality cannot be "conceived" because it is given only in immediate perception. If one were to suspect a philosophical influence, the emphasis upon the immediacy and purity of the perceptual act is much more akin to Bergson. The "Notes" was written during the period when, as the essays of *The Necessary Angel* reveal, Stevens was most attracted to Bergson's ideas. There is also an intimation of Bergson in the concluding three lines, which appear to accept the distinction between appearance and reality. The sun in its ultimate reality is unknowable: it "must bear no name," and its nature is left in the undefined "difficulty of what it is to be." This would appear to be a rejection of one of Stevens' earliest themes, the possibility of penetrating to a reality behind appearances.[2] Here, that possibility is seemingly discarded in favor of accepting the "idea" or image as the knowable limit of reality. It should be noted, however, that the sun is Stevens' usual symbol of the creative source of physical reality, the agent of change; and its creative character is suggested here by the fact that while it should "bear no name," it is in fact named — but as an intangible agent rather than a static object of perception, a "gold flourisher."

The reader may feel that such fine discriminations evince more ingenuity on the part of the interpreter than subtlety on the part of the poet. The idealist habit of mind is something one comes to recognize in such passages only after some familiarity with Stevens' poetry. The implicit ambiguity of the passage is not accidental; it is exploited in the later poetry with an intensity that may strike one as almost hallucinatory. To cite only a few examples:

> It is possible that to seem — it is to be,
> As the sun is something seeming and it is.
>
> The sun is an example. What it seems
> It is and in such seeming all things are.
> ("Description Without Place," p. 339)
>
> The false and the true are one.
>
> The eye believes and its communion takes.
> The spirit laughs to see the eye believe
> And its communion take.
> ("Extracts from Addresses to the
> Academy of Fine Ideas," p. 253)

I wonder, have I lived a skeleton's life,
As a disbeliever in reality....
                ("As You Leave the Room," *O. P.,* 117)

Inescapable romance, inescapable choice
Of dreams, disillusion as the last illusion,
Reality as a thing seen by the mind,

Not that which is but that which is apprehended,

....

Everything as unreal as real can be,

In the inexquisite eye. ("An Ordinary Evening in
                New Haven," 468)

If it should be true that reality exists
In the mind: the tin plate, the loaf of bread on it,
The long-bladed knife, the little to drink and her

Misericordia, it follows that
Real and unreal are two in one:...
                ("An Ordinary Evening in New Haven," 485)

                We seek

The poem of pure reality, untouched
By trope or deviation, straight to the word,
Straight to the transfixing object, to the object

At the exactest point at which it is itself,
Transfixing by being purely what it is,
A view of New Haven, say, through the certain eye,

The eye made clear of uncertainty, with the sight
Of simple seeing, without reflection. We seek
Nothing beyond reality.
                ("An Ordinary Evening in New Haven," 471)

None of these excerpts should be read independently of its context as representing the poet's viewpoint. They have been cited merely to illustrate Stevens' many variations on the appearance-reality theme. The first passage seemingly accepts the reality of appearances, the second rejects them, the third denies knowledge of external reality however defined, the fourth exploits the unreality of appearances solipsistically, the fifth extends this theme by equating the unreality of appearances with the unreality of all mental life, and the last is a reworking of the "first idea" which is introduced with the sun image in "Notes." This last passage is interesting in that it describes the effort to capture physical reality by an intense perceptual act which perceives the object "at the exactest point at which it is itself."

Stevens goes on to explain that reality so captured includes "not merely the visible,/ The solid, but the movable, the moment." This notion of capturing more than the visible, of the movable as opposed to the solid, and of time narrowed to the "moment" seems to be what Bergson called "the image of the creation of matter by form, which the philosopher must have in mind in order to conceive...creative energy."[3] And in Stevens, the sun is customarily the symbol of the creative power of nature, of the "savage presence" which is transformed into the "barbarous strength" of the creative imagination.[4]

With this much cross reference, it should be evident that the "inconceivable idea" of reality which introduces the "Notes" is a term capable of assuming all the ambiguous philosophical shuffling evident in other poems. But since the novice poet is told to regard the "idea" as an ignorant man, the reader is probably safest in following suit and assuming that an "idea" of the sun is simply an image derived from whatever reality lies beyond perceptual limits.

Poems ii and iii, however, are almost certainly appropriations of Bergsonian doctrine. In ii, Stevens introduces Bergson's notion of the necessity of renewed contact with external reality to supplant the unreality of the conceptualizing intellect. Coupled with this is the Bergsonian emphasis upon process. Thus the desire for reality is initiated by an awareness of change—"the effortless weather turning blue." Behind this lies Bergson's theory that reality is process ("real duration") and cannot be grasped by the intellect because mental conceptions are static, the artificial formulations by which the mind tries unsuccessfully to contain a fluid reality. Duration can only be immediately experienced, and in this, the acute perception of change is primary. Stevens summarizes the matter in two comments in "Adagia"; "The world is a force, not a presence," and "Conceptions are artificial. Perceptions are essential" (*O. P.,* 164, 172).

Poem iii is a development of these notions in which, as in the prose comments upon Bergson cited earlier, the *élan vital* hovers indistinctly on the periphery.

> The poem refreshes life so that we share,
> For a moment, the first idea...It satisfies
> Belief in an immaculate beginning
>
> And sends us, winged by an unconscious will
> To an immaculate end. We move between these points:
> From that ever-early candor to its late plural
>
> And the candor of them is the strong exhilaration
> Of what we feel from what we think, of thought
> Beating in the heart, as if blood newly came,

An elixir, an excitation, a pure power.
The poem, through candor, brings back a power again
That gives a candid kind to everything.

We say: At night an Arabian in my room,
With his damned hoobla-hoobla-hoobla-how,
Inscribes a primitive astronomy

Across the unscrawled fores the future casts
And throws his stars around the floor. By day
The wood-dove used to chant his hoobla-hoo

And still the grossest iridescence of ocean
Howls hoo and rises and howls hoo and falls.
Life's nonsense pierces us with strange relation. (pp. 382–83)

In the first stanza, the "immaculate beginning" is equivalent to what Stevens elsewhere calls "pure reality," that is, a reality undistorted by the mind. The "first idea," however, is not identified with such reality; it is merely a means of satisfying "belief" in it. The "late plural" in the second stanza refers to the mind's imagined concepts of reality, which eventually become static and stale, devoid of the immediacy of perception and feeling. Only by repeated return to pure perception can one recover the "unconscious will" which unites thought and feeling in the immediate moment and which supplies an "elixir" of life, a "pure power"—terms strongly suggestive of Bergson's *élan vital*. As in Bergson, the grasp of this mysterious power restores man's affinity with all creation, signifies the awakening of a primitive magic which has been lost by man's evolution to the level of intellect, and brings new possibilities into being. As Bergson explains,

> That this is an original tendency, we can all verify when a sudden shock arouses the primitive man dormant within us all. What we feel in these cases is the sensation of an efficient presence; the nature of this presence is of little consequence, the essential point is its efficiency:...we begin to count for something in the universe.[5]

We begin to count for something, of course, because we have been united with the impulse which moves through all creation. And the earliest manifestation of this impulse in man Bergson finds in the magic rituals of the primitive savage. The parallel notion is symbolized by the appearance of the Arabian and his primitive astronomy in stanza five. The extension of the same force to the animal realm and thence to the source of animate life, the ocean, is indicated in the concluding two stanzas. The final figure, the rise and fall of the sea, repeats what is one of Bergson's best known metaphors for the forward surge of the vital impetus, followed by its lapse back into the matter that constrains it. In one passage he elaborates upon the figure at some length.

Life as a whole, from the initial impulsion that thrust it into the world, will appear as a wave which rises and which is opposed by the descending movement of matter.... At one point alone it passes freely, dragging with it the obstacle which will weigh on its progress but not stop it. At this point is humanity; it is our privileged situation. On the other hand, this rising wave is consciousness, and, like all consciousness, it includes potentialities without number.... The matter that it bears along with it, and in the interstices of which it inserts itself, alone can divide it into distinct individualities. On flows the current, running through human generations, sub-dividing itself into individuals.[6]

In addition to the wave figure, the explanation of the single impulse dividing itself into the plurality of individual consciousness is like Stevens's description of a single reality evolving into its "late plural." Similarly, the notion that man at the apogee of the current is privileged to claim "potentialities without number" might explain the significance of the Arab's peculiar activity. His stars are astrological indications of unrealized possibilities, and his scattering them about may be intended to illustrate their plenitude.

The fourth poem of the section is a good example of Stevens's habit of exploiting an epistemological dualism as support for his argument. On this occasion the dualism affords an explanation of Christian myth and, implicitly, Stevens's criticism of it.

The first idea was not our own. Adam
In Eden was the father of Descartes
And Eve made air the mirror of herself,

Of her sons and of her daughters. They found themselves,
In heaven as in a glass; a second earth;
And in the earth itself they found a green—

The inhabitants of a very varnished green.
But the first idea was not to shape the clouds
In imitation. The clouds preceded us

There was a muddy centre before we breathed.
There was a myth before the myth began,
Venerable and articulate and complete.

From this the poem springs; that we live in a place
That is not our own, and, much more, not ourselves
And hard it is in spite of blazoned days.

We are the mimics. Clouds are pedagogues.
The air is not a mirror but bare board,
Coulisse bright-dark, tragic chiaroscuro

And comic color of the rose, in which
Abysmal instruments make sounds like pips
Of the sweeping meanings that we add to them. (pp. 383–84)

The fifth stanza has been widely quoted as illustrating Stevens' awareness of the alienation of modern man. While that theme is certainly present in Stevens and is employed here, the context in which it appears makes certain essential qualifications. The first stanza states that Cartesian dualism began not with Descartes but Adam, that is, with the first human consciousness of a physical world external to the mind and hence "not our own." As a consequence Eve created for herself and her descendants a more suitable spiritual world, a "second earth" in heaven, and in comparison to heaven the real world seemed a poor artifact, a "very varnished green." The attempt to people heaven with spiritual forms, "to shape the clouds/ In imitation," was wholly unreal, however. Thus the concluding three stanzas reassert a familiar theme: the physical world is man's only reality, it is not a reflection of a higher reality, and the poet's heavenly rhetoric is a pathetically empty rhetoric played upon "abysmal instruments."

It is obvious that the famous stanza of this poem, stanza five, takes on an ambiguous meaning when read as part of the total argument. It is not clear whether the explanation that poetry is a compensation for a reality that "is not our own" is to be accepted or rejected. The previous poem had argued that poetry restores "a candid kind to everything," and the poems to follow return to this view. While Stevens usually exploits the dualism which he here associates with Descartes, it would seem in view of the context that he is rejecting the notion. But he is arguing rather that poetry motivated by the acceptance of Cartesian dualism is fatally limited to vapid spirituality if it rejects the "first idea." Once the poet accepts reality as a wholly completed myth, "varnished" and beyond his power to alter, his poetry will become futile rhetoric. Certainly the attitude toward the Christian myth that was motivated by such acceptance is clear enough. It is demonstrated by other poems of the same period. There is a very similar passage, for example, in "The Pure Good of Theory":

> Man, that is not born of woman but of air,
> That comes here in the solar chariot,
> Like rhetoric in a narration of the eye—
>
> We knew one parent must have been divine,
> Adam of beau regard, from fat Elysia,
> Whose mind malformed this morning metaphor,
> While all the leaves leaked gold. His mind made
>   morning,
> As he slept. He woke in a metaphor: this was
>   a metamorphosis of paradise,
> Malformed, the world was paradise malformed...
>   . . . .
> To say the solar chariot is junk
> Is not a variation but an end. (pp. 331–32)

It is apparent that Adam's view of the world as a "malformed meta-phor" and Eve's vision of its "very varnished green" are the result of accept-ing the doctrine that the first idea was not our own, but the completed myth of God. Further evidence comes from the much later "Ordinary Evening in New Haven," which is essentially a revision of the "Notes." Here again the Cartesian viewpoint is treated as the natural manifestation of consciousness, but it is also a commitment to despair, to "disillusion as the last illusion":

> Everything as unreal as real can be
>
> In the inexquisite eye. Why, then inquire
> Who has divided the world, what entrepreneur?
> No man. The self, the chrysalis of all men?
>
> Became divided in the leisure of blue day
> And more, in branchings after day. One part
> Held fast tenaciously in common earth
>
> And one from central earth to central sky
> And in moonlit extensions of them in the mind
> Searched out such majesty as it could find. (p. 468-69)

This conclusion is revised in the next poem of the same sequence (vi), which begins with the contrary proposition, "Reality is the beginning not the end." The argument culminates in poem x, where the mind that retreats to a conceptual world is described as fixed, dead, and "imprisoned in con-stant change." By contrast, the free spirit accepts reality as "a permanence composed of impermanence" (p. 472). Here again the resolution is pure Bergson: it is his invariable contrast between the mind imprisoned within the static forms of the conceptualizing intellect, and the man who is intui-tively able to pierce those molds and immerse himself in real duration—a "permanence composed of impermanence."

> He who installs himself in becoming sees in duration the very life of things, the funda-mental reality. The Forms, which the mind isolates and stores up in concepts, are then only snapshots of the changing reality. They are moments gathered along the course of time; and, just because we have cut the thread that binds them to time, they no longer endure.[7]

For the conceptual mind change is a prison because it is trapped by its interpretation of change as successive states, and "with these successive states...you will never constitute movement."[8]

To return, then: poem iv of "Notes," if understood as a rejection of Cartesian dualism, assumes a logical relationship to poem v, which de-scribes the predicament of the modern poet, who, deprived of unreal spiritual myths, tries unsuccessfully to establish his supremacy over his physical world. The point of the poem lies in the contrast between the animal's instinctive dominance of his environment and the poet who is defeated by the isolated world of his intellect.

> The bear,
> The ponderous cinnamon, snarls in his mountain
>
> At summer thunder and sleeps through winter snow.
> But you, ephebe, look from your attic window,
> Your mansard with a rented piano. You lie
> In silence upon your bed. (p. 384)

A few symbolic touches are used to indicate the cause of the poet's difficulty. To live under a roof is Stevens' usual indication of withdrawal from reality to the world of the mind. (Compare the later reference to "Cinderella fulfilling herself beneath the roof," p. 405.) The novice poet resides in the highest or most intellectual part, the attic, and he tries to play a rented instrument rather than his own. Because of his intellectual viewpoint he feels himself inadequate to dominate the reality he is supposed to have in his care.

> You look
> Across the roofs as sigil and as ward
> And in your center mark them and are cowed...
>
> These are the heroic children whom time breeds
> Against the first idea—to lash the lion,
> Caparison elephants, teach bears to juggle. (pp. 384–85)

The animals have previously been described as beasts who fearlessly dominate their environment. Like them, the novice poet must learn to dominate reality, even the beasts themselves, by his opposing imagination. Unlike Adam and Eve, whose recourse was to retreat from an alien reality into a conceptual heaven, the heroic poet confronts and recreates the first idea in satisfying human terms. The next poem, vi, illustrates how this can be accomplished, how the artist transforms reality into his own uniquely human sense of reality, which would otherwise go unrealized.

> Not to be realized because not to
> Be seen, not to be loved nor hated because
> Not to be realized. Weather by Franz Hals,
>
> Brushed up by brushy winds in brushy clouds,
> Wetted by blue, colder for white. Not to
> Be spoken to, without a roof, without

First fruits, without the virginal of birds,
The dark-blown ceinture loosened, not relinquished.
Gay is, gay was, the gay forsythia

And yellow, yellow thins the Northern blue.
Without a name and nothing to be desired,
If only imagined but imagined well.

My house has changed a little in the sun.
The fragrance of the magnolias comes close,
False flick, false form, but falseness close to kin.

It must be visible or invisible,
Invisible and visible or both:
A seeing and unseeing in the eye.

The weather and the giant of the weather,
Say the weather, the mere weather, the mere air:
An abstraction blooded, as a man by thought. (p. 385)

The example of the Hals painting is intended to illustrate how "mere weather," with its invisible aspects of a changing reality may be represented concretely. Wind, wet, and cold are depicted by brush technique and color. The seasonal change is suggested by the loosening of the clouds, and a nuance of spring gaiety is introduced by tints of yellow based upon association of gaiety, yellow, and forsythia. In the same manner the poet tries to express the intangible change of sun on his house by finding an imagined correlative, the scent of magnolias. The touch is an artificial addition, a "false flick," but it approximates the invisible quality of the change. The conclusion contains the first appearance of the "abstraction" referred to in the section heading, and the meaning of the phrase, "an abstraction blooded," has occasioned some debate. It does not, as is sometimes supposed, refer to an abstraction in the usual sense of an abstract idea or universal which the poet embodies in particularity. Mr. Frank Dogget has explained correctly that it refers to "our environment,...the scene of our lives," which is unrealized until blooded by the "living mind of man."[9] It is, in short, the poet's sense of reality as distinguished from the merely physical. For example, in "Extracts from Addresses to the Academy of Fine Ideas," the weather is symbolic of that which contains both the external world and the poet:

> ...it is enough
> To believe in the weather, and in the things and men
> Of the weather and in one's self, as part of that
> And nothing more. (p. 258)

The interesting feature of the poem, however, is in Stevens' recourse to the invisible reality of change. Here the influence of Bergson is probably derived from the book which Stevens cites in one of his essays, *Two Sources of Morality and Religion*. The book concerns the distinction between what Bergson called "static" and "dynamic" religion. Static religions (including Christianity) originated, according to Bergson, in man's natural instinct to resist reality. Without this instinct, man's evolution to the stage of intellect would have been accompanied by a paralyzing fear of his environment. As a protective measure, nature provided him with a "myth-making faculty," corresponding to animal instinct, which "is a defensive reaction of nature against what might be depressing for the individual and dissolvent for society, in the exercise of intelligence."[10] While intelligence and environment create "resistances," the myth-making faculty provides an instinctive power to "resist these resistances." It may be recalled that Stevens develops a similar theme in the first essay of *The Necessary Angel,* in which the imagination's ability to resist reality is said to be an innate and self-preserving function — "a violence from within that protects us from a violence without." Bergson goes on to explain the naturalistic basis of myth-making by contrasting the animal's instinctive dominance of his environment with the destructive intellect of man:

> For, look at any other animal. It avails itself of everything it finds useful. Does it actually believe itself to be the center of the world? Probably not, since it has no conception of the world as such, and besides, it has not the slightest inclination to speculate. But since it only sees...it obviously behaves as though everything in nature were combined solely with a view to its well-being. Such is its conviction, not intellectualized, but lived, a conviction which sustains the animal and is indistinguishable from its effort to live. You bring reflexion into play, however, and this conviction will vanish; man will perceive himself, will think of himself as a speck in the immensity of the universe. He would feel lost, if the effort to live did not at once project into his intelligence...the opposing image of things and events turning towards man; whether well or ill disposed, a certain intention of his environment follows him then everywhere.....[11]

This is precisely the situation described in poem v, in which the novice poet strives to equal the animal's instinctive resistance to his environment but is "cowed" by his intellectual awareness of his inadequacy. Like Bergson's mythmakers he will learn to dominate reality only by "resisting" the first idea.

It might appear that Bergson regards the mythmakers of static religions with approval, but anyone acquainted with his philosophy will recognize the prejorative implications of "static." Thus, as he goes on to explain, while mythmaking was a necessary stage in the evolutionary scheme, it represents a turning away from life's vital impetus. It attempts to formulate or fix the vital impetus in mythical conceptions. It must therefore be supplanted by a "dynamic" phase of religion, which, as one might expect, means a return to sensible reality for the recovery of the *élan vital,* and an evolution from the plane of intellect to intuition.

...why should man not recover the confidence he lacks, or which has been undermined by reflexion, by turning back for fresh impetus, in the direction whence that impetus came? Not through intelligence.... [since] it does not attain any reality. But we know that all around intelligence there lingers still a fringe of intuition, vague and evanescent. Can we not fasten upon it, intensify it, and above all, consummate it in action, for it has become pure contemplation only through a weakening in its principle, and, if we may put it so, by an abstraction practiced on itself?

A soul strong enough, noble enough to make this effort would.... be content to feel itself pervaded, though retaining its own personality, by a being immeasurably mightier than itself.... [12]

Again, this is precisely the alternative illustrated in poem vi by the Hals painting. The great artist resists reality by returning to it, and he finds there something more than the visible—the invisible reality of change. As in his prose discussion of Bergson's book, Stevens avoids explicit acceptance of the mystical aspects of the *élan vital,* but it might be noted that Bergson's reference above to the soul capable of absorbing the impetus as a "being immeasurably mightier than itself" is remarkably like the poet who has become Stevens' "giant" of his environment. There is also a similarity in Bergson's reference to an "abstraction" from reality, which must be revitalized by the exceptional man, and Stevens' "blooded" abstraction. As for the adaptation of these notions to the function of the artist. Bergson offers a striking parallel to Stevens' treatment of the Hals painting in *Creative Mind.*

What is the aim of art if not to show us, in nature and in the mind, outside of us and within us, things which did not explicitly strike our senses and our consciousness?... The poet is this revealing agent. But nowhere is the function of the artist shown as clearly as in...painting. The great painters are men who possess a certain vision of things which has or will become the vision of all men. A Corot, a Turner,—not to mention others—have seen in nature many an aspect that we did not notice. Shall it be said that they have not seen but created...? If we reflect deeply upon what we feel as we look at a Turner or a Corot, we shall find that, if we accept them and admire them, it is because we had already perceived without seeing. It was, for us...the pale and colourless vision of things that is habitually ours. The painter has isolated it.... [13]

Clearly, the talent manifested by Corot and Turner is identical with that of Franz Hals. He too is the "revealing agent," as Bergson says, of "things which did not explicitly strike our senses and our consciousness" ("Not to be realized because not to/ Be seen...."). And finally, he brings to life a "pale and colourless vision of things," making them no longer a mere abstraction, but an "abstraction blooded."

The influence of Bergson upon the Imagists with their cultivation of intense perceptions has been mentioned earlier, but Stevens is exploiting Bergsonian theory at this period in much greater detail and with a closer approach to the mystical core of the philosophy. The difficulty is that he cannot accept the core, and so he resorts as in this poem to a nebulous weaving about the core, to implications of an ultimate meaning that seems always about to be expressed, but which turns out to be inexpressible. It is called here an "abstraction"; more often it is a "revelation" or a "discovery," or a "transparence." It is a "new text of the world" which lies "at the center of the unintelligible" and which requires for its realization a "giant of nothingness," a "giant ever changing, living in change."[14]

The final four poems envision a society of man in which the poet replaces the priest. While this is a fairly common concept in romantic tradition, the hand of Bergson and his "dynamic religion" are evident here, too. Stevens suggests as much in his discussion of Bergson's saints in the essay "The Figure of the Youth as Virile Poet."[15] The similarities may be briefly indicated as a final example of Bergson's influence.

Bergson's theory of "dynamic religion" is an adaptation of the nineteenth-century, romantic hero to his philosophical scheme. Its ideal end is "a mystic society embracing all humanity and moving animated by a common will, toward a continually renewed creation of a more complete humanity."[16] The animating will is, of course, a manifestation of the *élan vital,* and the soul most fully in possession of the impetus is the inspired saint who, by his example, is capable of drawing society after him. Thus dynamic religion occurs whenever life "imparts a new impetus to exceptional individuals who have immersed themselves anew in it."[17] The appeal of the exceptional man is due not to any doctrine he imparts; his appeal is not to the intellect but to the emotions. It is therefore of the utmost importance that while he partakes of a higher nature, he sees himself in terms of a common human nature. Otherwise he will not be able to inspire inferior men with his example:

> ...so exceptional souls have appeared who sensed their kinship with the soul of Everyman, ...The reappearance of each one of them was like the creation of a new species, composed of one single individual, the vital impulse culminating at long intervals in one particular man, a result which could not have been obtained at one stroke by humanity as a whole.... The creative emotion which exalted these exceptional souls, and which was an overflowing of vitality, has spread far and wide about them; enthusiasts themselves, they radiated enthusiasm which has never been completely quenched....[18]

Such are the inspired mystics who form, according to Bergson, an "irresistible attraction" to which common men instinctively respond with a "certain stirring up of the soul, which you call emotion." A number of modern philosophers have pointed out the dangers of this doctrine by noting that Bergson himself lived to see France overrun by inspired German fanatics. Bergson was sure that the vital impetus would inspire man with a "love of humanity," but a force dependent upon a blind instinct which transcends both conventional morality and religion issues naturally in the simple worship of force.[19]

Poems viii, ix, and x conclude the first section of the "Notes" by developing the "idea of man" which the young poet must try to exemplify. The characteristics which Stevens stresses explain his remark in *The Necessary Angel* that poets may be "the peers" of Bergson's saints. In poem ix, the ideal man is: (1) the man who has evolved from the stage of intellect to that of pure intuition ("He comes,/ Compact in invincible foils, from reason...."); (2) he has returned to the "first idea," to nature (where he "reposes/ On a breast forever precious for that touch...."); (3) he heralds the creation of a new era (being a "foundling of the infected past"); (4) and his inspiration must be emotionally realized by the novice poet ("The hot of him is purest in the heart").

In poem x the ideal man is: (5) the man who radiates the enthusiasm and creative force of all exceptional men ("Happy fecundity, flor-abundant force"); (6) whose exceptional qualities entail his recognition of his common human nature ("In being more than an exception, part/ Though an heroic part, of the commonal"); (7) who is motivated by a love of humanity like all great leaders ("grown furious with human wish"); (8) and whose desire is to inspire his fellow men to realize his vision of a higher humanity ("to confect/ The final elegance").

To sum up: the first section of "Notes Toward a Supreme Fiction" establishes the intellectual framework of the poem. Stevens' version of the great poet is extricated from the mystical swathing of Bergson's saints in so far as possible, but the implication that the poet is somehow in possession of a higher state of being runs throughout. On the one hand he appears to be simply the man who has reached an ultimate, intuitive stage of evolution where he is rejoined with nature — nature being Stevens's substitute for religious aspiration. On the other hand, however, it is only the mystical core provided by the *élan vital* that can explain the peculiar ameliorative power attributed to the poet's unique vision of reality. Without the *élan vital* the whole elaborate system comes down simply to an emotional worship of nature.

The remaining sections do not resolve the problem. Section II, "It Must Change," is mainly an extended illustration of the various kinds of artistic synthesis productive of change. Section III, "It Must Give Pleasure," reverses this procedure by stressing the inadequacies of art that fails to achieve the required synthesis. The final three poems provide the general summary. Given the mutually exclusive dualism, perceptual reality on the one hand, conceptual unreality on the other, Stevens arrives at the climactic question of the poem: "What am I to believe?" The answer is, Believe in the synthesizing imagination, in which perception and emotion seem momentarily reconciled in an awareness of becoming, "a moving contour, a change not quite completed." This is to accept an irrational solution, a wholly mental "fiction," but perhaps the explanation will some day be provided.

> That's it: the more than rational distortion,
> The fiction that results from feeling. Yes, that.
>
> They will get it straight one day at the Sorbonne.
> We shall return at twilight from the lecture
> Pleased that the irrational is rational.... (p. 406)

But the solution, at least as Bergson explained it at the Sorbonne, was not one that Stevens ever accepted wholeheartedly. It remained one of the more intriguing possibilities of his later years, and as such it illuminates some of the obscurities of the later poetry.

Among those who regard the "Notes" as the ultimate resolution of Stevens' epistemological debates, Roy Harvey Pearce is the best representative. He is distinguished, moreover, by having been the only one to attempt a coherent paraphrase of all thirty-one of its poems. His thesis, which has had wide influence, is that Stevens' career shows a steady development from *Harmonium* to his greatest achievement, the "Notes" and "Esthetique du Mal."[20] Stevens' poetry between *Harmonium* and *Transport to Summer* represents "a steadily maturing view" and a corresponding development of style capable of handling the intellectual demands of his subject. In "Notes" he at last becomes "explicitly philosophical" and "realizes the possibilities of philosophic understanding and moral imagination."

> ...Stevens becomes explicitly philosophical—in the sense that he is concerned with realizing in aesthetic form certain epistemological, ontological, and moral propositions. The relation between the propositions and the poetry is this: that esthetic experience is the only means we have of initiating the inquiry by which we arrive at those propositions and is, moreover, the only means we have of realizing and believing in them. Thus Stevens' poetry is at once an expression and an exposition of a philosophical attitude. Since the authenticity of that attitude depends on origin in esthetic experience, it depends on the sensibility of the poet, a sensibility divorced—ideally—from any abstract system which would impose on it order from without, for order, esthetic order, "the structure of things," must be derived from a dynamic relationship between the individual imagination and the reality which it beholds. So the poet-esthete becomes the philosopher-moralist.[21]

In what sense a poet becomes a philosopher by depending upon his sensibility—divorced "from any abstract system" is not quite clear. One should notice how Stevens' own aesthetic theories have been taken over by Pearce, applied to the poem as a standard of critical judgment, and reduced to an explicit statement of the autonomy of art. Aesthetic problems demand aesthetic solutions, and aesthetic solutions are a matter of attitude, and attitude depends upon the unique sensibility of the poet. It is scarcely possible by this standard to avoid the conclusion with which Pearce ends his discussion.

> Here the poem ends, the possibilities of the reasoned abstract having been realized in the imagination which, as it works, adjusts itself to the distortions of reality, to change, and so adjusting discovers the rich pleasures of existence. Belief in the world of "Sunday Morning" is not only possible but necessary. It is the exercise of the creative imagination, working out a set of epistemological and ontological propositions, which has made for that possibility and that necessity. After such knowledge there can come only belief.[22]

This is a fairly good example of the kind of circular reasoning to which the notion of autonomous art necessarily forces the critic. Pearce is dealing with a poem which undertakes to argue the validity of aesthetic experience. The poem is, he finds, successful because the poet's ideas have been "realized in the imagination"—in short, it is successful if we assume the very point in question, the validity of aesthetic experience. Aside from this difficulty, there is the additional problem of explaining why the poet's "philosophical understanding" should make the "Notes" a distinguished poem. Stevens had been "realizing" philosophical propositions in his poetry for over twenty years. Presumably the ideas in "Sunday Morning" are realized in the imagination. Why then should the "Notes" be necessary for belief in the ideas of "Sunday Morning"? Apparently the nature of the philosophical propositions has something to do with the matter. Or perhaps there are simply more of them. One might suspect the latter since the nature of the philosophy involved is not indicated; the propositions are not specified or examined. Their function, as Pearce describes it, is, in fact, limited to providing the necessary calisthenic equipment on which the imagination performs its creative exercise: "It is the exercise of the creative imagination. . . . which has made for that possibility and that necessity." By this line of reasoning, Stevens might have used the "ontological propositions" of Zoroastrianism and the "epistemological propositions" of logical positivism with equal effectiveness. In reality, the philosophical complexity which Pearce considers so significant has, according to his conclusions, no significance at all. It is called upon to attest to the magnificence of the struggle, but it has no share in the victory.

The effort to make aesthetics the mediator in an epistemological dilemma is, as this study has been concerned to show, the peculiar inheritance of the Kantian tradition. What Kant illuminated for his successors, notably Coleridge and Schelling, was the opportunity to make art the bridge between unrelated metaphysical worlds. Philosophy had elevated art to a metaphysical absolute. In much the same way, the modern critic who declares philosophical propositions irrelevant to aesthetic considerations usually does so by appropriating philosophical assumptions for support. In the case of Stevens, the contradiction is peculiarly exposed because his aesthetic concerns clearly emerge from a philosophical context. If the philosophical context is irrelevant, there is no aesthetic problem; and Stevens is left with what is merely the specious appearance of a subject. To put it another way, it is as if one said that Stevens' subject was a metaphysical problem, but that in poetry the nature of a metaphysical problem is irrelevant — so long as it is solved aesthetically. It is hard to find a better illustration of the point than in Mr. Kermode's explanation of Stevens' philosophical interests.

> The poems, though philosophical, are never philosophy. They aspire to that condition of philosophical poetry which Coleridge thought to be within the power of Wordsworth, whose theme was also the interdependence of imagination and reality. Such poetry differs from philosophy in that it is "part of the *res* itself and not about it." The poem is not a comment but a fact never before realized, a contribution to reality.[23]

The final sequence, it will be noted, is a perfect expression of the idealistic heritage traced in this study. The doctrines of radical novelty and of the mind as the "true world-building power" come together in the conclusion that the poem is a created fact and facts cannot be questioned. They are part of reality.

Stevens was not quite so sure. Nor did he suppose that the modern poet was capable of the same kind of philosophical poetry that Coleridge had in mind, a poetry that required the existence of an Absolute. The modern poet had, rather, to look for alternatives. He could appropriate Bergson's *élan vital,* exploiting a mystique of the inexpressible; he could join Santayana in adopting a fictional world of the "celestial possible"; or he could simply accept poetry as "a vital self-assertion in a world in which nothing but the self remains, if that remains."[24]

It is of course possible to question how seriously Stevens regarded the whole subject. The possibility that his philosophizing was merely another reflection of his aestheticism has been raised. It is hard to question a man's intentions, but forty years of preoccupation with a single subject should be a convincing display of seriousness. At the very least, Stevens' poetry has exposed something of the philosophical heritage of modern aesthetic. It may be that as the poetry comes to be better understood the effort will seem more significant, not because it provides platitudinous solutions to the problems of the modern poet, but because it has insisted upon a fuller recognition of the problems.

Notes

Chapter 1

1. Wallace Stevens, *The Necessary Angel: Essays on Reality and the Imagination* (New York: Alfred A. Knopf, 1951), hereafter referred to as *N.A.*
2. The posthumous publications are in *Opus Posthumous,* ed. Samuel French Morse (New York: Alfred A. Knopf, 1957), hereafter referred to as *O.P.*
3. *N.A.,* vii.
4. Subsequent references will be to *The Collected Poems of Wallace Stevens* (New York: Alfred A. Knopf, 1955). For facts of separate publications, see Bibliography.
5. For epithets and variations, see Llewellyn Powys, "The Thirteenth Way," *Dial,* LXXVII (1924), 45–50; Harriet Monroe, "A Cavalier of Beauty," *Poetry,* XXIII (1924), 322–27; Gorham Munson, "The Dandyism of Wallace Stevens," *Dial,* LXXIX (1925), 413–17; Paul Rosenfeld, *Men Seen* (New York: Dial Press, 1925), 151–62; Alfred Kreymborg, *Our Singing Strength* (New York: Coward McCann, 1929), 500.
6. Edmund Wilson, "The All-Star Literary Vaudeville," *A Literary Chronicle: 1920–1950* (Garden City, New York: Doubleday and Co., 1956), 87.
7. Burnshaw's review, "Turmoil in the Middle Ground," has been reprinted in *The Sewanee Review,* LXIX (1961), 363–66, along with Burnshaw's rather abashed account of his unmerited fame. Stevens' poem in reply first appeared in *The New American Caravan.* It was revised and retitled "The Statue at the World's End" before being included in *The Man with the Blue Guitar.* The original version, with the original title, is reprinted by Morse in *O.P.,* 46–52.
8. Theodore Roethke, "Review of Wallace Stevens' *Ideas of Order,*" *The New Republic,* LXXXVII, 15 July 1936, 305.
9. Howard Baker, "Wallace Stevens and Other Poets," *Southern Review,* I (1935), 373–89.
10. See, for example, Morton Dauwen Zabel, "Two Years of Poetry: 1937–1939," *Southern Review,* V (1940), 568–608.
11. R. P. Blackmur, "Examples of Wallace Stevens," *The Double Agent* (New York: Arrow Editions, 1935), 68. The essay first appeared in *Hound and Horn,* V (1932), 223–55.
12. William Van O'Connor, *The Shaping Spirit* (Chicago: Henry Regnery Co., 1950); Robert Pack, *Wallace Stevens: An Approach to his Poetry and Thought* (New Brunswick, N.J.: Rutgers Univ. Press, 1958); Frank Kermode, *Wallace Stevens* (Writers and Critics Series, Edinburgh: Oliver and Boyd, 1960).
13. Hi Simons, "The Humanism of Wallace Stevens," *Poetry,* LXI (1942), 452.
14. Louis L. Martz, "Wallace Stevens: The World of Meditation," *Yale Review* XLVII (1958), 517–36.

15. Pack, *Wallace Stevens,* 3–18.
16. Samuel French Morse, "Wallace Stevens: Some Ideas about the Thing Itself," *Boston University Studies in English,* II (1956), 63.
17. A notable exception is J. V. Cunningham's "The Poetry of Wallace Stevens," *Poetry,* LXXXV (1949), 149–64, which considers both traditional and modern elements in Stevens' style and which points out Stevens' use of Wordsworthian blank verse.
18. Randall Jarrell, "Reflections on Wallace Stevens," in *Poetry and the Age* (New York: Vintage Books, 1955), 121–34.
19. John Ciardi, "Wallace Stevens' Absolute Music," *Nation* (16 Oct. 1954), 346–47.
20. "Adagia," *O.P.,* 178.
21. *N.A.,* Introduction, vii.
22. *N.A.,* 17.
23. The biographical facts have been widely published. Frank Kermode includes most of them in *Wallace Stevens,* 1–24. A convenient summary of studies on the Symbolist influence, a subject that has been repeatedly scrutinized, is Hi Simons' "Wallace Stevens and Mallarmé," *Modern Philology,* XLIII (1946), 235–59.
24. Joseph Wood Krutch, *The Modern Temper* (New York: Harcourt, Brace and Co., 1956), xi.
25. *N.A.,* 26.
26. Ibid., 14.
27. Ibid., 13, 14, 25, 35, 138.
28. Ibid., 139.
29. Krutch, *The Modern Temper,* 156–57.
30. See Tate's "Introduction to American Poetry, 1900–1950," *Modern Verse in English: 1900–1950,* eds. Lord David Cecil and Allen Tate (New York: The Macmillan Co., 1958), 39–40.
31. J. V. Cunningham, "Tradition and Modernity: Wallace Stevens," *Tradition and Poetic Structure* (Denver: Alan Swallow, 1960), 106–8.
32. Cecil, "Introduction to British Poetry, 1900–1950," *Modern Verse in English,* 31–32.
33. Hulme does attribute romantic vagueness to the "bad metaphysical aesthetic" of German idealism, which could not deal with art without "dragging in the infinite," but he does not develop the point in terms of romantic aesthetic theory. His objection to the infinite is that it leads to romantic "moaning" and bad style. See "Romanticism and Classicism," *Speculations: Essays on Humanism and the Philosophy of Art,* ed. Herbert Read (New York: Harcourt, Brace and Co., 1924), 111–40.
34. *O.P.,* 222.
35. See T. S. Eliot, "The Metaphysical Poets," *Selected Essays,* 1917–32 (New York: Harcourt, Brace and Co., 1932), 248. For Eliot's discussion of Richards' theory of "pseudostatement," see "Dante," 230–32.
36. *O.P.,* 223. Yvor Winters has noticed Stevens's resemblance to Poe. See "Wallace Stevens, or the Hedonist's Progress," *In Defense of Reason* (Denver: The Swallow Press, 1947), 434–35, 438–39.
37. *N.A.,* 44.
38. *O.P.,* 220.
39. Ibid., 219.
40. Ibid., 222.
41. George Santayana, *Interpretations of Poetry and Religion* (New York: Charles Scribner's Sons, 1900), 287. See also p. 251ff.
42. *O.P.,* 220.
43. "A Poet that Matters," *O.P.,* 251–52.

44. Ibid., 254.
45. *N.A.,* 30.
46. Ibid., 138–39.
47. Martz dates the change from 1940, after which he thinks Stevens developed toward the tradition of the meditative poets of the seventeenth century. "Wallace Stevens: The World as Meditation," *Yale Review* XLVII (1958), 517–36. Martz's argument will be considered later.
48. *N.A.,* 138.
49. "Two or Three Ideas," *O.P.,* 215.
50. *O.P.,* 241.
51. *N.A.,* 151.

Chapter 2

1. Kermode, *Wallace Stevens,* 25.
2. Pack, *Wallace Stevens,* 79ff.
3. William York Tindall, *Wallace Stevens,* (Minneapolis, Minn.: Univ. of Minnesota Press, 1961), 8.
4. I. A. Richards, *Coleridge on Imagination,* 1st ed. (London: Kegan Paul, Trench, Trubner & Co., 1934).
5. Oxford: Oxford University Press, 1953, 158.
6. M. H. Abrams, *The Mirror and the Lamp: Romantic Theory and the Critical Tradition* (New York: W. W. Norton & Co., 1958).
7. Modern discussions of the realist-idealist controversy now usually take for granted this meaning of "realism." The term should not be confused with its older metaphysical usage where it refers to a dualistic metaphysic such as found in Thomistic philosophy — specifically to a belief in the reality of universals as opposed to nominalism or conceptualism. Modern realism, like modern idealism, is a general term for a number of variants — "Naive realism," "ideal realism," "empirical realism," "transcendental realism," etc. To differentiate here among these positions will serve no useful purpose; it is sufficient to bear in mind that "realism," as it will be used here, refers simply to the belief in the independent existence of the world of objects.
8. John Henry Muirhead, "Idealism," *Encyclopaedia Britannica* (Eleventh Edition), Vol. 14, 281.
9. Wilbur M. Urban, "The Philosophy of Spirit: Idealism and the Philosophy of Value," in *Contemporary Idealism in America,* ed., Clifford Barrett (New York: MacMillan Co., 1932), 122.
10. H. H. Price, "British Philosophy Between the Wars," *Horizon,* XIX (1949), 65.
11. Kenneth Burke, *A Grammar of Motives* (New York: Prentice Hall, 1945), 172.
12. Ibid., 171–72.
13. Samuel T. Coleridge, *Biographia Literaria,* ed. J. Shawcross, 2 vols. (London: Oxford University Press, 1958), I, 202. Hereafter referred to as *Bio. Lit.* (1958).
14. Alfred North Whitehead, *Science and the Modern World* (Middlesex, England: Penguin Books, 1938), 110.
15. Coleridge, *Bio. Lit.* (1958) I, 88–89.
16. Ibid., 91–92.
17. Ibid., 174.
18. Samuel Taylor Coleridge, *Specimens of the Table Talk,* ed. Henry Nelson Coleridge, (New York: R. Worthington, 1884), 188. Hereafter referred to as *Table Talk.*
19. Coleridge, *Bio. Lit.* (1958) I, 100.

20. Immanuel Kant, *Critique of Pure Reason,* trans. Norman Kemp Smith (New York: The Modern Library, 1958), 54.
21. Coleridge, *Bio. Lit.* (1958) I, 174.
22. Ibid. 178.
23. Ibid., 184. I am indebted here to Arthur O. Lovejoy's *The Reason, the Understanding and Time* (Baltimore: Johns Hopkins Press, 1961), which provides the best account I know of the new German epistemology initiated by Kant and developed by his successors. Of the principle of the "I Am," the immediate identification of subject and object in self-consciousness, Professor Lovejoy writes: "In this alone we *experience* being, and find reality by being real. Upon this theme Schelling dwells with tedious iteration in his writings of 1795 and his *System of Transcendental Idealism* of 1800. Only the existence of the Self (as Descartes saw, without seeing the true implications of this insight) is beyond the reach of doubt, since here the object of the thought is identical with the thinking, and the thinking is its own evidence of its existence: 'I am! My Ego includes a being that is antecedent [*vorhergeht*] to all other thinking and representing. It is, because it is thought, and it is thought because it is: therefore, because it is, and is thought only in so far as it thinks itself....*Ich bin, veil ich bin!*'" For this passage and Lovejoy's discussion of Coleridge and Schelling see pp. 48–49 and passim. Coleridge's paraphrase of Schelling in the twelfth chapter of the *Biographia* is well known. Professor Lovejoy provides the following passage from Coleridge's *Anima Poetae* which is less well known and a clearer example of the manner in which Coleridge, like Schelling, argues that the certainty of perceptual knowledge is contingent upon its identification with the "I Am": "I think of the wall. Here I necessarily think of the idea and the thinking I as two distinct and opposite things. Now let me think of myself, of the thinking being. The idea becomes dim — so dim that I scarcely know what it is; but the feeling is deep and steady, and this I call I — identifying the percipient and the perceived." *Anima Poetae,* ed. E. H. Coleridge (London: William Heinemann, 1895), 15. It will be noticed that the identification involves a loss of a distinct idea with a compensatory emphasis upon feeling.
24. Etienne Gilson, *The Unity of Philosophical Experience* (New York: Charles Scribner's Sons, 1950), 196.
25. Coleridge, *Bio. Lit.* I, 179.
26. Ibid., 186.
27. Ibid., 184.
28. "Thus all human knowledge begins with intuitions, proceeds from thence to concepts, and ends with ideas. Although in respect of all three elements it possesses a priori sources of knowledge, which on first consideration seem to scorn the limits of all experience, a thoroughgoing critique convinces us that reason, in its speculative employment, can never with these elements transcend the field of possible experience, and that the proper vocation of this supreme faculty of knowledge is to use all methods, and the principles of these methods solely for the purpose of penetrating to the innermost secrets of nature, in accordance with every possible principle of unity — that of ends being the most important — but never to soar beyond its limits, outside which there is *for us* nothing but empty space." *The Critique of Pure Reason,* 318–319. It should be noted that the discussion here is limited to Kant's formal theory of knowledge. In his treatment of the moral consciousness in the *Critique of Practical Reason* this position is modified somewhat. Kant's moral philosophy is excluded from the *Critique of Pure Reason,* however, as having "no place in transcendental philosophy," p. 38.
29. Lovejoy, *The Reason, the Understanding, and Time,* 4.
30. Kant's struggle with this problem is evident throughout the three *Critiques* and is on some points contradictory. A good summary of the problem occurs in the "Preface to

the Second Edition," in the *Critique of Pure Reason,* 20–22. This is the often quoted passage in which Kant argues that although we cannot know we are free, we can yet *"think* freedom," concluding that he has "found it necessary to deny *knowledge,* in order to make room for *faith."*

31. Coleridge, *Table Talk,* 72.
32. Samuel Taylor Coleridge, *Aids to Reflection and the Confessions of an Inquiring Spirit* (London: George Bell, 1893), 224 n.
33. Samuel Taylor Coleridge, *Biographia Literaria: Or Biographical Sketches of My Literary Life and Opinions; and Two Lay Sermons* (London: George Bell and Sons, 1894), Appendix C, 347. Hereafter referred to as *Bio. Lit. and Two Lay Sermons* (1894).
34. Coleridge, *Table Talk,* 101.
35. Coleridge, *Bio. Lit. and Two Lay Sermons* (1894), Appendix C, 340.
36. Coleridge, *Bio. Lit.* (1958) I, 202.
37. Coleridge, *Bio. Lit.* (1958) I, 202; II, 258.
38. Coleridge, *Anima Poetae,* 136.
39. Burke, *Grammar of Motives,* 199.
40. Erich Heller, *The Hazard of Modern Poetry* (Cambridge: Bowes & Bowes, 1953), 32, 35, and passim.
41. ... "even as natural philosophers we must arrive at the same principle from which as transcendental philosophers we set out; that is, in a self-consciousness in which the principium essendi does not stand to the principium cognoscendi in the relation of cause to effect.... Thus the true system of natural philosophy places the sole reality of things in an ABSOLUTE, which is at once causa sui et effectus...." Coleridge, *Bio. Lit.* I, 187.
42. Ibid., lxxii.
43. Coleridge, *Bio. Lit. and Two Lay Sermons* (1894), Appendix E, 367.
44. Coleridge, *Table Talk,* 59.
45. Coleridge, *Bio. Lit.* (1958) I, 20.
46. Ibid., 188.
47. Coleridge, *Bio. Lit.* (1958) II, 259.
48. Ibid., I, 92.
49. Coleridge, *Bio Lit. and Two Lay Sermons* (1894), Appendix C, 347.
50. C. M. Bowra, *The Romantic Imagination* (Oxford, Clarendon Press, 1950), 283.
51. Coleridge, *Bio. Lit. and Two Lay Sermons* (1894), Appendix C, 347.
52. Gustave Flaubert, *La Tentation De Saint Antoine* in *Oeuvres Complètes de Gustave Flaubert,* ed. Louis Conard (Paris: 1910), 176.
53. For the continuity of this tradition as a continental development see Eric Heller, *The Hazard of Modern Poetry.*
54. I. A. Richards, *Coleridge on Imagination,* 166
55. Ibid., 165–66.
56. Kant named the fallacy with which Coleridge is here charged the "transcendental illusion." (See the *Critique of Pure Reason,* pp. 161–62.) Kant, however, was attacking the view that through dialectic the mind could attain to knowledge of a supersensible reality. Richards' position is a good deal more extreme, since he begins by rejecting the objective reality of all ideas for the position that *"all* views of Nature are taken to be projections of the mind, and the religions as well as science are included among myths" (*Coleridge on Imagination,* p. 177). Belief in any idea is thus justified in terms of practical necessity or psychological need rather than "truth." The standard of practical necessity gives scientific "statements of fact" priority over all other ideas in that belief in them may be unconditional and mandatory; whereas belief in other ideas must be provisional or "severely limited," and subject to the sanctions of science. It is this fundamental distinction between ideas ("beliefs" or "myths") and scientific "facts," which

enables Richards to turn Coleridge's metaphysical struggle into a psychological study—and semantic analysis—of ideas deriving from "the imaginative fact of mind." To justify this radical reinterpretation of Coleridge, Richards repeatedly stresses that as a philosopher, Coleridge too often mistook his ideas for facts about an external reality. Thus, with some injustice, he appropriates Coleridge's own remark that a madman is one who "mistakes his thoughts for persons and things." Richards comments: "Other myths do not derive from knowledge in the sense in which science is knowledge; though to suppose that they do and thus to take them as giving us knowledge, in this sense, in return, is the chief human failing, the process to which Coleridge should have pointed in his definition of madness" (p. 174). To which Coleridge might well have replied that he did not have to mistake his ideas for facts in order to believe them. He was far enough from the twentieth century that he could still believe in the objective reality of ideas *as* ideas. It is worth observing that Richards is now regarded as the Cambridge philosopher who along with G. E. Moore, laid the groundwork for the Cambridge school of logical positivism. His reinterpretation of Coleridge along lines so strikingly sympathetic to logical positivism (for example, his commitment to the analytical semantic method and his distinction between "statements of fact" and "emotive meanings") is one of the most curious examples of the modern interaction between philosophic and aesthetic traditions. Richards himself was, of course, well aware of this philosophical incongruity. As he says in introducing his treatment of Coleridge, "I write then as a Materialist trying to interpret before you the utterances of an extreme Idealist. . . ." (p. 19).

57. Richards, *Coleridge on Imagination,* 21-22.
58. Abrams, *The Mirror and the Lamp,* 222.
59. Ibid., 183.
60. Ibid., 178-79.
61. Ibid., 335.
62. Ibid., 313-14.
63. Ibid., 52.
64. Ibid., 119.

Chapter 3

1. "Angel Surrounded by Paysans," *The Collected Poems of Wallace Stevens,* 496. Hereafter referred to as *C.P.*
2. Allen Tate, "The Angelic Imagination: Poe as God," *The Forlorn Demon* (Chicago: Regnery, 1953), 56-78.
3. Frank Kermode, *The Romantic Image* (New York: Macmillan Co., 1957), 154.
4. *N.A.,* 27.
5. Irving Babbitt, *On Being Creative* (Boston: Houghton Mifflin, 1932), 96.
6. *N.A.,* 151.
7. Coleridge *Bio. Lit.* (1958) II, 262.
8. *O.P.,* 240-41.
9. Ibid., 200.
10. Richards, *Coleridge on Imagination,* 59.
11. Kant is notoriously unquotable. His full argument can be found in *Critique of Pure Reason,* pp. 128-130, from which the following excerpts have been taken merely to establish the problem and Kant's solution: "Let us suppose that there is nothing antecedent to an event, upon which it must follow according to rule. All succession of perception would then be only in the apprehension, that is would be merely subjective, and would never enable us to determine objectively which perceptions are those that really

precede and which are those that follow. We should then have only a play of representations, relating to no object; that is to say, it would not be possible through our perception to distinguish one appearance from another as regards relations of time. . . .

". . . .On the contrary, the appearances must determine for one another their position in time, and make their time-order a necessary order. In other words, that which follows or happens must follow in conformity with a universal rule upon that which was contained in the preceding state.

". . . .This rule, by which we determine something according to succession of time, is, that the condition under which an event invariably and necessarily follows is to be found in what precedes the event."

12. A. C. Ewing, *Idealism: A Critical Survey* (London: Methuen & Co., 1934), 110. See also, Arthur O. Lovejoy's *The Reason, the Understanding, and Time,* 148–50 and passim.

13. Immanuel Kant, *Critique of Judgement,* trans. James C. Meredith (Oxford: Clarendon Press, 1952), 180–81.

14. Ibid., 185.

15. Ibid., 184.

16. Babbitt, *On Being Creative,* 130.

17. Ibid., 5.

18. *N. A.,* 115.

19. *O. P.,* 227.

20. *N. A.,* 36.

21. Ibid., 138, 139, 171.

22. Ibid., 14.

23. Ibid., 147–48.

24. Martz, "Wallace Stevens: The World as Meditation," 518.

25. *O. P.,* 202.

26. *O. P.,* 246.

27. Abrams, *The Mirror and the Lamp,* 224.

28. Ibid., 225.

29. Coleridge, *Bio. Lit.* (1958) I, 64.

30. One sometimes reads in modern criticism that Coleridge's notion of universals is Aristotelian, but such a possibility is precluded by Coleridge's faculty psychology. Were the Aristotelian theory accepted, there would be no justification for the secondary imagination either as a creative faculty or as a self-sufficient one. Babbitt may have initiated this misconception by remarking that Coleridge's theory of universals "seems at times Aristotelian"; he is careful to add, however, that Coleridge "does not succeed in disengaging his theory of the imagination sufficiently from the transcendental mist." See *On Being Creative,* pp. 129–130. Mr. R. S. Crane apparently overlooks this qualification in arguing that Coleridge's theory of the imagination does not necessarily imply a monistic position. See his "Cleanth Brooks, or, The Bankruptcy of Critical Monism," *Modern Philology,* XV (1948), pp. 226–45. Coleridge himself in *Table Talk* twice refers to the distinction between Aristotelian universals and Platonic ideas to illustrate his distinction between Understanding and Reason. "I believe that Aristotle never could get to understand what Plato meant by an idea. . . . .With Plato ideas are constitutive in themselves.

"Aristotle was, and still is, the sovereign lord of the understanding; the faculty judging by the senses. He was a conceptualist, and never could raise himself into that higher state, which was natural to Plato, and has been so to others. . ." (p. 101). "Plato's works are preparatory exercises for the mind. He leads you to see that propositions involving in themselves contradictory conceptions, are nevertheless true; and which, therefore, must belong to a higher logic—that of ideas. They are contradictory only in the Aristotelian logic, which is the instrument of the understanding" (p. 59). This same distinction underlies his later remark in the *Lay Sermons* that the only "ideas" are products of Pure Reason and Imagination and can never be contemplated by the Understanding except through a "false and falsifying perspective" *Bio. Lit. and Two Lay Sermons* (1894) Appendix A, 336.

31.   Burke, *Grammar of Motives,* 224.
32.   Ibid., 225.
33.   *N. A.,* 164–65.
34.   Coleridge *Bio. Lit.* (1958), II, 5–6.
35.   *Bio. Lit.,* II, 42.
36.   *N. A.,* 165.
37.   Ibid., 141.
38.   Ibid., 165.
39.   *N. A.,* 44.
40.   *N. A.,* 153–54.
41.   In a subsequent essay of the same period, "The Relations between Poetry and Painting," the notion of a miraculous logic or reasoning is restated more affirmatively. "The point is that the poet does his job by virtue of an effort of the mind. In doing so, he is in rapport with the painter, who does his job, with respect to the problems of form and color, which confront him incessantly, not by inspiration, but by imagination or by the miraculous kind of reason that the imagination sometimes promotes." *N. A.,* 165.

   Again, in "A Collect of Philosophy," having distinguished philosophers who utilize reason from poets who utilize imagination, Stevens takes up the problem of explaining how some philosophical concepts can also be poetic. "The probing of the philosopher is deliberate, as the history of the part that logic has played in philosophy demonstrates. Yet one finds it simple to assume that the philosopher more or less often experiences the same miraculous shortenings of mental processes that the poet experiences. The whole scheme of the world as will may very well have occurred to Schopenhauer in an instant. The time he spent afterward in the explication of that instant is another matter....It remains true, however, that the probing of the philosopher is deliberate. On the other hand, the probing of the poet is fortuitous." *O. P.,* 197. This passage offers perhaps the best illustration of the historical motive underlying the distinction between reason and imagination. The philosopher, using reason, is logical, methodical, deliberate; that is, his mind moves *mechanically* from cause to effect, and this cannot be equivalent to a creative act. To be freely creative, the mind must come upon the same concepts immediately, fortuitously and by the "miraculous shortenings of mental processes" characteristic of the poet.

42.   I. A. Richards, *Principles of Literary Criticism,* (New York: Harcourt, Brace and Co., 1948), 11.
43.   Richards, *Principles of Literary Criticism,* 13.
44.   Richards was fully aware of this. He was also aware that by referring aesthetic value to psychological origins, he was preserving the mental basis required by idealist assumptions. The one point upon which empiricst and idealist could agree was that both the writing of poetry and the experience of poetry involve the mind, whatever else they may involve. By isolating poetry on psychological ground, he argued, it should be possible to avoid endless philosophical controversy concerning poetry's relation to the external world. Unfortunately what proposed to be a compromise turned out to mean the triumph of scientific empiricism: "The view that we are bodies...and that the mind is a system of impulses should not be described as Materialism. It might equally well be

called Idealism. Neither term in this connection has any scientific, any strictly symbolic meaning or reference. Neither stands for any separable, observable group of things, or character in things. Each is primarily an emotive term used to incite or support certain emotional attitudes. Like all terms used in the vain attempt (vain because the question is nonsensical) to say what things are, instead of to say how they behave, they state nothing.... That the Materialist and the Idealist believe themselves to be holding views which are incompatible with one another is but an instance of a very widespread confusion between scientific statement and emotive appeal, with which we shall in later chapters be much concerned. The Mind-Body problem is strictly speaking no problem; it is an imbroglio due to failure to settle a real problem, namely, as to when we are making a statement and when merely inciting an attitude." Pp. 83-84. In short, the Idealist will have no problems at all — if he will just consent to be an empiricist. It will be recalled that in a passage quoted earlier, Stevens remarks that if poetry could escape the Logical Positivists and the romantics, it would still have to contend with Freud, who might permit it to exist as a "science of illusions." Some critics have regarded the remark as delightfully ironic. More likely, it represents a better than common understanding of the alternatives open to the idealist tradition. At least Mr. Richards was an early and distinguished proponent of the science of illusion.

45. Kant, *The Critique of Judgement,* 38.
46. Coleridge, *Bio. Lit.,* II, 254.
47. *N. A.,* 28-29.
48. Burke, *Grammar of Motives,* 224.
49. *N. A.,* 149.
50. Murray Krieger, *The New Apologists for Poetry* (Minneapolis: Univ. of Minnesota Press, 1956), 17.
51. James Benziger, "Organic Unity: Leibnitz to Coleridge," *PMLA,* LXVI (1951), 24, 29.
52. *N. A.,* 23. See the parallel passage from Coleridge, cited above, p. 27.
53. Martz, "Wallace Stevens: The World of Meditation," 518, 521.
54. See above, p. 45.
55. Morse, "Wallace Stevens: Some Ideas About the Thing Itself," 58, 60.

Chapter 4

1. *N. A.,* 56.
2. *N. A.,* 173.
3. Pack, *Wallace Stevens,* 99-100.
4. I. A. Richards, *Principles of Literary Criticism* (New York: Harcourt, Brace and Co., 1948), 275.
5. Richards, *Principles of Literary Criticism,* 281-82.
6. Ibid., 279.
7. *N. A.,* 6-7.
8. *N. A.,* 4.
9. Kermode, *Wallace Stevens,* 88.
10. Pack, for example, interprets the passage to mean that "if our fictions are to approach the truth they must be based on reality" and that the fiction of the poem is thus an approach to an "absolute reality." *Wallace Stevens,* 106-7.
11. *N. A.,* 9.
12. *N. A.,* 24-25. The passage is reminiscent of Henry Adams' habit of cultivating apparent contradictions to support his skepticism. No distinction is made between physical and metaphysical levels of interpretation. Also, it does not follow that because physics

resolves matter into vibrations the impenetrability of matter is simply illusion. Even physicists continue to use doors.

13. Ibid., 25.
14. *O. P.,* 241.
15. *N. A.,* 32.
16. Ibid., 32–33.
17. "The poet or painter who lacks form, lacks everything, because he lacks *himself.* Poetical material permeates the souls of all: the expression alone, that is to say, the form, makes the poet. And here appears the truth of the view which denies all content to art, just the intellectual concept being understood as content. In this sense, when we take "content" as equal to "concept" it is most true, not only that art does not consist of content, but that *it has no content."* Benedetto Croce, *Aesthetic: As Science of Expression and General Linguistic,* trans. Douglas Ainslie (New York: Noonday Press, 1953, rev. ed.), 25.
18. Croce, *Aesthetic,* 15.
19. Richards quotes what is probably the definitive criticism of Croce by Giovanni Papini in *Four and Twenty Minds:* "If you disregard critical trivialities and didactic accessories, the entire aesthetic system of Croce amounts merely to a hunt for pseudonyms of the word 'art,' and may indeed be stated briefly and accurately in this formula: art = intuition = expression = feeling = imagination = fancy = lyricism = beauty. And you must be careful not to take these words with the shadings and distinctions which they have in ordinary or scientific language. Not a bit of it. Every word is merely a different series of syllables signifying absolutely and completely the same thing." *Principles of Literary Criticism,* p. 255, note.
20. Henri Focillon, whose book *The Life of Forms in Art* Stevens describes as "one of the really remarkable books of the day" (*N. A.,* 46), is sometimes mentioned as an important influence. Focillon propounds what is essentially Crocean aesthetic, substituting for the words of a poem the "forms" of the visual arts. Stevens, in fact, quotes a passage in which this transference is implied: "Human consciousness is in perpetual pursuit of a language and style. To assume consciousness is at once to assume form. Even at levels far below the zone of definition and clarity, forms, measures and relationships exist." Using Croce's notion of form as a manifestation of consciousness, Focillon brings the organic theory of art to what must surely be its ultimate development. Art is provided with its own *élan vital* and elevated to biological status. Forms in art exhibit such remarkable biological functions as volition, growth, and reproduction, according to Focillon. At the next stage of evolution we may have to take art outside and shoot it.
21. Whitehead, *Science and the Modern World,* 172–73.
22. Henri Bergson, *Creative Evolution,* trans. Arthur Mitchell (New York: Random House, 1944), 296.
23. Bergson, *Creative Evolution,* pp. 218–19.
24. Hulme, *Speculations,* 213.
25. Whitehead, *Science and the Modern World,* p. 173–74.
26. Bergson, *Creative Evolution,* xvi–xvii.
27. Professor Lovejoy's comment on this point bears repeating. "It may at first sight appear an embarrassing circumstance for a philosopher to have a message to convey which is, by his own confession, incapable of being put into words. But in point of fact, as the history of both philosophy and religion shows, there are few things which render a doctrine more attractive to many minds than an air of ineffability. Certainly the writings of most of Bergson's disciples show how greatly they have felt the fascination of this quality of mystical unutterableness. The adepts of this philosophy have often the air of

going about with monitory fingers on lips and an expression of wondering rapture." *The Reason, the Understanding, and Time,* 40.

28. Bergson, *Creative Evolution,* 373.
29. Ibid., 372.
30. Ibid., 210, 212.
31. *O. P.,* 268.
32. Ibid., 213.
33. *N. A.,* 49.
34. Ibid., 50–51.
35. Bergson, *Creative Evolution,* 141, 147–48.
36. Bergson, describing the power of the artist's intuition to "grasp what it is that intelligence fails to give us" and thereby to "regain the intention of life," concludes: "...by its own work, it will suggest to us the vague feeling, if nothing more, of what must take the place of intellectual molds....Then by the sympathetic communication which it establishes between us and the rest of living, by the expansion of our consciousness which it brings about, it introduces us into life's own domain...endlessly continued creation." *Creative Evolution,* 194–95.
37. *N. A.,* 171.
38. Ibid., 174.
39. *O. P.,* 187.
40. In England, the counterpart of the American school was labeled "Oxford idealism," of which the most influential members were F. H. Bradley and Bernard Bosanquet.
41. *N. A.,* 26.
42. William James, *The Philosophy of William James,* ed. Horace M. Kallen (New York: Modern Library, 1923), See Kallen's "Introduction," 3, 28.
43. William James, *The Will to Believe, and Other Essays in Popular Philosophy* (New York: Longmans Green and Co., 1897), 14–15.
44. Ibid., 27.
45. "The Pure Good of Theory," *C. P.,* 332.
46. James, *The Will to Believe,* 18–19.
47. The passage is quoted by Kallen, *The Philosophy of William James,* 29.
48. William James, *Radical Empiricism and a Pluralistic Universe* (New York: Longmans, Green and Co., 1943), 214.
49. For the argument that idealist epistemology leads to absolute idealism, see Lecture II, "Monistic Idealism," Ibid., pp. 41–82. The section dealing with Royce and Bradley (pp. 61–73) is overly technical for purposes of quotation. Its conclusion may indicate the direction of James's argument: "Any other picture than this of post-Kantian absolutism I am unable to frame. I see the intellectualistic criticism destroying the immediately given coherence of the phenomenal world, but unable to make its own conceptual substitutes cohere, and I see the resort to the absolute for a coherence of a higher type. The situation has dramatic liveliness, but it is incoherent throughout....May not the remedy lie rather in revising the intellectualist criticism than in first adopting it and then trying to undo its consequences by an arbitrary act of faith in an unintelligible agent. May not the flux of sensible experience itself contain a rationality that has been overlooked, so that the real remedy would consist in harking back to it more intelligently, and not advancing in the opposite direction away from it and even away beyond the intellectualist criticism that disintegrates it, to the pseudo-rationality of the supposed absolute point of view. I myself believe that this is the real way to keep rationality in the world...."
50. William James, *Pragmatism:* (New York: Longmans, Green and Co., 1948) 17–19.

51. Ibid., 32.
52. James, *A Pluralistic Universe,* 123.
53. Those interested in the problem in all its multifariousness might consult Arthur O. Lovejoy, *The Revolt Against Dualism: An Inquiry Concerning the Existence of Ideas* (La Salle, Illinois: Open Court Publishing Co., 1955). For Professor Lovejoy's objections to James' "short and easy" solution, see pp. 56–58.
54. James, *The Will to Believe,* 56.
55. James, *A Pluralistic Universe,* 339, note.
56. Eliot, *Selected Essays, 1917-1932,* 367.
57. George Santayana, *Apologia Pro Mente Sua* in *The Philosophy of George Santayana,* ed. Paul Arthur Schilpp (New York: Tudor Publishing Co., 1951), 499.
58. Santayana, *Apologia Pro Mente Sua,* 497.
59. George Santayana, *The Winds of Doctrine and Platonism and the Spiritual Life* (New York: Harper and Brothers, 1957), 13–14.
60. George Santayana, *Realms of Being* (New York: Charles Scribner's Sons, 1942).
61. Santayana, *Apologia Pro Mente Sua,* 527.
62. Ibid.
63. Ibid., 523.
64. Ibid., 531.
65. Ibid., 532.
66. Ibid.
67. Ibid., 500–501.
68. Ibid., 529.
69. Ibid., 542.
70. "Humanism and Post-Humanism in the Philosophy of Santayana," in Schilpp, *The Philosophy of George Santayana,* 309–10.
71. *N. A.,* 166.
72. Ibid., 174.
73. Ibid., 79.
74. *O. P.,* 237.
75. *Collected Poems,* 508–510.
76. Santayana, *Apologia Pro Mente Sua,* 525.

Chapter 5

1. *C. P.,* 244–45. Subsequent page references will be cited in text.
2. "A Note on Les Plus Belles Pages," *O. P.,* 293–294.
3. "Two or Three Ideas," *O. P.,* 205.
4. James, *Pragmatism,* 122–23.
5. James, *A Pluralistic Universe,* 174–75.
6. James, *Pragmatism,* 266.
7. Ibid., 142–43.
8. James, *A Pluralistic Universe,* 191–92.
9. Ibid., 193.
10. *O. P.,* 213.
11. James, *Pragmatism,* 20.
12. James, *A Pluralistic Universe,* 331.
13. Ibid., 59.
14. James, *A Pluralistic Universe,* 290–291.
15. *N. A.,* 59.

16. For similar usage, see "Anecdote of Canna," which satirizes the grandiose dreams of the abstracting mind, "the mighty thought, the mighty man"; or the treatment of the generalizing "Chieftain" in "Bantams in Pine-woods," *C. P.,* 55.

17. For this usage, see the "white pigeon" of "Le Monocle de Mon Oncle" (p. 17) and a later poem, "A Rabbit as King of the Ghosts" (p. 209). In the latter poem, the rabbit is described as having "nothing to think of," because he has retired into a wholy conceptual world where he sits as king, unaware of his small and precarious place in the real scheme of things.

18. James, *Pragmatism,* 361–63.

19. *O. P.,* 22. The poem was first published in 1919.

20. William James, *Talks to Teachers on Psychology; and to Students on Some of Life's Ideals* (New York: Henry Holt and Co., 1912), 292–293.

21. James, *A Pluralistic Universe,* 175–76.

22. James, *Talks to Teachers,* 270.

23. "Tradition and Modernity: Wallace Stevens," in *Tradition and Poetic Structure,* 112.

24. O'Connor, *The Shaping Spirit,* 139.

25. Compare, for example, the description of the "collapsing edifice" of tradition in "The Public Square," in which the last vestige to remain is "the moon...with its porcelain leer." See also "Esthetique du Mal" in which the loss of Christian faith creates "Panic in the face of the moon." *C. P.,* 109, 320.

26. *N. A.,* 26.

27. Stevens' parodies are rarely obvious, but like his symbolism, they depend upon fairly conventional literary associations. In "Notes toward a Supreme Fiction," for example, he satirizes a Canon's dream of his spiritual ascent to heaven. The description merely suggests the Miltonic rhetoric of Satan's ascent from hell.

> ...he was the ascending wings he saw
> And moved on them in orbits' outer stars
>
> ....
>
> Forth then with huge pathetic force
> Straight to the utmost crown of night he flew. (p. 403)

In the same manner, he parodies the nineteenth-century romantics, whose voices compose a single "heavenly gong" by parodying Shelley's "be-thou's" in "Ode to the West Wind."

> Bethou me, said sparrow, to the crackled blade,
> And you, and you, bethou me as you blow (p. 393)

28. "Two or Three Ideas," *O. P.,* 206–7.

29. In a later parallel to this passage in "Academic Discourse at Havana," the tropics are treated as an escape from both Christianity and romanticism:

> Canaries in the morning, orchestras
> In the afternoon, balloons at night. That is
> A difference, at least, from nightingales,
> Jehovah and the great sea-worm. (*C. P.,* 142)

30. *O. P.,* 152.

31. I have followed here the 1950 edition of *Harmonium,* p. 60. In the 1923 edition and in *C. P.* the third line is misprinted, "Which was, and if, chief motive, first delight..."

32. This same explanation of the nonsensical and bizarre elements in Stevens' early poetry is provided in several shorter poems such as "A High-Toned Old Christian Woman" and "The Weeping Burgher." In the latter, the burgher-poet explains that he has adopted the "belle design of foppish line" as a stylish "excess" in order to cure his grief for the "sorry verities" of the past.

33. This is the passage, for example, which led R. P. Blackmur to conclude in 1932 that Crispin's quest ends in failure because, "He has been brought back to social nature, has gone to seed." The essay, "Examples of Wallace Stevens," is reprinted in *The Achievement of Wallace Stevens,* eds. Ashley Brown and Robert S. Haller (Philadelphia: J. B. Lippincott Co., 1962), 52–80. For Blackmur's conclusion see pp. 77–78.

34. The essays are included under the subtitle "Talks to Students" in *Talks to Teachers on Psychology; and to Students on Some of Life's Ideals.* The cited passage is found on p. 294.

35. *Talks to Teachers,* 257.

36. Ibid., 257–58.

37. Ibid., 262–63.

38. Ibid., 274–75.

39. Ibid., 266.

40. Ibid., 231–32.

41. Ibid., 234.

Chapter 6

1. Critical studies of the poem include: R. P. Blackmur, "Wallace Stevens: An Abstraction Blooded," *Form and Value in Modern Poetry* (Garden City, New York: Doubleday & Co., 1957), 213–17; R. H. Pearce, "Wallace Stevens: The Life of the Imagination," *PMLA,* LXVI (1951), 561–82; Robert Pack, *Wallace Stevens,* 94–115; B. Heringman, "Wallace Stevens: The Use of Poetry," *ELH,* XVI (1949), 325–36; L. Frankenberg, *The Pleasure Dome* (Boston: Houghton Mifflin, 1949), 197–267; Frank Kermode, *Wallace Stevens,* 111–19; Frank Doggett, "This Invented World: Stevens' Notes toward a Supreme Fiction,'" *ELH,* XXVIII (1961), 284–99; and Harold Bloom, "Notes toward a Supreme Fiction: A Commentary," in Marie Borroff (ed.), *Wallace Stevens: A Collection of Critical Essays* (Englewood Cliffs, New Jersey: Prentice-Hall, 1963), 76–95.

2. See, for example, "The Man Whose Pharynx Was Bad," *C. P.,* 96.

3. Henri Bergson, *Two Sources of Morality and Religion,* trans. R. Ashley Audra and Cloudesley Brereton (New York: Henry Holt and Co., 1935), 243. As mentioned earlier, Stevens refers to this book and quotes Bergson in "The Noble Rider and the Sound of Words" and "The Figure of the Youth as Virile Poet." These essays were first published in 1942 and 1944 respectively; "Notes" first appeared in 1943.

4. See "The World as Meditation," *C. P.,* 520–21.

5. Bergson, *Two Sources of Morality and Religion,* 165.

6. Bergson, *Creative Evolution,* 293–94.

7. Ibid., 344–45.

8. Ibid., 334.

9. Frank Doggett, "This Invented World," 294.

10. Bergson, *Two Sources of Morality and Religion,* 194.

11. Ibid., 166–67. Bergson's rather striking remark that "a certain intention of his environment follows him then everywhere," might be compared with an equally striking passage in "An Ordinary Evening in New Haven":

> There were looks that caught him out of empty air.
> *C'est toujours la vie qui me regarde*...This was
> Who watched him, always, for unfaithful thought.
>
> This sat beside his bed, with its guitar,... (p. 483)

The personification of this mysterious intention is, according to Bergson, the primitive form of mythmaking.

12. Ibid., 200–201.
13. Bergson, *Creative Mind,* 159–60.
14. See "Things of August," *C. P.,* pp. 494–95, and "A Primitive like an Orb," *C. P.,* p. 443.
15. *N. A.,* 50–51.
16. Bergson, *Two Sources of Morality and Religion,* 75.
17. Ibid., 91.
18. Ibid., 86.
19. See Irwin Edman's "Foreword" to *Creative Evolution,* xvi; and H. B. Parkes, "Bergson," in *The Pragmatic Test* (San Francisco: Colt Press, 1941), 157–58.
20. "Wallace Stevens: The Life of the Imagination," 561–62.
21. Ibid., 575. It should be mentioned that Pearce's version of Stevens' development involves an error in dating. He apparently failed to notice that "Notes" did not make its first appearance in *Transport to Summer* but was published separately five years earlier. Thus the other poems in the volume, which Pearce finds "rush toward Stevens' masterworks" postdate the "Notes" by as much as five years. Kermode, who expands the same thesis, acknowledges his debt to Pearce without noting the error.
22. Ibid., 575–76.
23. Kermode, *Wallace Stevens,* 83.
24. *N. A.,* 171.

Bibliography

Abrams, M. H. (ed.). *Literature and Belief.* (English Institute Essays.) New York: Columbia University Press, 1958.

———. *The Mirror and the Lamp: Romantic Theory and the Critical Tradition.* New York: W. W. Norton and Company, 1958.

Arnett, Willard E. *Santayana and the Sense of Beauty.* Bloomington: Indiana University Press, 1955.

Ayer, A. J. *The Problem of Knowledge.* Baltimore: Penguin Books, 1962.

Babbitt, Irving. *On Being Creative.* Boston: Houghton Mifflin, 1932.

———. *Rousseau and Romanticism.* Boston: Houghton Mifflin Company, 1947.

Baker, Howard. "Wallace Stevens and Other Poets," *Southern Review,* I (Autumn, 1935), 373-89.

Barrett, Clifford (ed.). *Contemporary Idealism in America.* New York: Macmillan Company, 1932.

Benziger, James. "Organic Unity: Leibnitz to Coleridge," *Publications of the Modern Language Association,* LXVI (March, 1951), 24-48.

Bergson, Henri. *Creative Evolution.* Translated by Arthur Mitchell with a Foreword by Irwin Edmans. (The Modern Library.) New York: Random House, 1944.

———. *Creative Mind.* Translated by Mabelle L. Andison. New York: Philosophical Library, 1946.

———. *Matter and Memory.* Translated by Nancy Margaret Paul and W. Scott Palmer. Garden City, New York: Doubleday and Company, 1959.

———. *The Two Sources of Morality and Religion.* Translated by R. Ashley Audra and Cloudesley Brereton. New York: Henry Holt and Company, 1935.

Bewley, Marius. "The Poetry of Wallace Stevens," *Partisan Review,* XVI (Sept., 1949), 895-915.

Blackmur, R. P. "Examples of Wallace Stevens," *The Double Agent.* New York: Arrow Editions, 1935, pp. 68-102.

———. "Wallace Stevens: An Abstraction Blooded," "On Herbert Read and Wallace Stevens," and "Lord Tennyson's Scissors: 1912-1950," *Form and Value in Modern Poetry.* Garden City, New York: Doubleday and Company, 1957, pp. 213-18, 219-224, 369-88.

Borroff, Marie (ed.). *Wallace Stevens: A Collection of Critical Essays.* Englewood Cliffs, New Jersey: Prentice-Hall, 1963.

Bowra, C. M. *The Romantic Imagination.* Oxford: Clarendon Press, 1950.

Bradley, F. H. *Essays on Truth and Reality.* Oxford: Clarendon Press, 1950.

Brown, Ashley, and Haller, Robert S. (eds.). *The Achievement of Wallace Stevens.* Philadelphia: J. B. Lippincott Company, 1962.

Burke, Kenneth. *A Grammar of Motives.* New York: Prentice-Hall, 1945.

Burnshaw, Stanley. "Wallace Stevens and the Statue," *Sewanee Review,* LXIX (Summer, 1961), 355–66.

Cecil, David, and Tate, Allen (eds.). *Modern Verse in English, 1900–1950.* New York: Macmillan Company, 1958.

Ciardi, John "Wallace Stevens' Absolute Music," *Nation,* CLXXIX (Oct. 16, 1954), 346–47.

Coleridge, Samuel Taylor. *Aids to Reflection and the Confessions of an Inquiring Spirit.* London: George Bell, 1893.

——. *Anima Poetae.* Edited by Ernest Hartley Coleridge. London: William Heinemann, 1895.

——. *Biographia Literaria.* Edited with an introduction by J. Shawcross. Rev. ed. 2 vols. London: Oxford University Press, 1958.

——. *Biographia Literaria: Or Biographical Sketches of My Literary Life and Opinions; and Two Lay Sermons.* George Bell and Sons, 1894.

——. *Specimens of the Table Talk of Samuel Taylor Coleridge.* Edited by Henry Nelson Coleridge. New York: R. Worthington, 1884.

Crane, R. S. "Cleanth Brooks; or the Bankruptcy of Critical Monism," *Modern Philology,* XV (May, 1948), 226–45.

Croce, Benedetto. *Aesthetic: As Science of Expression and General Linguistic.* Translated by Douglas Ainslie. Rev. ed. New York: The Noonday Press, 1956.

Cunningham, G. Watts. *The Idealistic Argument in Recent British and American Philosophy* New York: The Century Company, 1933.

Cunningham, J. V. "The Poetry of Wallace Stevens," *Poetry,* LXXV (Dec., 1949), 149–64.

——. "Tradition and Modernity: Wallace Stevens," *Tradition and Poetic Structure.* Denver: Alan Swallow, 1960, pp. 106–24. (A revision of "The Poetry of Wallace Stevens.")

Doggett, Frank. "This Invented World: Stevens' 'Notes Toward a Supreme Fiction,' " *English Literary History,* XXVIII (Sept., 1961), 284–99.

——. "Wallace Stevens' Later Poetry," *English Literary History,* XXV (June, 1958), 137–58.

Drew, Elizabeth, and Sweeney, John L. *Directions in Modern Poetry.* New York: W. W. Norton and Company, 1940.

Duffey, Bernard. A review of Robert Pack's *Wallace Stevens. American Literature,* XXXI (May 1959), 211.

Eliot, T. S. *Selected Essays, 1917–32.* New York: Harcourt, Brace and Company, 1932.

Ewing, Alfred C. *Idealism: A Critical Survey.* London: Methuen and Company, 1934.

Ferm, Vergilius (ed.). *A History of Philosophical Systems.* Paterson, New Jersey: Littlefield, Adams and Company, 1961.

Flaubert, Gustave. *La Tentation De Saint Antoine.* Vol. VII of *Oeuvres Complètes de Gustave Flaubert.* Edited by Louis Conard. Paris, 1910.

Focillon, Henry. *The Life of Forms in Art.* Revised translation by Charles Beecher Hogan and George Kubler. 2nd English ed., enl. New York: Wittenborn, Schultz, 1958.

Foster, Richard. *The New Romantics: A Reappraisal of the New Criticism.* Bloomington: Indiana University Press, 1962.

Frankenberg, Lloyd. "Wallace Stevens," *Pleasure Dome.* Boston: Houghton Mifflin, 1949, pp. 197–267.

Frye, Northrop. "The Realistic Oriole: A Study of Wallace Stevens," *The Hudson Review,* X (Autumn, 1957), 353–70.

Gilson, Etienne. *The Unity of Philosophical Experience.* New York: Charles Scribner's Sons, 1950.

Heller, Erich. *The Hazard of Modern Poetry.* Cambridge: Bowes and Bowes, 1953.

Heringman, Bernard. "Wallace Stevens: The Use of Poetry," *English Literary History,* XVI (Dec. 1949), 325–36.

Hulme, T. E. *Speculations: Essays on Humanism and the Philosophy of Art.* Edited by Herbert Read. New York: Harcourt, Brace and Company, 1924.

James, William. *The Letters of William James.* Edited by Henry James. Boston: Little, Brown, and Company, 1926.

————. *The Philosophy of William James.* Edited with an Introduction by Horace M. Kallen. (The Modern Library.) New York: Random House, 1923.

————. *Pragmatism.* New York: Longmans, Green and Company, 1948.

————. *Radical Empiricism and a Pluralistic Universe.* New York: Longmans, Green and Company, 1943.

————. *Talks to Teachers on Psychology; and to Students on Some of Life's Ideals.* New York: Henry Holt and Company, 1912.

————. *The Will to Believe and Other Essays in Popular Philosophy.* New York: Longmans, Green and Company, 1897.

Jarrell, Randall. "Reflections on Wallace Stevens," *Poetry and the Age.* New York: Vintage Books, 1955, pp. 121–34.

Kant, Immanuel. *Critique of Judgement.* Translated by James C. Meredith. Oxford: Clarendon Press, 1952.

————. *Critique of Pure Reason.* Translated by Norman Kemp Smith. Abr. ed. (The Modern Library.) New York: Random House, 1958.

Kermode, Frank. *The Romantic Image.* New York: Macmillan Company, 1957.

————. *Wallace Stevens.* (Writers and Critics Series.) Edinburgh: Oliver and Boyd, 1960.

Kreymborg, Alfred. *Our Singing Strength: An Outline of American Poetry 1620–1930.* New York: Coward McCann, 1929.

Krieger, Murray. *The New Apologists for Poetry.* Minneapolis: University of Minnesota Press, 1956.

Krutch, Joseph Wood. *The Modern Temper.* New York: Harcourt, Brace and Company, 1956.

Lovejoy, Arthur O. *The Reason, the Understanding, and Time.* Baltimore: Johns Hopkins Press, 1961.

————. *The Revolt Against Dualism: An Inquiry Concerning the Existence of Ideas.* La Salle, Illinois: Open Court Publishing Company, 1955.

Martz, Louis L. "Wallace Stevens: The World as Meditation," *Yale Review,* XLVII (Summer, 1958), 517–536.

Miller, Oscar W. *The Kantian Thing-in-Itself or The Creative Mind.* New York: Philosophical Library, 1958.

Monroe, Harriet. "A Cavalier of Beauty," *Poetry* XXIII (March, 1924, 322–27.

————. *A Poet's Life: Seventy Years in a Changing World.* New York: Macmillan Company, 1938.

Moore, George Edward. *Principia Ethica.* Cambridge: University Press, 1960.

Morse, Samuel F. "Wallace Stevens: Some Ideas about the Thing Itself," *Boston University Studies in English,* II (Spring, 1956), 55–64.

Muirhead, John Henry. "Idealism," *Encyclopaedia Britannica.* 11th ed. Vol. XIV.

Munson, Gorham. "The Dandyism of Wallace Stevens," *Dial,* LXXIX (Nov., 1925), 413–17.

O'Connor, William Van. *The Shaping Spirit.* Chicago: Henry Regnery, 1950.

Parkes, Henry Bamford. "Bergson," *The Pragmatic Test: Essays on the History of Ideas.* San Francisco: The Colt Press, 1941, pp. 135–59.

Pack, Robert. *Wallace Stevens: An Approach to his Poetry and Thought.* New Brunswick, New Jersey: Rutgers University Press, 1958.

Pearce, Roy Harvey. "Wallace Stevens: The Life of the Imagination," *Publications of the Modern Language Association,* LXVI (Sept., 1951), 561–82.

Powys, Llewellyn. "The Thirteenth Way," *Dial,* LXXVII (July, 1924), 45–50.

Price, H. H. "British Philosophy Between the Wars," *Horizon,* XIX (Jan., 1949), 54–74.

Richards, I. A. *Coleridge on Imagination.* (2nd ed.) London: Routledge and Kegan Paul, 1955. [1st ed. London: Kegan Paul, Trench, Trubner & Co., 1934.]

——. *Principles of Literary Criticism.* New York: Harcourt, Brace and Company, 1948.

Riddel, Joseph N. "Wallace Stevens' 'Visibility of Thought,'" *Publications of the Modern Language Association,* LXXVII (Sept., 1962), 482–98.

Roethke, Theodore. Review of Wallace Stevens' *Ideas of Order. The New Republic,* LXXXVII (July 15, 1936), 305.

Rosenfeld, Paul. "Wallace Stevens," *Men Seen.* New York: Dial Press, 1925, pp. 151–62.

Royce, Josiah. *The Spirit of Modern Philosophy.* Boston: Houghton, Mifflin and Company, 1892.

Russell, Bertrand. *The Problems of Philosophy.* London: Oxford University Press, 1952.

Santayana, George. *Interpretations of Poetry and Religion.* New York: Charles Scribner's Sons, 1900.

——. *Realms of Being.* New York: Charles Scribner's Sons, 1927–40.

——. *Reason in Art.* Vol. IV of *The Life of Reason.* New York: Collier Books, 1962.

——. *The Sense of Beauty: Being the Outlines of Aesthetic Theory.* New York: Charles Scribner's Sons, 1896.

——. *Winds of Doctrine and Platonism and the Spiritual Life.* New York: Harper and Brothers, 1957.

Schilpp, Paul Arthur (ed.). *The Philosophy of George Santayana.* New York: Tudor Publishing Company, 1951.

Simons, Hi. " 'The Comedian as the Letter C': Its Sense and Its Significance," *Southern Review,* V (Winter, 1940), 453–68.

——. "The Genre of Wallace Stevens," *Sewanee Review,* LIII (Autumn, 1945), 566–79.

——. "The Humanism of Wallace Stevens," *Poetry,* LXI (Nov., 1942), 448–52.

——. "Wallace Stevens and Mallarmé," *Modern Philology,* XLIII (May, 1946), 235–59.

Stallknecht, Newton P. "Absence in Reality: A Study in the Epistemology of the Blue Guitar," *Kenyon Review,* XXI (Autumn, 1959), 545–62.

Stevens, Wallace. *The Auroras of Autumn.* New York: Alfred A. Knopf, 1950.

——. *The Collected Poems of Wallace Stevens.* New York: Alfred A. Knopf, 1955.

——. *Esthétique du Mal.* Cummington, Massachusetts: Cummington Press, 1944.

——. *Harmonium.* New York: Alfred A. Knopf, 1923. (Second edition, with additional poems, 1931)

——. *Ideas of Order.* New York: Alfred A. Knopf, 1936.

——. *The Man with the Blue Guitar and Other Poems.* New York: Alfred A. Knopf, 1937.

——. *The Necessary Angel: Essays on Reality and the Imagination.* New York: Alfred A. Knopf, 1951.

——. *Notes Toward a Supreme Fiction.* Cummington, Massachusetts: Cummington Press, 1942.

——. *Opus Posthumous.* Edited, with an Introduction, by Samuel French Morse. New York: Alfred A. Knopf, 1957.

——. *Owl's Clover.* New York: Alfred A. Knopf, 1936.

——. *Parts of a World.* New York: Alfred A. Knopf, 1942.

——. *Poems.* Selected and with an Introduction by Samuel F. Morse. New York: Vintage Books, 1959.

————. *Transport to Summer* (including *Notes Toward a Supreme Fiction* and *Esthétique du Mal*). New York: Alfred A. Knopf, 1947.

Tate, Allen. "The Angelic Imagination: Poe as God," *The Forlorn Demon*. Chicago: Regnery, 1953, pp. 56–78.

————. "Wallace Stevens," *Sixty American Poets, 1896–1944*. Washington: Library of Congress, 1945.

Tindall, William York. *Wallace Stevens*. (University of Minnesota Pamphlets on American Writers, no. 11.) Minneapolis: University of Minnesota Press, 1961.

Vaihinger, Hans. *The Philosophy of "As If."* Translated by C. K. Ogden. 2nd ed. London: Kegan Paul, Trench, Trubner and Company, 1935.

Vazakas, Byron. "Three Modern Old Masters: Moore, Stevens, Williams," *New Mexico Quarterly*, XXII (Winter, 1952), 431–44.

Whitehead, Alfred North. *Process and Reality: An Essay in Cosmology*. New York: Macmillan Company, 1960.

————. *Science and the Modern World*. Middlesex, England: Penguin Books, 1938.

Wilson, Edmund "The All-Star Literary Vaudeville," *A Literary Chronicle: 1920–1950*. Garden City, New York: Doubleday and Company, 1956, pp. 76–92.

————. *Axel's Castle: A Study in the Imaginative Literature of 1870–1930*. New York: Charles Scribner's Sons, 1955.

Winters, Yvor. "Wallace Stevens, or the Hedonist's Progress," *In Defense of Reason*. Denver: Swallow Press and William Morrow and Company, 1947, pp. 431–59.

Zabel, Morton Dauwen. "Two Years of Poetry: 1937–1939," *Southern Review*, V (Winter, 1940), 568–608.

Index